KU-712-031

# What's new in economics?

027.9.93

30130503945113

# What's new in economics?

*edited by*
John Maloney

The South East Essex
College of Arts & Technology
Carnarvon Road  Southend on Sea  Essex  SS2 6LS
Tel: Southend (0702) 220400  Fax. Southend (0702) 432320

Manchester University Press
Manchester and New York

*Distributed exclusively in the USA and Canada by*
*St. Martin's Press*

Copyright © Manchester University Press 1992

While copyright in the volume as a whole is vested in Manchester
University Press, copyright in individual chapters belongs to their
respective authors, and no chapter may be reproduced wholly or in part
without the express permission in writing of both author and publisher.

*Published by* Manchester University Press
Oxford Road, Manchester M13 9PL, UK
*and* Room 400, 175 Fifth Avenue,
New York, NY 10010, USA

*Distributed exclusively in the USA and Canada
by* St. Martin's Press, Inc.,
175 Fifth Avenue, New York, NY 10010, USA

*A catalogue record for this book is available from the British Library*

*Library of Congress cataloging in publication data*

What's new in economics? / edited by John Maloney,
    p.    cm.
    Includes index.
    ISBN 0–7190–3280–6. — ISBN 0–7190–3281–4 (pbk.)
    1. Economics.   I. Maloney, John, 1948–   .
    HB171.W537    1991
    330—dc20                                    91-18500

ISBN 0 7190 3280 6 *hardback*
    0 7190 3281 4 *paperback*

Printed in Great Britain
by Bell & Bain Limited, Glasgow

## ESSEX COUNTY LIBRARY

330 WHA.                               X FF90671

# Contents

*John Maloney*

# Introduction

Whatever it may say about the quality of contemporary research, it is a sad loss to economics undergraduates that much of the work appearing in the specialist journals is pitched above their level. As things stand, they have four options. They can try to catch the general drift of an advanced paper, look for the part where the author confesses his 'intuition', and familiarise themselves with its conclusions. They can content themselves with the theoretical advances of the day before yesterday, those which have filtered into a textbook after the double lag of absorption by the author and preparation by the publisher. They can resort to survey articles and literature reviews, though they will all too often find impenetrable mathematics replaced by a literary terseness so cryptic and concentrated as to send them scurrying back to the original with something like relief. Or they can simply avoid those journals, or those papers, which they find too difficult. Yet in doing so they will be avoiding nearly all of what is new and important in economics.

Most keen students in universities and polytechnics probably do some juggling between all four of these inadequate options. This situation is hardly satisfactory, and this book sets out to remedy it. Its purpose is to bring down to second- and third-year undergraduate level the most important recent advances in the main branches of economics. The aim is both to supplement the reading of students doing specialist options in particular fields, and to give a broad overview of recent developments for the more general reader, be he or she an undergraduate, a professional economist looking for a refresher course, or anyone interested in the subject who wants to raise the dividend from an existing investment in basic theory.

All the essays in this book reflect, to some degree, the reunification of macroeconomics and microeconomics after decades of division under opposing ideological regimes. The macro story has been the incorporation of once exogenous elements into the main body of theory. First the division of aggregate nominal demand between prices and output was endogenised by the Phillips curve. Then expectations were endogenised by the 'rational expectations' postulate that agents' forecasts be consistent with the predictions of the model itself. It could be debated at length whether the *objective* of the rational expectations revolution was to reintegrate macro- and microeconomics or whether it began as a limited attempt to tidy up an awkward corner of arbitrariness and perversity in the otherwise trim macroeconomic garden. Whatever the answer, the story of the rational expectations revolution and its apogee in new classical economics (rational expectations plus immediately clearing markets) is told here in the chapters by Michael Artis (macroeconomic theory) and Kent Matthews (macroeconomic policy). Both chapters also focus on the school which made most of the running in the 1980s, the rational expectations Keynesians (consistent expectations but sticky prices in the goods and labour markets). The spread of ideas to those in power has speeded up since Keynes derided the fixation of the great upon the work of defunct economists. Monetarism, in terms of its greatest influence within the economics profession, was a 1960s doctrine. Its dominance around the world peaked at the end of the 1970s. The new classical 'policy ineffectiveness proposition' was a child of the 1970s which came to power in the 1980s. People who are now expressing hopes, or fears, of a 'Keynesian revival' can only (unless hopelessly ill-informed) be talking of the application to policy in the 1990s of a theoretical development which has already occurred.

David Gowland's chapter on monetary economics charts the shift of emphasis from the crudities of the credit multiplier model (a 'troglodyte' which, in Dr Gowland's view, still infests too many textbooks) to the modern monetary economics which starts with the bank as a profit-maximising firm. Others have claimed that this revision has shifted the centre of gravity of monetary economics from the macro to the micro sphere. This semantic question does not detain Dr Gowland's chapter. Nor need heat be expended on whether international trade theory belongs to macroeconomics, microeconomics, both or neither. Keith Bain's chapter shows how, like monetary economics, much international trade theory is moving onto an imperfectly competitive basis. Governments can and do deploy trade policy in a strategic fashion which, as Dr Bain shows, makes the field a natural target for game theory. Here the link is with international monetary economics: see Lynne Evans' strong emphasis on the game-theoretic aspects of international policy coordination.

Game theory, in fact, has a part to play in most of the chapters in this book. One thinks of Eric Rasmussen's characterisation of game theory as the Argentina of economic analysis, econometrics being the Japan. (All four held the promise of enormous riches in the 1930s: but econometrics and Japan were to enjoy explosive growth while Argentina and game theory remained forlornly on the starting line.) If the present book is anything to go by, game theory has now exploded too, though to use this fact as the optimal forecast for the Argentine economy might be thought to show excessive contempt for econometrics.

Game theory, and imperfect competition as a rigorous domain where substantive predictions can be made and tested, are the themes of much of Roger Clarke's chapter on industrial economics. Readers will notice there is no chapter entitled 'microeconomic theory'. This was a deliberate editorial decision. The theory of the firm and the theory of rational choice under uncertainty do possess some overlap, as a reading of Adrian Darnell's and Roger Clarke's chapters will demonstrate. But modern microeconomics does exist in a somewhat bifurcated state: we have chosen to demarcate along the 'fault' and let the potential for bridge-building speak for itself.

Adrian Darnell's chapter is, among many other things, a pointer to the growth of experimental economics over the last few years. A fairly sure prediction is that lottery experiments, indifference maps and regret theory will continue to loom large on the microeconomic research agenda, and that new ways of either measuring utility or coping with the intrinsic difficulties of measuring utility will be eagerly sought after. Here welfare economics will have work to do though, as Peter Jackson's essay shows, welfare economists are on several frontiers at once. The Rawls vs. Nozick contest continues, albeit through the great men's respective seconds, over what is a just initial allocation of resources, what is a just distribution when trading has taken place, and to what extent the latter can claim sanction from the justice of the former.

Last but not least, Zafiris Tzannatos's chapter on labour economics shows how far the subject has gone since its early post-war days as a refuge from frontier theorising. Even now labour economics does not exactly revel in technique in the way that some other branches of the subject do. Like monetary economics, it continues to attract more than its share of economists in the noble tradition of Marshall and Keynes – who recognise that economics without rigour may be worse than no economics at all, but are prepared to admit that theorising for its own sake does not, in the social sciences, have the unexpected applications, delayed pay-offs and lucky by-products which so enviably resolve the natural scientist's internal tug of war between the pleasures of precision and the need to do good.

# 1

*Adrian Darnell*

# Decision-making
# under uncertainty

## Introduction

The microeconomic theory of consumer choice under conditions of certainty is well developed, and has not been the subject of any significant advances in recent years. However, the theory of consumer choice under conditions of uncertainty has developed rapidly over the last decade and, while there are excellent reviews of that literature,[1] a volume such as this would be deficient were it not to address this subject.

Uncertainty is pervasive in almost all decision-making environments; however, the traditional textbook presentation of microeconomic theory typically focuses upon the static theory from which the familiar results of demand and supply functions and cost and expenditure functions are derived. Most 'modern' approaches to microeconomic theory use the technique of duality, and, while this represents a marked change in analytical technique, it has not, of itself, generated any new results; rather, it has certainly provided a much neater and, in many instances, simpler analytic tool.[2]

## Choice under uncertainty

Uncertainty may be seen to be present in almost all decisions, though its role may range from the trivial to the very important. It is to be noted, for example, that, whatever the purchase, the consumer is always uncertain as to the *precise* quality of the good; very good information may exist but that information is always less than perfect. The impact of quality uncertainty is relatively trivial in, for example, the purchase of a pound of

1

apples, but is not at all trivial in the case of a second-hand car purchase where the size of the financial outlay is so much larger.[3] The role of uncertainty is equally important when issues such as search behaviour, investment, insurance, and bargaining are considered.[4]

In all the above examples the classical approach of the expected utility model has proved useful and the main body of this chapter is an exposition of that theory, and a discussion of its weaknesses and the subsequent theoretical developments. However, it is important first to discuss precisely what is meant by the expression 'uncertainty'.

## The nature of 'uncertainty'

At a tautological level, 'uncertainty' is a 'lack of certainty'; thus an 'uncertain' environment is one in which the individual decision-maker is not absolutely sure of the consequences of any particular action. In an uncertain world, individuals make decisions according to some behavioural rule but the outcome(s) of those decisions is (are) not known with certainty at the time the decision is taken. The outcome of any action is determined by which 'state of the world' actually pertains. Clearly, then, there is a time dimension to such a world, since decisions and outcomes are separated in time.

Decision-makers always choose their particular course of action given a relevant set of information and that information set concerns, of necessity, the future, which is inherently unknowable with certainty. Knight (1921) discussed the way in which individuals are able to gather and describe information of an uncertain future and distinguished between 'risk' and 'uncertainty': to Knight, 'risk' describes that situation in which the individual is able to attach 'degrees of belief', or 'probabilities', to all potential states of the world, and 'uncertainty' describes that situation in which the individual is unable to attach any such probabilities.

Almost all recent developments in the field of 'behaviour under uncertainty' have concentrated upon 'behaviour in Knightian risky situations' as opposed to 'behaviour in Knightian uncertain situations'. It is, nevertheless, helpful to discuss, albeit briefly, theories of behaviour under Knightian uncertainty.

## Decision-making under knightian uncertainty

There is no agreed 'best' procedural rule for decision-making in a world of pure uncertainty, though several rules have been proposed and examined (see, for example, Arrow, 1951). Suppose that there are $M$ mutually exclusive and exhaustive possible states of the world, denoted by the set $S = \{S_j; j = 1, 2, \ldots, M\}$; suppose further that the individual is faced with making one choice, $C_i$, of a set of $N$ possible choices, denoted by $C = \{C_i, i = 1, 2, \ldots, N\}$. One state of the world pertains, but, at the time of making the decision, that state is not known. Given choice $C_i$, and state of the world $S_j$, the individual is 'rewarded' with utility $U_{ij}$; this utility measure is actually a von Neumann–Morgenstern utility index, a concept which will be explained in more detail below. The following rules have been proposed:

### (1)   The Maximin rule

The maximin rule first identifies the worst possible outcome for each choice, and then picks that choice $C_i$ which maximises the minimum outcomes:

$$\underset{i}{\text{Max}} \underset{j}{\text{Min}}\, U_{ij} \text{ determines the optimal choice}$$

This is clearly a rule which applies to a pessimistic individual!

### (2)   The Maximax rule

In stark contrast to the pessimism of the minimax rule, the maximax approach first identifies the very best outcome for each choice, and then picks that choice which results in the greatest of the best outcomes:

$$\underset{i}{\text{Max}} \underset{j}{\text{Max}}\, U_{ij} \text{ determines the optimal choice}$$

The maximax rule applies to the optimists of society.

### (3)   The Hurwicz rule

The Hurwicz rule is a combination of (1) and (2), and is formally described as:

$$\underset{i}{\text{Max}} \left[ \alpha . \underset{j}{\text{Min}}\, U_{ij} + (1 - \alpha) . \underset{j}{\text{Max}}\, U_{ij} \right]$$

determines the optimal choice, where $\alpha$ is some positive fraction and describes the degree of pessimism utilised by the decision-maker: the greater is $\alpha$ the more pessimistic the decision-maker.

### (4) The Minimax regret rule

This concerns the extent of regret experienced by the individual who, having chosen $C_i$ irrevocably, then learns that the actual state of the world is $S_j$. In such a situation, the individual experiences regret, $R_{ij}$, given by:

$$R_{ij} = \max_k U_{kj} - U_{ij}$$

The minimax regret rule then chooses that action for which the maximum regret is minimized:

$$\underset{i}{\text{Min}} \underset{j}{\text{Max}} R_{ij} \text{ determines the optimal choice.}$$

This rule has a number of significant drawbacks, not least of which is that, by comparing the regrets, $R_{ij}$, it effectively disregards the level of utility. Although there are many objections to this rule, it is suggestive of an approach to risky decision-making which will be described later.

### (5) The principle of insufficient reason

This proposal effectively transforms Knightian uncertainty into Knightian risk: by arguing that in a world of pure uncertainty the individual cannot identify any one outcome (state of the world) as more likely than any other, it is therefore reasonable to assign equal probabilities to all outcomes. Thus, if there are $M$ possible states, each is assigned probability $(1/M)$, and the decision-making then proceeds as if in a risky world.

In any particular decision-making example, it is possible that there are as many 'best' choices as there are rules, and this only illustrates the very great uncertainty in a world of Knightian uncertainty. The situation of Knightian risky situations is less complex, and it is to this world that we now turn. To avoid semantic distinctions, in what follows a Knightian risky situation will also be described using the simple and common label of 'uncertainty'.

## Decision-making and the expected utility model

The classical expected utility model is set within the following framework: a decision-maker is faced with a set of *lotteries* and must choose amongst them. A lottery (or a prospect) is a list of consequences and an associated list of probabilities; the consequences are mutually exclusive and, for each given course of action, the consequences exhaust the possibilities.[5] One implication of this is that for each lottery the associated probabilities sum to unity. For the purposes of this exposition, the concept of probability will not be discussed; it may be thought of as a subjective degree of belief or as an 'objective' relative frequency concept.

The development of the axiomatic theory of consumer choice under uncertainty dates from the work of von Neumann and Morgenstern (1947 and 1953). Their approach shows that an individual whose preferences satisfy certain axioms (detailed below) will, in an uncertain environment, choose that course of action as though 'expected utility' were being maximised. Their axiomatic approach has been the subject of criticisms[6] and the outcome of that debate has been to identify that the crucial von Neumann–Morgenstern axioms are those of ordering, continuity and independence.

The individual is assumed to have preferences defined over all conceivable lotteries. The ordering axiom simply requires that preferences be complete, transitive and reflexive over the set of conceivable lotteries. The continuity axiom requires the following:

Suppose that $a$, $b$ and $c$ are any three lotteries such that $a$ is preferred to $b$ and $b$ is preferred to $c$; then there exists some positive fraction, $\theta$, such that the lottery which mixes $a$ and $c$ with probabilities $\theta$ and $1 - \theta$, $\theta a + (1 - \theta)c$, is indifferent to $b$.

The independence axiom may be formulated as follows:

Suppose that $a$ and $b$ are any two lotteries such that $a$ is preferred, or is indifferent, to $b$ (that is, $a$ is weakly preferred to $b$). Then, for any third lottery, $c$, the lottery given by $\theta a + (1 - \theta)c$ is weakly preferred to the lottery $\theta b + (1 - \theta)c$ for all $0 < \theta < 1$.

Given these axioms it is then possible to derive a function $U(.)$ which denotes the individual's preference ordering.

This axiomatic approach has not gone unchallenged (given the wide-ranging evidence which contradicts its predictions) and much recent work has sought to identify the potential revisions to those axioms which might improve the theoretical foundations of choice under uncertainty. Writing in 1980, Deaton and

Muellbauer, observed that: 'certainly, those who still do not accept the expected utility approach do not seem to be able to support their position with generally convincing objections to the axioms. Consequently, we are able to present . . . "the" theory of choice under uncertainty' (p. 381, original emphasis). Since 1980, the pace of development has been rapid, and the optimism expressed in the view that there exists 'the' theory would appear, with hindsight, to have been misplaced.

The earliest approach to decision-making under uncertainty, developed by mathematicians concerned with the theory of probability, was that if a particular lottery (gamble) has a set of consequences (pay-offs) given by $x = \{X_i; i = 1, 2, \ldots, n\}$ and an associated set of probabilities $\{p_i; i = 1, 2, \ldots, n\}$, then the relevant measure of the attractiveness of that gamble is given by its mathematical expectation: $\Sigma p_i x_i$. That this one statistic is not sufficient was demonstrated by the mathematician Nicholas Bernoulli in 1728 in an example now known as the St Petersburg Paradox. Though this is well known, it is repeated here.

Suppose there is a simple game involving two players, A and B; player A tosses a 'fair' coin repeatedly until a head occurs; if a head first occurs on the $r$'th throw then player A pays B the sum of £$(2)^{r-1}$; what is the largest sure gain that player B is willing to forgo in order to participate in one play of the game?

This game, with an unlimited number of throws, offers the pay-off £$(2)^{r-1}$ with probability $(1/2)^r$; player B is guaranteed to be paid some amount, and the expected value of the payment is given by $(1/2) + (1/2) + (1/2) + (1/2) + \ldots = \Sigma(1/2)$, which is not finite. On this analysis, a potential player B will prefer playing to any sure finite gain. However, very few individuals would actually be willing to pay other than a very modest 'entry fee' to play once. The large gains which might be enjoyed, and which contribute to the infinite expected value, have very small probability attached to them; the probability is concentrated on the small gains. If the game is modified and restricted to a finite number of throws, say $N$, player B can no longer be guaranteed to be paid anything, since there is now a probability of receiving nothing, given by:

$$1 - \sum_{r=1}^{N} (1/2)^r$$

The expected value of the game is given by $N/2$ but even this expected value may differ markedly from an individual's assessment of the worth of the gamble. As a concrete example, suppose $N = 16$: the expected value of the game is then finite and equal to £8, but the probability of winning less than the expected value or less is large, and equal to $1/2 + 1/4 + 1/8 + 1/16 +$ the probability of winning nothing; this is equal to 0.937515, and few individuals would be willing to stake £8 to play even this modified game once.[7]

The response to this 'paradox' was provided by Daniel Bernouilli (Nicholas Bernouilli's cousin), who proposed that the *expected utility of the game*, rather than the *expected value of the game*, was the determining statistic. They observed that a gain of, say, £4 is not necessarily 'worth' twice a gain of £2, but is, in fact, 'worth' rather less than twice that of £2. This imposes a utility function defined on money which is characterised by a diminishing marginal utility of money. On the basis of this approach, the relevant statistic with which to value a game is the expected utility, given by $\Sigma U(x_i) \cdot p_i$.

The *certainty equivalent* of any particular game may now be defined as that sure gain which yields the same utility as does the game (where the 'utility of a game' is evaluated as the expected utility). Thus, if an individual currently holds a stock of wealth given by $W$, then the certainty equivalent, $\tau$, of any particular game is computed by solving the following equation:

$$U(W + \tau) = \Sigma U(W + x_i)p_i.$$

As an example, suppose that the utility function is given by a simple logarithmic form $U(.) = \ln(.)$, and that $W = £100,000$; then the solution to this equation, for the Petersburg gamble, is $\tau = £9.28$; if the opening wealth stock is very much larger, say £1,000,000, then $\tau = £10.94$, and if the stock of wealth is very much smaller, say $W = £10,000$, then $\tau = £7.62$. The individual would clearly be prepared to pay up to the certainty equivalent in order to play the game, but would not be willing to pay more. It is to be noted that not all functions $U(.)$ can be used to 'solve' the St Petersburg Paradox; if $U(.)$ is characterised by an increasing marginal utility of money, then the certainty equivalent may be infinite. Clearly, then, the shape of the utility function is important, and it is to this that we now turn.

### *The shape of the utility function and attitudes towards risk*

Suppose that the utility function $U(.)$ is a monotonic increasing function and suppose the individual is offered a gamble which presents a $p_1:p_2$ chance of either $x_1$ or $x_2$ (where $x_1 < x_2$). Then the expected value of the gamble, $E(x)$, is given by $E(x) = x_1p_1 + x_2p_2$; $E(x)$ is the weighted average of $x_1$ and $x_2$ and lies, therefore, between them; the larger is $p_1$ (equivalently, the lower is $p_2$) the closer is $E(x)$ to $x_1$ (and vice versa). The expected utility of the gamble differs from the expected value of the gamble and is given by the weighted average of $U(x_1)$ and $U(x_2)$, with weights given by the probabilities (thus $E(U) = U(x_1)p_1 + U(x_2)p_2$); this is shown as $E(U)$. Clearly, given the monotonic increasing property of $U(.)$, the larger is $p_2$ the greater is $E(U)$; as $p_2$ increases so $p_1$ decreases, and this process may be seen as a transference of probability from a lower-valued to a higher-valued outcome, a process which produces a preferred gamble; this illustrates the phenomenon of stochastic dominance: if two gambles differ only in the probabilities attached to *given* pay-offs and gamble B may be obtained from gamble A by transferring probability from a lower to a higher outcome, then gamble B is preferred and is said to *stochastically dominate* gamble A; this is the analogue of 'more is better'. Stochastic dominance follows directly from the monotonic increasing property of the utility function.

$U(.)$, although it has been labelled a 'utility function' is not to be thought of as identical to the familiar utility function of consumer theory; in fact this function is quite distinct from the traditional function of consumer theory, and is accordingly given a unique label: $U(.)$ is a von Neumann–Morgenstern utility function and the most critical difference between it and the usual utility function is that $U(.)$ is a cardinal, not an ordinal, function. $U(.)$ is a monotonic increasing function, but the decisions which result from its use are invariant only to linear monotonic increasing transformations, that is transformations which retain the shape of the function.[8] The choices resultant from a von Neumann–Morgenstern utility function are sensitive to the *shape* of the function, and only a linear monotonic increasing function preserves shape. Figures 1.1 and 1.2 illustrate how the shape of the function determines behaviour:

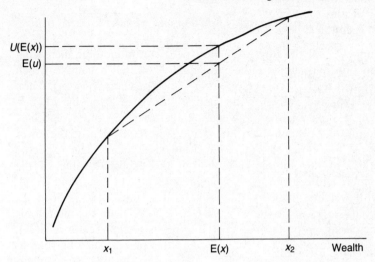

Fig 1.1   Concave von Neumann–Morgenstern utility function

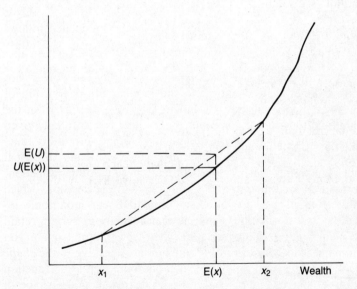

Fig 1.2   Convex von Neumann–Morgenstern utility function

From the above discussion it is important to distinguish between the expected utility of the gamble, $E(U)$, and the utility of the expected value of the gamble, $U(E(x))$. The very shape of the function dictates both the size and sign of this difference. The expected utility, $E(U)$, has already been defined and is shown on the diagrams; the utility of the expected value of the gamble, $U(E(x))$ is also shown on the diagrams. Clearly, the difference $U(E(x)) - E(U)$ may be positive or negative. If the utility function is a concave function (which requires a diminshing marginal utility of wealth), then this difference is necessarily positive, and the individual prefers the sure gain of $E(x)$ to the gamble (see Figure 1.1). Such an individual is described as *risk averse*. However, the size of this difference, which measures the extent of the individual's preference for the sure gain to the gamble, is critically dependent upon the shape of the function. From this analysis it is clear that a risk-averse individual will not participate in a 'fair game', defined as one for which the entry fee is equivalent to the expected value of the game, since the utility of the expected value (the entry fee) exceeds that of the gamble itself.

If the individual is *risk loving*, then the utility function is convex, which is equivalent to an increasing marginal utility of wealth (see Figure 1.2). For such an individual any gamble will be preferred to the sure gain of the expected pay-off, as is seen from the fact that the difference $U(E(x)) - E(U)$ is negative.

While the concavity (convexity) of the utility function illustrates risk aversion (loving), it does not provide an immediate measure of the degree of risk aversion; clearly the rate at which the marginal utility changes, that is the second derivative of $U$, $U''$, provides important information, but it is not a useful numerical indicator of the degree of aversion, since the utility function is only unique up to a monotonic increasing transformation, and, therefore, $U''$ is not uniquely defined for a given set of preferences; to avoid this, $U''$ can be 'normalised' by dividing by the first derivative, $U'(.)$, to obtain:

$$R_A(.) = -U''(.)/U'(.).$$

$R_A(.)$ is the Arrow–Pratt measure of absolute risk aversion.[9]

These concepts have proved useful in explaining why some individuals both gamble (that is, accept risk) and insure (that is, seek to avoid risk): Friedman and Savage (1948) demonstrated that an individual whose von Neumann–Morgenstern utility function is concave for low values of wealth, but convex at high levels, explains neatly why an individual both gambles and insures (see Figure 1.3).

If the individual begins with wealth $W^*$ and faces a 50:50 chance of losing $W^* - W_1$, the expected value of this prospect is $E_1$; clearly it pays the individual to forgo an insurance premium of up to $W^* - Z$ against the loss. Suppose also that for some very small fee, say $W^* - W_2$, the individual can buy a raffle ticket which will yield a gain of $W_3 - W^*$ with a very small probability. As drawn, the expected value of the gamble is given by $E_g$ and this would induce the purchase of the raffle ticket.[10]

### Linearity in probabilities

The standard expected utility hypothesis shares many assumptions with the traditional static, deterministic, choice theory. *Inter alia* it is assumed that the individual can place all the objects of choice in a preference ordering which is transitive, and that the chooser is capable of carrying out all the necessary mathematical opreations. Of the assumptions used in the expected utility

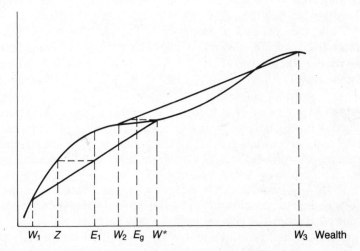

Fig 1.3 Concave and convex von Neumann–Morgenstern utility function

model, the strongest arises from the maximand: the preference function which is the key to choice under uncertainty is the expected utility, $\Sigma U(x_i)p_i$. It is to be noted that this maximand may be seen as a generalisation of the expected value of the outcomes given by $\Sigma x_i p_i$ since expected utility drops the assumption of linearity in the pay-offs $(x_i)$ but retains linearity in the probabilities $(p_i)$. Linearity in probabilities implies that, while any transfer of probability from one outcome to another affects the expected utility, the effect is independent of the initial probabilities and depends only on the outcomes.

The implications of the property of linearity in probabilities may be conveniently illustrated in the case of three outcomes. Let the outcomes be denoted by $x = \{x_i\}$ and the associated probabilities by $\{p_i\}$, where $\Sigma p_i = 1$. In the case $n = 3$ we have, then, that $p_1 + p_2 + p_3 = 1$; thus we may write one of the probabilities uniquely in terms of the other two: $p_2 = 1 - p_1 - p_3$. This device allows a diagrammatic representation in $(p_3, p_1)$ space, having eliminated the $p_2$ term. Since $0 \le p_i \le 1$ for each $i$, and $p_3 + p_1 \le 1$, the $(p_3, p_1)$ space is limited to the unit triangle, as drawn in Figures 1.4 and 1.5.[11] In order to draw the indifference curves in this space, consider a given set of pay-offs, $\{x_i\}$, for which $x_1 < x_2 < x_3$; the maximand, the expected utility, is given by:

$$E(U) = \sum U(x_i)p_i = U(x_1)p_1 + U(x_2).(1 - p_1 - p_3) + U(x_3)p_3.$$

An indifference curve is given by $E(U) = \beta$, some constant. Thus:

$$p_3[U(x_3) - U(x_2)] - p_1[U(x_2) - U(x_1)] + U(x_2) = \beta;$$

therefore,

$$p_3 = \{\beta - U(x_2)\}/[U(x_3) - U(x_2)]$$
$$+ p_1[U(x_2) - U(x_1)]/[U(x_3) - U(x_2)],$$

i.e. in $(p_3, p_1)$ space, the indifference curves defined over the probabilities, for given pay-offs, are all straight parallel lines with a common slope[12] given by $[U(x_2) - U(x_1)]/[U(x_3) - U(x_2)]$. Since it has been assumed that $x_1 < x_2 < x_3$, it follows that $U(x_1) < U(x_2) < U(x_3)$ and hence the slope is positive. To examine the direction of preference, consider the following:

$$E(U) = \sum U(x_i)p_i$$
$$= U(x_1)p_1 + U(x_2) \cdot (1 - p_1 - p_3) + U(x_3)p_3.$$

If $p_1$ is considered fixed, the greater is $p_3$ the lower is $p_2$, and, since this represents a reduction in the probability of a lower outcome $(x_2)$ and an increase in the probability of a higher outcome $(x_3)$, the transfer of probability results in a gamble which is preferred; equally, if $p_3$ is considered fixed, the greater is $p_2$ the lower is $p_1$, and, since this effectively reduces the probability of a lower outcome $(x_1)$ by transferring probability to a higher outcome $(x_2)$, this transfer of probability also results in a gamble which is preferred. This argument simply illustrates the concept of *stochastic dominance*, explained above. Thus, given the ordering $x_1 < x_2 < x_3$, as $p_1$ falls (for given $p_3$), so the lotteries become more preferred; similarly, as $p_3$ increases (for given $p_1$) the lotteries become more preferred. Hence, any movement of probabilities in the north-western direction are movements in the direction of increasing preference.

Thus the indifference curves are all parallel straight lines and the more north-westerly are the indifference curves the more preferred are those lotteries. Moreover, the common slope may be seen to reflect the individual's attitude to risk, and this is best illustrated by introducing the *iso-expected value lines*, which are given by the solution to the equation:

$$E(x) = \sum x_i p_i$$
$$= x_1 p_1 + x_2 \cdot (1 - p_1 - p_3) + x_3 p_3 = \alpha, \text{ some constant.}$$

From this equation we obtain:

$$p_3 = (\alpha - x_2)/[x_3 - x_2] + p_1[x_2 - x_1]/[x_3 - x_2];$$

i.e. in $(p_3, p_1)$ probability space, the iso-expected value lines are all parallel straight lines, with slope given by $[x_2 - x_1]/[x_3 - x_2]$.

The relative slope of the indifference curves and iso-expected value lines may be examined through the following expression. If the von Neumann–Morgenstern utility function is given by $U$, and $U$ is a concave function over the region of pay-offs considered here (that is, the individual is risk averse in the region $(x_1, x_3)$, then the slope of the utility function is a decreasing function:

$$[U(x_3) - U(x_2)]/[x_3 - x_2] < [U(x_2) - U(x_1)]/[x_2 - x_1],$$

which implies that:

$$[U(x_2) - U(x_1)]/[U(x_3) - U(x_2)] > [x_2 - x_1]/[x_3 - x_2].$$

The left-hand expression is seen as the common slope of the indifference curves, and the right-hand expression is seen as the common slope of the iso-expected value lines; thus the indifference curves are steeper than the iso-expected value lines for an individual who is risk averse over the outcomes $x_1$, $x_2$ and $x_3$ where $x_1 < x_2 < x_3$ (and the more risk averse the individual, the steeper are the indifference curves). For an individual who is risk loving over these outcomes the reverse is true, and, for a risk-neutral individual, the indifference curves and the iso-expected value lines have the same slope. These possibilities are given in Figures 1.4 and 1.5.

If a north-east movement along an iso-expected value line

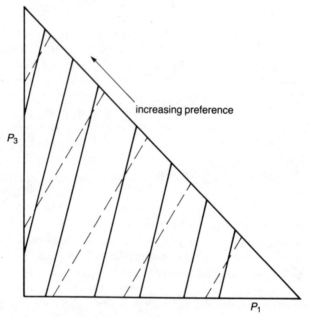

Dashed lines are iso-expected value lines
Solid lines are indifference curves

Fig 1.4   Indifference curves of a risk averter

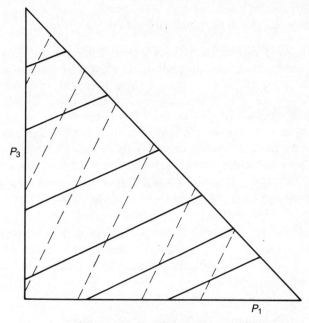

Dashed lines are iso-expected value lines
Solid lines are indifference curves

Fig 1.5   Indifference curves of a risk lover

is considered, this leaves the expected value of the gamble unchanged, by definition, but does so by increasing the probabilities of both $x_1$ and $x_3$ (the extreme outcomes) at the expense of the median pay-off. Such a reallocation of probability is a *mean-preserving spread* or a 'pure increase in risk' (see Rothschild and Stiglitz, 1970). Given a risk-averse individual, a north-east movement along an iso-expected value line will lead to a lower indifference curve, and a pure increase in risk is, thus, less preferred by the individual. For a risk lover, pure increases in risk are preferred.

Linearity in probabilities is a powerful prediction of the expected utility model, and constitutes a binding restriction on the individual's behaviour. Consider a given set of pay-offs $\{x_i, i = 1, 2, \ldots, n\}$ and two lotteries over the pay-offs, $P$ and $P^{**}$, where $P = \{p_i\}$ and $P^{**} = \{p_i^{**}\}$; consider the $q : 1 - q$

15

probability mix of $P$ and $P^{**}$, $Q$, where $Q = qP$ $(1 - q)P^{**}$
Linearity in the probabilities implies that:

$$E(U|Q) = \sum U(x_i)[qp_i + (1 - q)p_i^{**}]$$
$$= qE(U|P) + (1 - q)E(U|P^{**})$$

Thus, an expected utility maximiser will behave according to the *independence axiom*:

> if the lottery $P$ is preferred to $P_1$ (i.e. $E(U|P) > E(U|P_1)$), then the mixture $qP + (1 - q)P^*$ will be preferred to $qP_1 + (1 - q)P^*$ for all $0 < q < 1$ and all lotteries $P^*$.

To illustrate this axiom, suppose that lottery $P$ is a gain of £100,000 with certainty, and that $P_1$ is a lottery which yields £500,000 with probability 0.6 and £0 with probability 0.4; suppose further that $P^*$ is a simple lottery which yields £$x$ with certainty. A coin is tossed which, if it lands a head, yields the lottery $P^*$, and if it lands tails yields either lottery $P$ or lottery $P_1$; we thus have the following:

GAME 1:
coin lands tails:     £100,000 with certainty (lottery $P$)
coin lands heads:     £$x$ with certainty (lottery $P^*$).

GAME 2:
coin lands tails:     £500,000 with probability 0.6
                      and £0 with probability 0.4 (lottery $P_1$)
coin lands heads:     £$x$ with certainty (lottery $P^*$).

You are now asked, *before the coin is tossed*, which game you wish to play. If you prefer $P$ to $P_1$ then the axiom of independence says that Game 1 is preferred to Game 2, *whatever the amount* x; that is, your choice over the two games is independent of $x$. The reasoning is as follows: either the coin lands heads, in which case your choice becomes irrelevant, or it lands tails, in which case you are back to the original choice between $P$ and $P_1$. The introduction of the third lottery, $P^*$, is irrelevant to this choice, and therefore it is only 'rational' to prefer Game 1 since $P$ is preferred to $P_1$ when the choice is confined to them without the 'contamination' of $P^*$. Any other behaviour is deemed 'irrational', and in this sense the expected utility model provides not only description, but also prescription. It is important to note that this argument is itself independent of what kind of coin is used: the coin may be unbiased (so that the probability of a head is 0.5), or it may be biased so that we can say, generally, that the probability of a head is $q$, where $q$ is some positive fraction.

Tests of the expected utility-maximising model, through tests of the linearity prediction, are particularly easy to construct; most tests do, however, reject this restriction and hence form a rejection of the underlying model.

## Tests and violations of the linearity (independence) property

One of the earliest, and best-known, tests of linearity was performed by Allais (see Allais, 1953 and 1979). Consider further the coin-tossing example. Retaining the lotteries $P$, $P_1$ and $P^*$ as above, letting £$x$ equal £0, and defining the pay-off vector by $x = \{x_1; x_2; x_3\} = \{0; 100,000; 500,000\}$ expressed in pounds, the probability vectors are given by:

$$P: \{0 \quad 1 \quad 0\}$$
$$P_1: \{0.4 \quad 0 \quad 0.6\}$$
$$P^*: \{1 \quad 0 \quad 0\}.$$

Now introduce a fourth lottery $P^{**}$, where $P^{**}$ yields £100,000 with certainty so that the probability vector is given by:

$$P^{**}: \{0 \quad 1 \quad 0\}$$

Now imagine a biased coin-tossing game, where the probability of a head is 0.25; the coin-tossing generates a 'probability mixture' so that two games are now produced: in Game 1, if the coin lands tails you always win lottery $P^{**}$ and if it lands heads you obtain either lottery $P$ or $P_1$; in Game 2, if the coin lands tails you always win lottery $P^*$ and if it lands heads you again obtain either lottery $P$ or $P_1$. The probabilities are thus given by:

Game 1:
$Q_1$ £100,000 with cetainty
$\quad (0.25P + 0.75P^{**})$
$\quad$ versus
$Q_2$ £0 with 0.10 probability
$\quad$ £100,000 with 0.75 probability

      £500,000 with 0.15 probability
      $(0.25P_1 + 0.75P^{**})$

Game 2:
$Q_3$  £0.00 with probability 0.75
    £100,000 with probability 0.25
    $(0.25P + 0.75P^*)$
    versus
$Q_4$  £0.00 with probability 0.85
    £500,000 with probability 0.15
    $(0.25P_1 + 0.75P^*)$

*Before the coin is tossed*, you are asked, if playing Game 1, whether you prefer $Q_1$ to $Q_2$, and if playing Game 2, whether you prefer $Q_3$ to $Q_4$.

In the unit $(p_3, p_1)$ triangle, these four gambles form a parallelogram; thus, using the expected utility-maximisation model, if gamble $Q_1$ is preferred to $Q_2$, then the indifference curves are steep, as shown in Figure 1.6. Since the indifference curves are

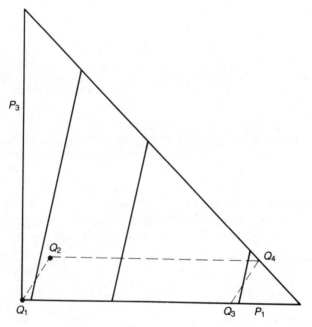

Fig. 1.6

parallel, it follows that gamble $Q_3$ will be preferred to $Q_4$; however, experimental work has identified systematic violations of this prediction: the modal preference (if not the majority) is for $Q_1$ in the first gamble, while it is for $Q_4$ in the second.[13] Such evidence clearly refutes the linearity in probabilities property of the expected utility model; this phenomenon is known as the 'Allais Paradox' and may be seen as a special case of the 'common consequence effect'.

A choice of $Q_1$ and $Q_4$ (or $Q_2$ and $Q_3$) implies indifference curves which are not parallel.[14] Indeed, for such choices to consistent with a preference ordering it is necessary to posit that the indifference curves actually 'fan out'. This phenomenon is known as the 'common consequence effect' since there is a common consequence of $P^{**}$ in $Q_1$ and $Q_2$ and of $P^*$ in $Q_3$ and $Q_4$. In terms of the simple coin-flip experiment, the common consequence effect suggests that the greater the gain in the event of a tail, the more risk averse do individuals become regarding the outcomes in the event of a head (see Figure 1.7). Thus, if, in the $Q_1$, $Q_2$ pair, the lottery $P^{**}$ involves very large outcomes, the individual may be unwilling to bear any further risk in the (unlucky) event that $P^{**}$ is not received and will then prefer the sure thing of lottery $P$ (£100,000) to the lottery of $P_1$ which involves a risk of gaining nothing (that is, the individual will choose $Q_1$ over $Q_2$); if in the $Q_3$, $Q_4$ pair, the lottery $P^*$ involves relatively low outcomes, then in the (lucky) event that $P^*$ is not received, the individual may be more willing to bear risk and thus prefer the lottery $P_1$ over the sure thing of $P$, namely a gain of £100,000 (that is, the individual will choose $Q_4$ over $Q_3$). What is important in this process is the individual's willingness to bear risk.

### The common ratio effect

Another class of systematic violations of the independence axiom arises in the following example, which illustrates the 'common ratio effect':

$S_1$: £X with probability $p$
    £0 with probability $1 - p$
versus
$S_2$: £Y with probability $q$
    £0 with probability $1 - q$

19

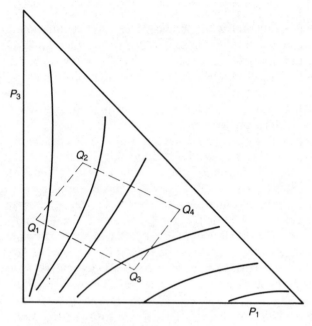

As drawn, $Q_1$ is preferred to $Q_2$
and $Q_4$ is preferred to $Q_3$.

Fig 1.7 Fanning-out of indifference curves, and the consequence effect

and
$S_3$:   £$X$ with probability $\theta p$
       £0 with probability $1 - \theta p$
versus
$S_4$:   £$Y$ with probability $\theta q$
       £0 with probability $1 - \theta q$

where $p > q$, $0 < X < Y$ and $0 \leq \theta \leq 1$.[15] Denoting the common
outcome vector by $\{x_1; x_2; x_3\} = \{0; X; Y\}$, the lotteries then
have the following probability structure:

|  | OUTCOMES | PROBABILITIES |
|---|---|---|
| $S_1$ | $\{0; X; Y\}$ | $\{1 - p; p; 0\}$ |
| $S_2$ | $\{0; X; Y\}$ | $\{1 - q; 0; q\}$ |
| $S_3$ | $\{0; X; Y\}$ | $\{1 - \theta p; \theta p; 0\}$ |
| $S_4$ | $\{0; X; Y\}$ | $\{1 - \theta q; 0; \theta q\}$ |

20

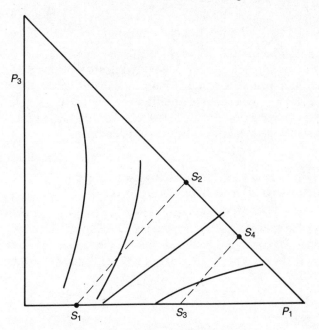

Fig 1.8  The common ratio effect

These may be plotted in the $(p_1, p_3)$ triangle as in Figure 1.8.

The expected utility model indicates that if the indifference curves are relatively steep then the choices will be for $S_1$ and $S_3$, or if the indifference curves are relatively flat then the choices will be for $S_2$ and $S_4$. However, experimental work has discovered the tendency for individuals to choose $S_1$ and $S_4$, which is yet further evidence that the indifference curves are not linear, but rather fan out. Additional evidence on this issue has also been collated, replacing the gains of £$X$ and £$Y$ with losses of identical magnitude.[16] Defining the common outcome vector by $\{x_1; x_2; x_3\} = \{-Y; -X; 0\}$ (in order to preserve the ranking of the elements of the outcome vector), the probability structure is then:

```
       OUTCOMES      PROBABILITIES
S₁  {-Y; -X; 0}    {0; p; 1 - p}
S₂  {-Y; -X; 0}    {q; 0; 1 - q}
```

21

$S_3$ $\{-Y; -X; 0\}$ $\{0; \theta p; 1 - \theta p\}$
$S_4$ $\{-Y; -X; 0\}$ $\{\theta q; 0; 1 - \theta q\}$

These may be plotted in the $(p_1, p_3)$ triangle as in Figure 1.9.

The typical choice is for $S_2$ and $S_3$, again providing evidence for indifference curves which fan out. Given the wealth of evidence against linear parallel indifference curves, this chapter now turns to a discussion of the characteristics of models which have been developed in response to these phenomena.

## Preferences giving rise to non-linear or non-parallel indifference curves[17]

The violations of the independence axiom illustrated above all suggest a re-working of the axioms whereby the ordering and continuity axioms are retained, but the independence axiom is rejected. In the $(p_3, p_1)$ triangle there will then be a family of

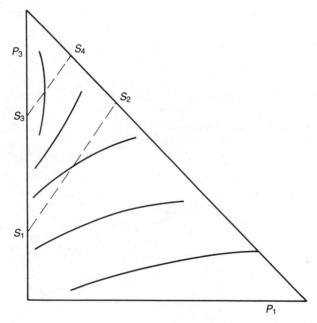

Fig 1.9   The common ratio effect and negative pay-offs

indifference curves, but these will be neither straight nor parallel, necessarily. From the first diagram of violation of the independence axiom (Figure 1.7), the observed choices of $Q_1$ and $Q_4$ demand that $Q_1$ lies on a higher indifference curve than does $Q_2$ and that $Q_4$ lies on a higher indifference curve than does $Q_3$; this requires that the indifference curves *relevant to the choices here examined* fan out and are not parallel. It should be stressed that the fanning out of indifference curves does not imply that the independence axiom is *always* violated; rather, what the fanning out hypothesis suggests is *a tendency for the independence axiom to be violated in a well-defined direction*. It may be seen that the fanning out of indifference curves is sufficient to provide an explanation for the common consequence and both forms of the common ratio effect. If indifference curves do fan out, what requirements are placed upon them?

### The properties of fanning indifference curves

Recalling the original discussion of the $(p_3, p_1)$ triangle, it was noted there that movements in the north-westerly direction reflected a shift of probability from a low outcome $(x_1)$ to a higher outcome $(x_3)$, and through the requirement of stochastic dominance were necessarily movements in a preferred direction. Thus the requirement that the direction of preference is in the north-westerly direction is merely a consequence of the stochastic dominance requirement. Given any lottery in the triangle, it is stochastically dominated by lotteries in the north-westerly direction, while it itself dominates lotteries in the south-easterly direction; hence, the areas in which indifferent lotteries lie must be in the south-west and north-east directions; thus an immediate corollary of stochastic dominance is that the indifference curves slope upwards from the south-west to the north-east.

This may be explained using the concept of the local utility function. Suppose that pay-offs (consequences) are monetary, and denoted by the $n$-dimensional vector $x$; then the set of all possible consequences is simply some range of monetary values. Let the set of all possible lotteries over the pay-off vector $x$ be denoted by $P = (p_1, p_2, \ldots, p_n)$; it is then possible to construct the local utility function, denoted by $U(x, P)$, which describes the utility index of a given set of consequences in a small neighbourhood around a given lottery. The standard expected utility model may be written using the preference function $V(P) = \Sigma U(x_i)p_i$; written in this form, 'the utility of $x_i$, $U(x_i)$' may be seen as $\partial V/\partial p_i$,[18] the partial derivative of $V(P)$ with respect to $p_i$. The familiar results of the expected utility model may then be cast in the following terms:

> *Stochastic dominance preference*: $V(P)$ exhibits global stochastic dominance preference if and only if the coefficients on the $p_i$ are increasing functions of $x_i$; that is, global stochastic dominance implies and is implied by a monotonic increasing function $U(.)$.
> *Risk aversion*: $V(P)$ exhibits global risk aversion if and only if the coefficients on the $p_i$ are concave in $x_i$; that is, global risk aversion implies and is implied by the concavity of the monotonic increasing function $U(.)$.
> *Comparative risk aversion*: $V^*(P) = \Sigma U^*(x_i)p_i$ is at least as risk averse as $V(P)$ if and only if the coefficients on $p_i$ in $V^*(.)$ are at least as concave as the coefficients on $p_i$ in $V(.)$.

Now, for a given set of consequences, $x$, consider the more general preference function $V(P) = f(x, P)$ where $f$ is not linear in probabilities but is differentiable; thus $V(P)$ is a preference function which denies linear indifference curves and explicitly allows fanning-out. The partial derivative of $f$ with respect to $p_i$, $\partial f/\partial p_i$, is denoted by $f_i$ and has, as arguments, the consequences $x$ and the lottery $P$.

Taking a total derivative:[18]

$$dV = \sum f_i . dp_i.$$

Suppose that the vector of consequences is so ordered that $x_i < x_{i+1}$ for all $i = 1, 2, \ldots, n - 1$. Now let the probability $p_i$ fall by $dp_i$ and $p_{i+1}$ increase by an identical amount, all other probabilities remain constant:

$$dV = f_i . dp_i + f_{i+1} . dp_{i+1};$$

but

$$-dp_i = dp_{i+1} > 0$$

hence

$$dV = (f_{i+1} - f_i) . dp_{i+1}$$

and so $dV > 0$ if and only if $(f_{i+1} - f_i) > 0$.

Since this reallocation of probability results in a stochastically dominating lottery, the preference function $V(P)$ exhibits stochastic dominance if and only if its derivatives $f_i$ are increasing in $x_i$.

Now consider the following:

$$dV = \sum f_i \cdot dp_i.$$

Along an indifference curve, $dV = 0$. Suppose that only the probabilities on the consequences $x_{i-1}$, $x_i$ and $x_{i+1}$ change, and do so as a mean preserving reallocation of probabilities:

$$x_{i-1} \cdot dp_{i-1} + x_i \cdot dp_i + x_{i+1} \cdot dp_{i+1} = 0;$$

since $dp_{i-1} + dp_i + dp_{i+1} = 0$, the above equation may be written as:

$$(x_{i-1} - x_i) \cdot dp_{i-1} + (x_{i+1} - x_i) \cdot dp_{i+1} + x_i = 0;$$

similarly:

$$dV = (f_{i-1} - f_i) \cdot dp_{i-1} + (f_{i+1} - f_i) \cdot dp_{i+1} + x_i = 0.$$

Thus the slope of the iso-expected value line in $(p_{i+1}, p_{i-1})$ space is given by:

$$(x_i - x_{i-1})/(x_{i+1} - x_i)$$

and the slope of the indifference curve is given by:

$$(f_i - f_{i-1})/(f_{i+1} - f_i).$$

If the slope of the indifference curve is greater than that of the iso-expected value line, a mean preserving reallocation of probabilities results in lower utility; such preferences reflect local risk aversion and this is illustrated in Figure 1.10.

Thus the individual is made worse off after a mean preserving reallocation of probabilities if and only if:

$$(f_i - f_{i-1})/(f_{i+1} - f_i) > (x_i - x_{i-1})/(x_{i+1} - x_i)$$

i.e. if and only if:

$$(f_i - f_{i-1})/(x_i - x_{i-1}) > (f_{i+1} - f_i)/(x_{i+1} - x_i).$$

That is, the preference function $V(P)$ exhibits risk aversion if and only if the derivatives $f_i$ are concave in $x_i$.

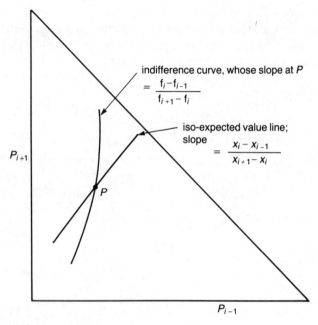

Fig. 1.10

The above two results are provided in order to demonstrate what properties are required of the derivatives of a general, non-linear preference function (which gives rise to the fanning-out of indifference curves) to ensure stochastic dominance preference and risk aversion.[19] The results only hold, of course, for infinitesimal changes in the probabilities and are thus *local* to a given lottery; the standard techniques of calculus may be used to extend these local results to global results, but this is not of importance here.

Given this simple correspondence between the coefficients $\{U(x_i)\}$ of an expected utility preference function and the derivatives, $f_i$, of the more general preference function $V(P)$, the derivatives $f_i$ are called 'local von Neumann–Morgenstern utility indices'.

The concept of the local von Neumann–Morgenstern utility function has allowed the retention of much of the tradition of the expected utility-maximisation model and this flexible form approach has proved most useful in extending the analysis of choice under uncertainty to non-expected utility models.[20] It has proved especially useful in the analysis of the 'fanning-out' of indifference curves, but it has not proved capable of providing an analysis of 'preference reversal phenomena'.

## Preference reversal

The preference reversal phenomenon was first reported in 1971 by psychologists (see Lichtenstein and Slovic, 1971); the phenomenon concerns bets of the form;

$P$:  £$X$ with probability $p$
    £$x$ with probability $1 - p$
versus
£:  £$Y$ with probability $q$
    £$y$ with probability $1 - q$

The structure of the bets is $X > x$ and $Y > y$, $p > q$ and $Y > X$. The former bet is known as the $P$(robability)-bet and the latter is the £-bet since in the former the probability of winning the higher return is greater, while in the latter there is the possibility of the highest win ($Y$). Whether the expected utility model or a non-expected utility model is used, the prediction is that the individual will consistently choose that bet which has the higher certainty equivalent. However, the evidence first presented in 1971 demonstrated that individuals systematically violate this prediction; later studies confirmed this violation, even in work by economists who sought to deny the existence of this phenomenon (see Grether and Plott, 1979).

Let the certainty equivalent of the $P$-bet be $CEP$, while that of the £-bet be $CE£$; then the preference reversal phenomenon occurs when $CE£ > CEP$ *but* the $P$-bet is strictly preferred to the £-bet. Such preferences are cyclic: the individual is indifferent between the £-bet and the sure amount $CE£$, $CE£$ is preferred to $CEP$ and the individual is indifferent between $CEP$ and the $P$-bet and so transitivity of preferences would dictate that the £-bet is preferred to the $P$-bet, yet individuals actually prefer the $P$-bet! In response to this phenomenon, economists have developed models of choice under uncertainty which admit intransitivity;

the major responses utilise the concepts of 'disappointment' or 'regret':[21] once some uncertainty has been resolved, the individual actually feels worse off if the outcome is worse than that expected, and experiences elation if the outcome is better than expected.

Consider an uncertain event in which the outcome is either a gain of £100,000, with probability 0.95, or nothing, with probability 0.05; in the event of the 5 per cent chance, the individual feels bitterly disappointed. In contrast, suppose there were a 0.95 probability of losing £100,000 and a 0.05 probability of neither losing nor gaining anything; then, were the 5 per cent chance to occur, the individual would feel highly elated. In comparing the two situations, the 0.05 chance results in the *status quo* for the individual – there is no change in net wealth in either situation – yet the implications for feelings of well-being are quite different.

Suppose attention is confined to a simple pairwise choice, and the consequence is either $x$ or $y$; suppose that $x$ is the outcome; then $r(x, y)$, if positive, denotes the level of satisfaction (rejoice) perceived when the outcome is $x$ and the alternative choice would have resulted in $y$; if $r(x, y)$ is negative then it measures the regret at outcome $x$ when the alternative choice would have resulted in $y$. Suppose the choice is defined over a common outcome set $x = \{x_1, x_2, \ldots, x_n\}$ and the choice concerns two statistically independent lotteries, $P = \{p_1, p_2, \ldots, p_n\}$ and $Q = \{q_1, q_2, \ldots, q_n\}$; then, in choosing $P$, the probability that $x_i$ is received *and* $x_j$ *is not received* is given by the product of probabilities $p_i \cdot q_j$ (this follows from the assumption that the lotteries are statistically independent). Then the expected satisfaction is given by the double sum:

$$\sum\sum p_i \cdot q_j \cdot r(x_i, x_j).$$

Assuming that choice is determined by minimising expected regret (equivalently, by maximising expected satisfaction), $P$ will be chosen if

$$\sum\sum p_i \cdot q_j \cdot r(x_i, x_j) > \sum\sum p_i \cdot q_j \cdot r(x_j, x_i)$$

and $Q$ will be chosen otherwise.

Defining the function $\Phi(x_i, x_j) = r(x_i, x_j) - r(x_j, x_i)$, the decision rule may be stated as:

$$P \text{ is chosen if } \sum\sum p_i \cdot q_j \cdot \Phi(x_i, x_j) > 0$$

and Q is chosen otherwise.

It is to be noted that, by definition:

$$\Phi(x_i, x_i) = 0, \text{ and}$$
$$\Phi(x_i, x_j) = -\Phi(x_j, x_i);$$

that is, $\Phi$ is a skew-symmetric function. Note that it is not necessary to assume that the satisfaction (regret) function $r(x_i, x_j)$ is itself skew-symmetric.

As a special case, consider the particular form:

$$r(x_i, x_j) = U(x_i);$$

then

$$\Phi(x_i, x_j) = U(x_i) - U(x_j)$$

then $P$ is chosen if and only if:

$$\sum\sum p_i . q_j . \Phi(x_i, x_j) > 0;$$

i.e. if and only if $\Sigma\Sigma p_i . q_j[U(x_i) - U(x_j)] > 0$.

Since $\Sigma p_i = 1 = \Sigma q_j$, we have:

$P$ is chosen if and only if:

$$\sum p_i U(x_i) - \sum q_j U(x_j) > 0,$$

which is, of course, the decision rule which arises from the expected utility model. Using a general form for the regret/ rejoice function, $r$, leads, however, to a preference function which does not, necessarily, exhibit transitivity of preferences.

Suppose that attention is confined to a simple outcome set of only three elements: $x = \{x_1, x_2, x_3\}$. Consider the statistically independent lotteries $P = \{p_1, p_2, p_3\}$ and $Q = \{q_1, q_2, q_3\}$; then the individual is indifferent between $P$ and $Q$ if and only if:

$$\sum\sum p_i . q_j \Phi(x_i, x_j) = 0.$$

Expanding this expression, using the properties $\Phi(x_i, x_j) = -\Phi(x_j, x_i)$ and $\Phi(x_i, x_i) = 0$, we have the following:

$$q_1[(1 - p_3)\Phi(x_2, x_1) + p_3(\Phi(x_3, x_1) - \Phi(x_3, x_2))]$$
$$- q_3[(1 - p_1)\Phi(x_3, x_2) + p_1(\Phi(x_3, x_1) - \Phi(x_2, x_1))]$$
$$- [p_1\Phi(x_2, x_1) - p_3\Phi(x_3, x_2)]$$
$$= 0.$$

29

Thus, considering a given lottery $P$, and fixing the outcome set, $x$, the above equation defines all those lotteries $Q$ to which $P$ is indifferent. Since $P$ and $x$ are both fixed, the above may be written simply as:

$$a . q_1 + b . q_2 + c = 0;$$

where $a$, $b$, and $c$ are fixed parameters determined by $P$ and $x$; this equation clearly defines a straight line; thus the lotteries which are indifferent to $P$ lie on a straight line through $P$, the slope of which is determined by $P$ and $x$. If such indifference curves are constructed for all lotteries, $P$, then it may be shown that no three such lines are linearly independent; thus *either* the indifference curves intersect at some point, *or* all indifference curves are parallel lines (the limiting case illustrated above when, as a special case of regret theory, the model is equivalent to the more traditional expected utility model). In the case that the lines intersect at a point, two cases are to be considered: (i) the point of intersection lies within the probability triangle and (ii) the point of intersection lies outside the triangle.

If the point lies within the probability triangle, then Figure 1.11 reflects this. The indifference curve through $P$ divides the triangle into those lotteries preferred to $P$ and those to which $P$ is preferred. Suppose the preference direction is north-westerly as shown; then the lottery $P^*$ is preferred to $p$. Suppose that the indifference curve through $P^*$ is downward sloping; hence the indifference curve through $P^*$ must have a north-easterly direction of preference as shown. If $P^{**}$ is now introduced as a lottery preferred to $P^*$, it must lie north-east of the indifference curve through $P^*$ and have an indifference curve which intersects with the indifference curves associated with both $P$ and $P^*$. As drawn, the direction of preference associated with the indifference curve of $P^{**}$ must be south-easterly and so we have the following:

$P^{**}$ is preferred to $P^*$
$P^*$ is preferred to $P$
$P$ is preferred to $P^{**}$.

Thus, in the case of the intersection lying within the triangle, cyclic non-transitive behaviour is admitted. However, on closer examination, this possibility may be seen as unlikely, in the case of consequences with only three elements, if the assumption of *increasingness* is adopted.

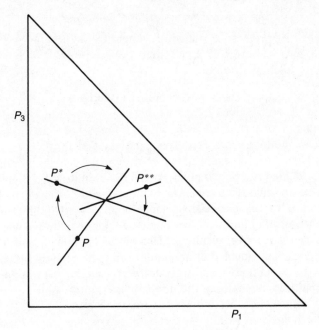

Fig 1.11   Cyclic behaviour and expected regret

For the indifference curves to intersect within the triangle, it must be the case that not all indifference curves have the same slope (that is, intransitive behaviour is only admitted when the preference function fails to exhibit stochastic dominance). The condition for a positive slope is that:

$$\frac{[(1 - p_3)\Phi(x_2, x_1) + p_3(\Phi(x_3, x_1) - \Phi(x_3, x_2))]}{[(1 - p_1)\Phi(x_3, x_2) + p_1(\Phi(x_3, x_1) - \Phi(x_2, x_1))]} > 0.$$

Now the triangle probability diagram is drawn with an ordered outcome vector, so that $x_1 < x_2 < x_3$, and let us suppose that the individual has a complete and transitive ordering over the elements of $x$ when they are available with certainty such that $x_i$ is preferred to $x_{i-1}$ for $i = 2$ and 3. Thus it is the case that the individual enjoys satisfaction when $x_i$ is received and $x_{i-1}$ ($<x_i$) would have been available had the alternative choice been made; similarly, the individual regrets the choice when the lower payoff, $x_{i-1}$, is received when $x_i$ was to be had. Thus we may say that $r(x_i, x_{i-1}) > 0$ and $r(x_{i-1}, x_i) < 0$; thus:

31

$$\Phi(x_i, x_{i-1}) = r(x_i, x_{i-1}) - r(x_{i-1}, x_i) > 0.$$

Hence the preference function generates indifference curves which have a positive slope (that is, the preference function exhibits stochastic dominance) if:

$$\Phi(x_3, x_1) - \Phi(x_3, x_2) > 0$$

and

$$\Phi(x_3, x_1) - \Phi(x_2, x_1) > 0.$$

These inequalities may be seen to rest upon an intuitively appealing assumption, the assumption of *increasingness*: the satisfaction of receiving $x_i$ and not receiving $x_j$ is the greater the greater is the satisfaction of $x_i$ (with certainty) and the lower is the satisfaction of receiving $x_j$ (with certainty). Thus $\Phi(x_i, x_k) > \Phi(x_j, x_k)$ if and only if the individual prefers $x_i$ to $x_j$ (and vice versa). From this assumption we may conclude that $\Phi(x_3, x_1) - \Phi(x_2, x_1) > 0$; manipulating the assumption, the following is derived:

if and only if $x_i$ is preferred to $x_j$:

$$\Phi(x_i, x_k) > \Phi(x_j, x_k)$$
$$-\Phi(x_i, x_k) < -\Phi(x_j, x_k)$$
$$\Phi(x_k, x_i) > \Phi(x_k, x_j)$$

Hence $\Phi(x_3, x_1) > \Phi(x_3, x_2)$; thus the preference function of expected regret exhibits stochastic dominance given the intuitively appealing assumption of increasingness. If this assumption holds, regret theory is unable to offer any explanation of preference reversal in the case of three consequences; however, if four or more consequences are considered, then preference reversal can arise, even when there is a transitive ordering over the pure consequences (that is, over the consequences if they are received with certainty).

Nevertheless, even in the simple case of only three consequences when regret theory does not indicate preference reversal, it then generates indifference curves in $(p_3, p_1)$ space which fan out when the point of intersection lies outside the triangle to the south-west; the requirement is that the slope of the indifference curves is an increasing function of $p_3$, and the slope of the indifference curve is given by:

$$\frac{dq_3}{dq_1} = \frac{[(1 - p_3)\Phi(x_2, x_1) + p_3(\Phi(x_3, x_1) - \Phi(x_3, x_2))]}{[(1 - p_1)\Phi(x_3, x_2) + p_1(\Phi(x_3, x_1) - \Phi(x_2, x_1))]} > 0$$

Hence the derivative of this with respect to $p_3$ is given by:

$$\frac{\Phi(x_3, x_1) - \Phi(x_3, x_2) - \Phi(x_2, x_1)}{[(1 - p_1)\Phi(x_3, x_2) + p_1(\Phi(x_3, x_1) - \Phi(x_2, x_1))]}.$$

Given the assumption of increasingness, the denominator is positive; hence this derivative is positive if $\Phi(x_3, x_1) - \Phi(x_3, x_2) - \Phi(x_2, x_1) > 0$. If this condition holds, then the slope of the indifference curves increases as $p_3$ increases; that is, the curves fan out.

Thus, in the case of three consequences, regret theory *either* is capable of indicating preference reversal *or* generates indifference curves which fan out.

## Conclusions

The expected utility model for choice under uncertainty, developed from the work of von Neumann and Morgenstern, has been shown to be in conflict with much experimental evidence; that evidence has brought to light the phenomena of the common consequence effect, the common ratio effect and preference reversal. Expected utility predicts that such phenomena do not exist, and in response to this weakness the traditional model has been developed during the 1980s. Skew-symmetric bilinear utility theory, of which regret theory is an example, represents one of the more successful developments of the standard expected utility model; it is capable of generating the common consequence effect, the common ratio effect, the preference reversal phenomenon and other aspects of choice over lotteries. However, real-world environments within which agents face uncertainty do not, typically, present themselves in the simple, clean, fashion of the experiments upon which the criticisms of the expected utility model are based. The laboratory experimental work which gave rise to observations which contradicted expected utility theory is incontrovertible, but questions of the relevance of such phenomena and the relevance and applicability of the developments of expected utility to choice under uncertainty in the real world remain.

The expected utility model has proved most useful in analysing situations within both micro- and macroeconomic theory where uncertainty is of importance; these applications include the analysis of search behaviour, investment strategies, portfolio purchase, insurance and bargaining. The question of the relevance and applicability of the non-expected utility models of choice under uncertainty can only be judged in the context of its success (or otherwise) of providing meaningful analyses of precisely those situations where expected utility has proved itself. That work is yet to be carried out, but its foundation lies in the observations of lottery choice which refute the expected utility model and in the subsequent developments of that model; the refutations of the traditional model have been explained in this chapter, and the most promising development, that of skew- symmetric bilinear (SSB) utility theory, has been introduced. This is a fertile and rapidly changing area of economics; the dominant position of the expected utility model is being seriously questioned, and the proponents of non-expected utility models are continually refining their alternative approach.

For the non-expected utility research programme to dominate the expected utility model, it must be shown that the non-expected utility models are not merely a tautological response to experimental, laboratory, evidence regarding the choice over lotteries. To achieve this it is vital that future research demonstrates that the non-expected utility models:

(i) are not refuted by empirical observations and specifically are not refuted by those observations which refute the expected utility models;

(ii) are of use in theoretical examinations of familiar areas of economic enquiry – search theory, investment, etc. – which have already been successfully examined using expected utility models;

(iii) are immune to the charge that agents who behave according to non-expected utility model are, in a dynamic sense, inconsistent or 'irrational'.[22]

To the extent that this work is not complete, and some of it is at a very early stage, the 'jury is still hearing the evidence on non-expected utility theory'; it will be some time before a definitive verdict is available regarding the theory of choice under uncertainty.

## Notes

1 See, for example, Shoemaker (1982), Sugden (1986) and Machina (1987).

2 See, for example, the presentations of microeconomic theory using duality in Silberberg (1978) and Birchenhall and Grout (1984) and contrast that approach with the more traditional exposition as presented, for example, by Intrilligator (1971).

3 For an analysis of quality uncertainty and a market characterised asymmetric information, such as that for second-hand cars, see Akerlof (1970).

4 For a survey of individual search behaviour, see McKenna (1986); for an introduction to investment behaviour under uncertainty, see, for example, Hey (1981); for a survey of the recent literature on insurance, see Rees (1989), and for a survey of the recent literature on wage bargaining, see Lyons and Varoufakis (1989).

5 It is possible that a consequence is itself a lottery.

6 Some of which arise from a Knightian distinction between 'risk' and 'uncertainty'.

7 If $N = 8$, then the expected value is £4, but the probability of winning £4 or less is equal to 0.878906 which will, of itself, deter many individuals from staking the expected value as an entry fee. In this example, the probability of winning nothing is given by 0.003906; in the case in the text where $N = 16$, the probability of winning nothing is much smaller, and given by 0.000015.

8 This is in contrast to the static, deterministic, theory of the consumer, where any monotonic increasing transformation of the function leaves the final choices (the demand functions) unchanged.

9 For further details of measures of risk aversion, see, for example, Hey (1981), pp. 20–5.

10 For further details of this, see, for example, Chacholiades (1986), pp. 165–6.

11 The 'triangle diagram' is a most valuable device; Sugden (1986) attributes it to Machina, although Machina (1987) states that versions of it date from Marschak (1950).

12 It should be noted that the slope is invariant to a linear monotonic increasing transformation of the utility function, but not to a general monotonic increasing transformation.

13 See, for example, Allais (1953), Morrison (1967), Raiffa (1968) and Slovic and Tversky (1974).

**14** Research has shown that there is a marked tendency for individuals to choose $Q_1$ in the first pair, and $Q_4$ in the second; see, for example, MacCrimmon (1968), MacCrimmon and Larson (1979), Kahneman and Tversky (1979) and Chew and Waller (1986).

**15** The 'common ratio' label arises from the common ratio of Prob $(X)$ : Prob $(Y) = p : q$. This effect, by setting $p = 1$, has as a special case the certainty effect of Kahneman and Tversky (1979).

**16** See Kahneman and Tversky (1979).

**17** See, for examples of non-expected utility models, Edwards (1955), Karmarker (1978), Kahneman and Tversky (1979), Machina (1982), Chew (1983), Fishburn (1983) and Quiggin (1982); for discussion of these models, see the reviews of MacCrimmon and Larson (1979), Machina (1983), Sugden (1986), Weber and Camerer (1987) and Fishburn (1988).

**18** The terms in $dx_i$ do not appear since we are here working with a fixed set of consequences.

**19** The property of comparative risk aversion is translated into the property that $V^*(P)$ is at least as risk averse as $V(P)$ if and only if the partial derivatives with respect to $p_i$ of $V^*(.)$ are at least as concave as the corresponding derivatives of $V(.)$.

**20** See, for example, Machina (1982), Chew (1983), Fishburn (1984), Epstein (1985), Allen (1987) and Chew, Karni and Safra (1987).

**21** The major examples of this approach are to be found in Bell (1982 and 1985), Fishburn (1982) and Loomes and Sugden (1982).

**22** This is the subject of the recent paper by Machina (1989).

# References

Akerlof, G. A. (1970), 'The market for "lemons": quality uncertainty and the market mechanism', *Quarterly Journal of Economics*, 84, pp. 488–500.

Allais, M. (1953), 'Le comportement de l'homme rationel devant le risque, critique des postulates et axiomes de l'école Americaine', *Econometrica*, 21, pp. 503–46.

Allais, M. (1979), 'The foundations of a positive theory of choice involving risk and a criticism of the postulates and axioms of the American school', in M. Allais and O. Hagen (eds), *Expected Utility Hypotheses and the Allais Paradox*, Dordrecht: Reidel.

Allen, B. (1987), 'Smooth preferences and the approximate expected utility hypothesis', *Journal of Economic Theory*, 41, pp. 340–55.

Arrow, K. J. (1951), 'Alternative approaches to the theory of choice in risk-taking situations', *Econometrica*, 19, pp. 404–37.

Bell, D. E. (1982), 'Regret in decision making under uncertainty', *Operations Research*, 30, pp. 961–81.

Bell, D. E. (1985), 'Disappointment in decision making under uncertainty', *Operations Research*, 33, pp. 1–27.

Birchenhall, C. and Grout, P. (1984), *Mathematics for Modern Economics*, Deddington: Philip Allan.

Chacholiades, M. (1986), *Microeconomics*, New York: Macmillan.

Chew, S. H. (1983), 'A generalization of the quasilinear mean with applications to the measurement of income inequality and the Allais paradox', *Econometrica*, 51, pp. 1065–92.

Chew, S. H., Karni, E. and Safra, Z. (1987), 'Risk aversion in the theory of expected utility with rank dependent probabilities', *Journal of Economic Theory*, 42, pp. 370–81.

Chew, S. H. and Waller, W. (1986), 'Empirical tests of weighted utility theory', *Journal of Mathematical Psychology*, 30, pp. 55–72.

Deaton, A. and Muellbauer, J. (1980), *Economics and Consumer Behavior*. Cambridge: Cambridge University Press.

Edwards, W. (1955), 'The prediction of decisions amongst bets', *Journal of Experimental Psychology*, 50, pp. 201–14.

Epstein, L. (1985), 'Decreasing risk aversion and mean-variance analysis', *Econometrica*, 53, pp. 945–61.

Fishburn, P. C. (1982), 'Nontransitive measurable utility', *Journal of Mathematical Psychology*, 26, pp. 31–67.

Fishburn, P. C. (1983), 'Transitive measurable utility', *Journal of Economic Theory*, 31, pp. 293–317.

Fishburn, P. C. (1984), 'SSB utility theory: an economic perspective', *Mathematical Social Sciences*, 8, pp. 63–94.

Fishburn, P. C. (1988), *Nonlinear Preference and Utility Theory*, Baltimore, Md: Johns Hopkins University Press.

Friedman, M. and Savage, L. J. (1948), 'The utility analysis of choices involving risk', *Journal of Political Economy*, 56, pp. 279–304.

Grether, D. M. and Plott, C. R. (1979), 'Economic theory of choice and the preference reversal phenomenon', *American Economic Review*, 69, pp. 623–38.

Hey, J. D. (1981), *Economics in Disequilibrium*, New York: New York University Press.

Intrilligator, M. D. (1971), *Mathematical Optimization and Economic Theory*, Englewood Cliffs, NJ: Prentice-Hall.

Kahneman, D. and Tversky, A. (1979), 'Prospect theory: an analysis of decision under risk', *Econometrica*, 47, pp. 263–91.

Karmarker, U. S. (1978), 'Subjectively weighted utility: a descriptive extension of the expected utility model', *Organizational Behavior and Human Performance*, 21, pp. 61–72.

Knight, F. H. (1921), *Risk, Uncertainty and Profit*, New York: Houghton Mifflin.

Lichtenstein, S. and Slovic, P. (1971), 'Reversals of preferences between bids and choices in gambling situations', *Journal of Experimental Psychology*, 101, pp. 16–20.

Loomes, G. and Súgden, R. (1982), 'Regret theory: an alternative theory of rational choice under uncertainty', *Economic Journal*, 92, pp. 805–24.

Lyons, B. and Varoufakis, Y. (1989), 'Game theory, oligopoly and bargaining', in J. D. Hey (ed.), *Current Issues in Microeconomics*, London: Macmillan.

Machina, M. J. (1982), ' "Expected utility" analysis without the independence axiom', *Econometrica*, 50, 277–323.

Machina, M. J. (1983), 'Generalized expected utility analysis and the nature of observed violations of the independence axiom', in B. Stigum and F. Wenstop (eds), *Foundations of Utility and Risk Analysis with Applications*, Dordrecht: Reidel.

Machina, M. J. (1987), 'Choice under uncertainty: Problems solved and unsolved', *Journal of Economic Perspectives*, 1, pp. 121–54.

Machina, M. J. (1989), 'Dynamic consistency and non-expected utility models of choice under uncertainty', *Journal of Economic Literature*, 27, pp. 1622–68.

MacCrimmon, K. (1968), 'Descriptive and normative implications of the decision-theory postulates', in K. H. Borch and J. Mossin (eds), *Risk and Uncertainty: Proceedings of a Conference held by the International Economics Association*, London: Macmillan.

MacCrimmon, K. and Larson, S. (1979), 'Utility theory: axioms versus "paradoxes" ', in M. Allais and O. Hagen (eds), *Expected Utility Hypotheses and the Allais Paradox*, Dordrecht: Reidel.

McKenna, C. J. (1986), 'Theories of individual search behaviour', *Bulletin of Economic and Social Research*, 38, pp. 189–207.

Marschak, J. (1950), 'Rational behavior, uncertain prospects, and measurable utility', *Econometrica*, 18, pp. 111–41; see also 'Errata', *Econometrica*, 18, p. 312.

Morrison, D. G. (1967), 'On the consistency of preferences in Allais' paradox', *Behavioral Science*, 12, pp. 373–83.

Quiggin, J. (1982), 'A theory of anticipated utility', *Journal of Economic Behavior and Organization*, 3, pp. 323–43.

Raiffa, H. (1968), *Decision Analysis. Introductory Lectures on Choice under Uncertainty*, Reading, Mass.: Addison-Wesley.

Rees, R. (1989), 'Uncertainty, information and insurance', in J. D. Hey (ed.), *Current Issues in Microeconomics*, London: Macmillan.

Rothschild, M. and Stiglitz, J. E. (1970), 'Increasing risk: I. a definition', *Journal of Economic Theory*, 2, pp. 225–43.

Shoemaker, P. J. H. (1982), 'The expected utility model: its variants, purposes, evidence and limitations', *Journal of Economic Literature*, 20, pp. 529–63.

Silberberg, E. E. (1978), *The Structure of Economics: A Mathematical Analysis*, New York: McGraw-Hill.

Slovic, P. and Tversky, A. (1974), 'Who accepts Savage's axiom?', *Behavioral Science*, 19, pp. 368–73.

Sugden, R. (1986), 'New developments in the theory of choice under uncertainty', *Bulletin of Economic Research*, 38, pp. 1–24.

von Neumann, J. and Morgenstern, O. (1947), *Theory of Games and Economic Behavior*, 2nd ed, Princeton, NJ: Princeton University Press.

von Neumann, J. and Morgenstern, O. (1953), *Theory of Games and Economic Behavior*, 3rd ed, Princeton, NJ: Princeton University Press.

Weber, M. and Camerer, C. (1987), 'Recent developments in modelling preferences under risk', *OK Spektrum*, 9, pp. 129–51.

# Industrial economics

## Introduction

In this chapter we consider recent developments in industrial economics. Whilst it would be possible to pick a large number of areas in which important new developments have taken place, we shall, in what follows, focus on two broad areas: the theory of entry and the theory of the firm. In both areas we will meet a number of new ideas which have had considerable influence in recent years.

We begin by offering two different perspectives on the theory of entry. First, we look at the application of new game-theoretic/ oligopolistic ideas to the theory of *entry deterrence*, and we emphasise, in particular, the role that pre-entry commitment in production capacity may play in deterring entry. In contrast, we then consider the case where markets are *perfectly contestable* and there is free entry (and exit) in the market. In such markets, entry and exit conditions alone are sufficient to ensure that no monopoly power exists and it is argued that this implies that *potential* rather than *actual* competition can be used to regulate markets. We outline the theory and also consider some of the criticisms of it which have been made.

This is followed by a look at recent developments in the theory of the firm. Whilst some of these ideas (and, in particular, Williamson's work on transactions costs) have quite a long pedigree, we consider them sufficiently interesting to warrant attention here. First, we outline Williamson's ideas on transactions costs and internal governance, and (briefly) consider some applications of these ideas. Then we look at the principal–agent problem in the theory of the firm and consider ways in which this problem might be overcome. Taken together, these developments offer important new perspectives on firm organisation and the nature and scope of firms.

The final section of the chapter offers some brief conclusions.

## Strategy and entry

In this section we consider recent developments in the theory of strategic entry deterrence. This theory has developed beyond the traditional theory of *limit price* to consider a number of new ideas which can be important in entry deterrence. In what follows, we focus on some of these ideas; in particular, the ideas of *pre-entry commitments* and *credible threats*. We also show how these ideas can be applied to entry deterrence in the most often cited case – the case of investment in production capacity as a deterrent to new entry.

It is useful to begin by quickly reviewing the traditional *limit pricing* theory of entry deterrence: the so-called Bain–Sylos-Labini–Modigliani (BSM) model.[1] This argues that established firms seek to prevent new entry by limiting the price that they charge in the market. The basic idea is that established firms use their pre-entry output as a *signal* to potential entrants of what their post-entry output will be. Given this signal, established firms set an output which just makes entry unprofitable for potential entrants. Using this strategy, established firms maintain their market share in the long run and are able to make at least some monopoly profits in both the short and the long run.

The theory has two important elements. First, it assumes that there are barriers to entry in an industry in the sense that established firms can maintain price above unit cost without attracting entry. The BSM model assumes that such entry barriers take the form of economies of scale which dictate that entry must take place on a relatively large scale.[2] Second, it assumes that the established firms can influence potential entrant expectations as to the likely post-entry price. In the BSM model this is assumed in the so-called Sylos postulate that *entrants expect established firms to maintain their current output levels should entry take place*. Given this assumption, potential entrants can estimate to what extent their entry would lower market price and, thereby, determine whether entry would be worthwhile.

More important, established firms can set a limit price and output which (just) make entry unprofitable and thereby prevent entry taking place.[3]

A number of criticisms of this theory have been made in the literature. First, it assumes that established firms can effectively coordinate their actions in order to set the limit price. In non-collusive oligopoly situations, however, one would not expect firms to limit price. Second, it assumes that established firms opt to *effectively impede entry* (i.e. prevent entry taking place) rather than *ineffectively impede entry*.[4] The implicit assumption, therefore, is that the firms adopt a longer-term view in which they are concerned to maintain their market share (and their profits) in the long run. Third, the theory is essentially static and ignores the possibility, in a more dynamic context, that firms may seek to regulate the rate at which entry takes place rather than prevent entry absolutely (see Gaskins, 1971; and, for a recent survey, Gilbert, 1989). The limit price model, therefore, captures more dynamic entry-deterring strategies in only a rough and ready way.

Fourth, a central criticism of the theory concerns the Sylos postulate itself. Why should it be the case that entrants expect established firms to maintain their outputs should entry take place? From the point of view of incumbents, it is obviously better if entrants expect a more aggressive response (i.e. an increase in output) should entry take place. If the established firms can make entrants believe such a response is likely, they can set a price higher than the limit price under the Sylos postulate and not attract entry. On the other hand, entrants may think that, if they enter a market, established firms are more likely to accommodate rather than react aggressively to their entry. If this is the case then the BSM limit price will not prevent entry. The BSM model gives no firm basis for accepting the Sylos postulate and hence can be criticised for adopting an essentially arbitrary assumption over entrant expectations.

We now turn to more recent work on entry deterrence. This work has focused on a number of new strategic ideas which we discuss briefly here. First, it is noted that established firms can adopt a strategy with respect to new entry prior to entry taking place. In strategic terms, this gives established firms an *incumbency* or *first mover advantage* which they may use to prevent entry taking place.[5] Second, following the early work of Schelling (1960), it is argued that established firms may be able to make a *commitment* in the market which prevents entry taking place. According to this idea, the incumbents adopt some (irreversible) policy which has the effect of limiting their possible responses to entry. If, by so doing, they induce entrants to believe that they cannot make a profit from entry, then entry will be effectively deterred.

A third idea is that, in order for a commitment to work in deterring entry, it is necessary that it provide a *credible threat* to potential entrants. This point has been stressed, in particular, by Dixit (1980, 1982). He argues that a threat will be believed only if it is credible, i.e. if it would be optimal for established firms actually to carry out the threat if entry were to take place.[6] We consider below how the notion of credibility can affect the way in which a commitment is used as a deterrent to new entry.

In what follows, we concentrate explicitly on how investment in production capacity can be used to prevent entry, ignoring other possibilities.[7] This idea was initially developed by Spence (1977), who observed that established firms often install new capacity ahead of demand in a growing market or carry excess capacity in a static or declining market. Spence argued that established firms may hold excess capacity as a commitment to respond aggressively to entry should it take place. Such a strategy would be superior to limit pricing because it would leave price and output relatively free to maximise profits. In what follows, we review this basic argument and then consider the criticism and extension of the model put forward by Dixit to take account of the credibility argument.

It is probably easiest to consider Spence's model in diagrammatic terms (Figure 2.1).[8] Assume, for simplicity, that there is one established firm (firm 1) in the market and one potential entrant (firm 2). Assume also that both firms experience constant operating costs per unit of output, $w$, and constant capital costs per unit of capacity, $r$. In Figure 2.1, therefore, the horizontal line, $w$, represents constant operating costs and $(w + r)$ represents long-run average costs of production. Once a level of capacity, $k_1$, has been installed, however, average costs follow curve $AC$, as output falls below capacity and capital costs are spread over fewer units of output.

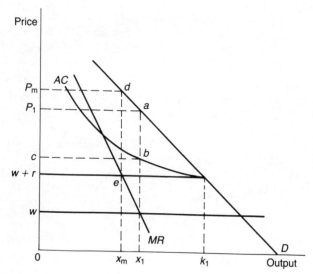

Fig. 2.1

Spence assumes that by holding excess capacity the incumbent firm can support a threat to use it should entry take place. Thus, he assumes that *the entrant expects the established firm to produce at full capacity should entry take place.* In this simple model, therefore, this implies that the incumbent should set capacity at $k_1$ such that no entry can take place. Note also that this would be the limit output under the Sylos postulate in the absence of economies of scale. In Spence's model, however, the incumbent holds capacity at this level while setting output at a lower level to maximise profits. It therefore sets output $Ox_1$ such that marginal revenue, *MR*, equals marginal cost, *w*. This enables it to make profits $p_1abc$ whilst at the same time preventing entry from taking place. This is clearly superior to the limit pricing strategy which allow only normal profits to be made.[9]

The basic assumption of Spence's model is that the entrant expects the established firm to produce at full capacity should entry take place. Dixit (1980), however, argues that this threat need not be credible as far as the entrant is concerned. The entrant may expect that, if it enters the market, it would be in the best interest of the incumbent to accommodate entry rather than fight, and hence the threat suggested by Spence would be empty.[10] If this is so, we need to consider how credible threats can affect the possibility of entry, and whether excess production capacity could be used to prevent entry in that case.

These issues are considered by Dixit (1980), who employs a similar model to that sketched above. Clearly, if the entrant (firm 2) enters the market, there may be considerable uncertainty as to the rules of the post-entry game and this, to a risk-averse firm, could act to deter entry in itself. Dixit, however, makes the strong assumption that both firms (correctly) anticipate that if entry occurs they will compete (non-cooperatively) in the market. More specifically, he assumes that they both expect that a Cournot–Nash equilibrium will emerge, i.e. each firm will maximise profits in equilibrium given the output of the other firm. Firm 1 (the incumbent) nevertheless has a first-mover advantage in that it can choose its level of investment (and capacity) prior to entry taking place, and thereby make an irrevocable commitment to at least some level of capacity. As we shall see, by manipulating capacity in this way, it can affect the terms of the post-entry game and thereby may prevent entry from taking place.

The analysis is illustrated in Figures 2.2 and 2.3. In Figure 2.2 we show firm 1's marginal cost curve for a level of capacity, $k_1$. If output $x_1 \leq k_1$, firm 1 has marginal cost $w$; whilst if $x_1 > k_1$ it must build more capacity to meet demand and its marginal cost is $w + r$. Firm 2, in contrast, starts from scratch and its marginal cost is $w + r$.[11] Whether $k_1$ is sufficient to meet its output requirements should entry occur depends on firm 2's output, $x_2$, and the corresponding position of firm 1's marginal revenue curve, $MR_1$. With $x_2$ low, $MR'$ is high and $k_1$ is insufficient; but, conversely, with $x_2$ high, $MR''$ is low and $k_1$ is sufficient.

The key insight in Dixit's paper is to recognise that investment and hence the level of marginal cost affects the reaction curve of firm 1. Specifically, if $x_1 \leq k_1$ then marginal cost is lower and firm 1 has a higher reaction curve than if $MC_1 = w + r$. This is shown in figure 2.3, where, if $MC_1 = w$, firm 1's reaction curve is $NN_1$ (showing the output it chooses to maximise profit given 2's output), whilst $MM_1$ is its reaction curve if $MC_1 = w + r$. Firm 2, in contrast, has just one reaction curve, $RR_1$. Since firm 1 can

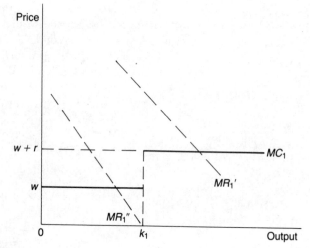

Fig. 2.2

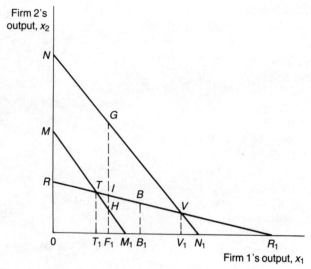

Fig. 2.3

choose its own reaction curve by the extent of its investment in capacity, this implies it can choose a point on 2's reaction cure in the range $TV$ by appropriate choice of capacity. If capacity $k_1 \leq T_1$ the post-entry equilibrium is at $T$; whilst if $k_1 \geq V_1$ the equilibrium is at $V$. For $T_1 < k_1 < V_1$, equilibrium is at an appropriate point on the line segment $TV$. Thus, for example, with capacity $F_1$, firm 1 has the discontinuous reaction function $NGHM_1$, thereby forcing a post-entry equilbrium at $I$. Within a limited range, therefore, the incumbent is able to use investment in capacity to influence *the terms of the post-entry game* and, amongst other things, prevent entry taking place.

Dixit derives two principal results from his analysis. First, he shows that Spence's excess capacity threat is not credible in the model he considers. Without threat of entry, firm 1 sets capacity $M_1$ to maximise profits with $x_2 = 0$ and $MC_1 = w + r$. With threat of entry, in contrast, firm 1 can choose a level of capacity between $T_1$ and $V_1$ but would not choose capacity above $V_1$ since it would not be credibly employed should entry take place. In Spence's model, output is set at $N_1$ where $x_2 = 0$ and $MC_1 = w$ and capacity greater than this is held. Clearly, therefore, if reaction curve $NN_1$ is negatively sloped (and $V_1 < N_1$) then Spence's excess capacity result cannot hold. Both firms recognise that firm 1 would accommodate firm 2's entry should it take place, and holding excess capacity above level $V_1$ (and hence $N_1$) is thus an empty threat.

Second, Dixit shows that the incumbent can use capacity to deter entry although it will always be fully employed. Various cases are possible (see Dixit, 1980, for details) but in one case, at least, entry can be effectively impeded. This arises when there is some point, $B$, along $TV$ at which the entrant's profits are zero. The incumbent then has the problem of whether to deter entry or allow it to take place (regulating the pay-offs in the post-entry game by choosing the appropriate level of capacity).[12] If it chooses to deter entry then it will set capacity, $k_1$, at (just more than) $B_1$ on the horizontal axis. Having deterred entry, firm 1 then finds it optimal to set output equal to $k_1$ to maximise its profits in the market.[13]

Dixit's analysis, therefore, shows that, if one considers credible threats (as he defines them), the incumbent firm will not use excess capacity to deter new entry.[14] Nevertheless, by making an appropriate investment in capacity prior to entry, the incumbent can make a credible threat that does prevent entry taking place. These arguments suggest, therefore, that investment in production capacity can be used to deter new entry, although in Dixit's analysis it is the more subtle use of investment to affect the terms of the post-entry game which prevents entry taking place.

## Contestable markets

In this section we consider a second recent development in entry theory: the theory of contestable markets. This theory has been developed, in particular, by Baumol, Panzar and Willing in their book *Contestable Markets and the Theory of Industry Structure* (1982), although a more useful introduction is given in Baumol's (1982) Presidential Address to the American Economic Association. Baumol and his co-authors argue that this theory, if not representing a revolution, at least represents 'an uprising in the theory of industry structure' and we consider this argument below. In what follows we outline the basic ideas of the theory in fairly general terms and consider some of the main results. We then consider some of the criticisms of the theory that have been made.

We begin with general ideas. In one sense, a perfectly contestable market can be viewed as a polar extreme case as regards entry conditions. In contrast to the literature on strategic entry deterrence which often considers barriers to entry in a market, a perfectly contestable market is one in which no barriers to entry (or exit) exist. More specifically, it is assumed that 'entry is absolutely free, and exit is absolutely costless' (Baumol, 1982, p. 3) in such a market.

The latter idea is the key point since it implies that an entrant incurs no *sunk costs* in entering an industry (over and above normal user costs and depreciation). Hence, an entrant is perfectly free to enter an industry should a profit opportunity arise because it knows it can leave again and recoup any entry costs that it has incurred. Perfectly contestable markets, therefore, are exposed to the possibility of 'hit and run entry' by potential entrants to the industry. This implies (as we discuss below) that such markets have certain desirable properties from a welfare point of view.

Let us be a little more specific about the assumptions of the theory. Basically, these assumptions come down to three:

(1) there are no barriers to entry in the market in the sense due to Stigler (1968);[15] that is new entrants compete on equal cost and demand terms to established firms;
(2) there is free entry and exit in the market in the sense of no sunk costs; and
(3) entrants are assumed to take the incumbent(s) price as fixed in considering possible entry. In a dynamic context, this assumption can be interpreted as implying that incumbents adjust price slowly relative to possible 'hit and run entry'.

Under these assumptions, any available profit opportunity can induce entry into the market. The entrant slightly undercuts the established firms in the market and makes a profit, and, if necessary, departs from the market if incumbents respond. Thus, with costless 'hit and run entry' equilibrium must involve zero economic profits. In contrast to the theory of perfect competition, however, perfect contestability can encompass a variety of circumstances, such as limited numbers of sellers, economies of scale, and product differentiation, which are explicitly ruled out under perfect competition. It is this fact which underlies the claim of Baumol and his co-authors that perfect contestability is a more general theory than the theory of perfect competition.

Baumol *et al.* suggest that perfect contestability is most useful for the welfare properties it implies. If markets are subject to 'hit and run entry', then all available profit opportunities are taken. This implies, amongst other things, that there will be *efficiency in production* in perfectly contestable markets since any production inefficiency represents a profit opportunity which will be competed away. Hence, in a perfectly contestable market, goods will be produced at least economic cost.

Second, equilibrium in a perfectly contestable market necessarily implies *efficiency in production and exchange* (i.e. marginal cost pricing), with the proviso that this need not apply if there is only *one* firm in the market. In the case of one firm (i.e. natural monopoly), price can exceed marginal cost in equilibrium so that full Pareto optimality need not obtain.

An intuitive explanation of these results is given by Baumol (1982) and we follow his treatment here. In the case of two or

49

more firms in the market, suppose that one firm (firm A) produces output, $y$, and earns profits, $\pi \geq 0$, in a situation where price exceeds marginal cost. If this is the case, then an entrant can enter the market and replicate firm A's output but produce a small extra increment of output, $dy$. Since A has one or more rivals, this extra increment of output can be taken from those rivals as well as itself without greatly shading price. Hence, the entrant finds it is able to make an extra profit on the marginal quantity of output it produces without a fully offsetting fall in profit arising from a fall in price. With two or more firms in the market it is always the case that entry is profitable in this way, so that, in a perfectly contestable equilibrium, price cannot exceed marginal cost.

It can also be shown, by a converse argument, that price can never be less than marginal cost in a perfectly contestable equilibrium and this applies for any number of firms in the market (see Baumol, 1982, for details).

In the case of one firm in the market with price above marginal cost, however, the above arguments need not hold. In this case, the incumbent firm can set price equal to average cost where the latter exceeds marginal cost and entry will not take place. The reader can easily verify this by drawing a falling average cost curve (with a marginal cost curve below it) which intersects market demand from below. The basic problem is that an entrant cannot draw sales from a rival firm in this case and therefore presses against the market demand curve. New entry by a firm is ruled out because, in trying to produce an increment of output greater than the incumbent firm, price is forced down to less than average cost and entry is not worthwhile. Hence, there need not be a first-best welfare outcome in this case. On the other hand, as noted by Baumol *et al.* welfare is maximised subject to a non-negative profit constraint. Such a solution thus involves at least a second-best welfare optimum.[16]

Clearly, these welfare results are important since they suggest that, regardless of the existing market structure, free entry (and exit) can produce a socially efficient allocation of resources. Hence, if perfect contestability were attainable, it would not be necessary to worry about concentrated markets, monopoly power, product differentiation, etc. It is also necessary, however, to consider how these results vary if markets are *imperfectly contestable* and we return to this issue below.

Baumol, Panzar and Willing also discuss the positive theory of perfectly contestable markets, although much of this work is concerned with multi-output analysis which we omit here.[17] They do show, however, that market structure is endogenously determined in a perfectly contestable equilibrium. In the single-output case, for example, if all firms have U-shaped average costs with an optimal scale of $x_1$ units of output and market demand is $x_2$ units of output (assuming price is set equal to average and marginal cost), then there will be $x_2/x_1$ firms in a perfectly contestable equilibrium. Hence, we find a determinate number of firms will arise in a perfectly contestable industry; determined by cost and demand conditions in that industry.

We now consider some of the problems and criticisms of the theory. One problem, which is immediately apparent from the preceding paragraph, concerns the *existence* of perfectly contestable equilibria. Since the number of firms in equilibrium can be quite small, obvious problems of indivisibility can arise. Thus, for example, if $x_1 = 100$ and $x_2 = 420$ in the preceding example, a perfectly contestable equilibrium will not exist because a non-integer number of firms ($n = 4.2$) is implied. Such a problem does not arise in perfect competition because each firm is small enough relative to market demand such that indivisibilities can be ignored. In contrast, the problem can be important in contestable markets where a small number of oligopoly firms may operate in a market.

Baumol, Panzar and Willig (1982) adopt an essentially pragmatic defence against this criticism, arguing that much of the problem can be removed by assuming flat-bottomed, long-run average cost curves. Figure 2.4 illustrates their argument by assuming that average costs fall up to a minimum efficient scale, $x_1$, and then become horizontal up to output $kx_1$. Clearly, if $k \geq 2$ then no problem of existence arise if output exceeds $x_1$, since industry average costs will be constant thereafter. If $1 < k < 2$, however, some small problems of existence can arise when firm numbers are samll. If we define $k = 1 + 1/w$, where $w$ is an integer, then it is straightforward to show that industry costs are constant for output equal to or greater than $wx_1$.[18] Baumol,

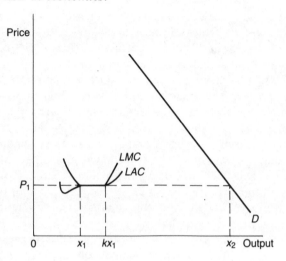

Fig. 2.4

Panzar and Willig, therefore, argue that problems of existence are unlikely to be of major importance as long as $k$ and $n$ are not too small.

A second criticism of the theory has been made by Weitzman (1983). Weitzman considers the claim that perfect contestability is a more general theory than perfect competition since it applies to markets with decreasing-cost technologies and limited numbers of firms. In contrast, Weitzman argues that, if entry and exit occur with no sunk costs, then, in fact, this must imply that costs are constant and not decreasing. Thus, the model does not have the wider applicability to decreasing-cost industries that Baumol, Panzar and Willig imply.

The basic argument that Weitzman makes is that costs are function of both the output flow rate *and* the period of production. Hence, with no sunk costs, a firm is always able to produce a given output at least unit cost by operating for a small enough unit of time. Thus, for example, if efficient production requires an output of 1,000 units a week but demand is for only 500 units a week, a firm can simply produce for half of the week at optimal scale and then costlessly disband production. With no sunk costs there would be no restriction in doing this and, in effect, the indivisibility giving rise to decreasing costs would be overcome by the divisibility of time.

Whilst this is quite a strong argument, Baumol, Panzar and Willig (1983) point out that it need not always apply. In the first place, Weitzman's argument implies some storing of goods and hence cannot apply where production and consumption take place at one and the same time; various service industries might fall into this category. Second, for some industries production takes place in batches and hence cannot be turned on and off at will; i.e. production takes place with an irreducible amount of time. In both cases, therefore, it is possible for there to be decreasing costs in the absence of sunk costs although this could not be generally so across all industries.

This gives rise to our third issue in perfect contestability theory–the problem of 'robustness' of the theory. In practice, it is unlikely that many industries (except, perhaps, some service industries, e.g. fast food takeaways) have no sunk costs, no barriers to entry, and relatively slow price responses by incumbent firms. This opens up the question, therefore, of what happens when some degree of imperfection in contestability arises. It has been argued by Schwartz and Reynolds (1983) and Schwartz (1986) that perfect contestability is *not robust* to small changes in its assumptions. We consider this argument below, focusing, in particular, on the work of Schwartz (1986).

Schwartz considers two types of imperfect contestability: the case of an exit lag and the case of some sunk costs. In the case of an exit lag, Schwartz assumes a model in which an incumbent firm sets price at time $-E$, entry to the market occurs at time $0$, price retaliation by the incumbent occurs at time $T$ and the entrant can exit the market (with no sunk costs) at time $x$:

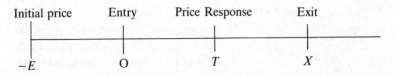

Clearly, if $X \leq T$ there is no exit lag and the potential entrant will not be discouraged from entering the market if price exceeds the competitive price. In this case, the incumbent will set the monopoly price at time $-E$, earn monopoly profits from $-E$ to

0, and then lose all its sales to 'hit and run entry' over time 0 to $T$.

In the case where $X > T$, however, a trade-off will operate, with the entrant being able to undercut the incumbent and make a positive profit until time $T$ but then suffering a loss until it can exit at time $X$. Schwartz shows that this trade-off depends on the length of the periods 0 to $T$ and $T$ to $X$ and on the price set initially by the incumbent firm. Given that a trade-off will arise, there will be some price that the incumbent can set which just makes entry unprofitable. If the incumbent sets this limit price, then entry will be deterred and some monopoly profits will be earned. Baumol, Panzar and Willig argue that this price rises smoothly between the competitive and the monopoly price as the exit lag increases. As noted above, however, the issue of robustness considers the rate at which price rises to the monopoly price. This issue is considered, in the case of sunk costs, further below.

An alternative model of imperfect contestability involves sunk costs. Assume that an entrant expects a proportion, $s$, of fixed costs to be lost should it exit the market. In this case, there is no exit lag and the entrant can leave at time $T$ when the incumbent firm makes its price retaliation. Schwartz again shows that there will be a trade-off in this case, with the entrant weighing profits prior to price retaliation against the sunk costs involved.[19] The incumbent firm can again set a limit price to deter entry which rises smoothly between the competitive and the monopoly price as $s$ increases.

Schwartz (1986) considers the robustness of his model in the case of some sunk costs, $s$. If the introduction of sunk costs into an otherwise perfectly contestable market causes the limit price to rise slowly above the competitive price, then the model is robust. Conversely, if the introduction of sunk costs causes price to rise rapidly to monopoly levels as $s$ increases, then the model is not rubust. These possibilities are shown, respectively, in curves $OBC$ and $OAC$ in Figure 2.5. Schwartz argues that, in fact, curves such as $OAC$ are the most likely outcome, and that this limits the practical usefulness of the contestability idea.

In order to get a feel for the magnitudes involved, Schwartz uses a numerical example for the sunk cost case (see Table 2.1). Assume that $T = 0.1$ (just over a month) or $T = 0.5$ (half a year) and consider a competitive rate of return, $r$, of either 10 or 20

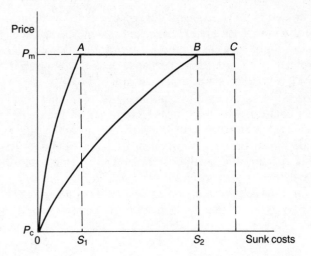

Fig. 2.5

Table 2.1 *Numerical example*

| $r$ | $T = 0.1$ | | $T = 0.5$ | |
|---|---|---|---|---|
| $r_m/r$ | 0.1 | 0.2 | 0.1 | 0.2 |
| 1.5 | 0.005 | 0.01 | 0.026 | 0.053 |
| 2.0 | 0.01 | 0.02 | 0.051 | 0.105 |
| 3.0 | 0.02 | 0.04 | 0.103 | 0.210 |

*Source*: Schwartz (1986).

per cent. Assume also that $r_m$ (the ratio of monopoly profits to fixed costs of production in Schwartz's model) represents the monopoly rate of return. Table 2.1 shows the proportions of sunk cost, $s$, sufficient for the limit price to equal the *full* monopoly price in the market. Thus, for example, with $T = 0.1$, $r = 0.1$ and $r_m/r = 2.0$, sunk costs as low as 1 per cent of fixed costs are sufficient for the incumbent to be able to set the monopoly price and deter entry. Whilst this figure rises with a longer lag to retaliation (e.g. the same case with retaliation at $T = 0.5$ implies

55

that sunk costs must be slightly over 5 per cent for the incumbent to set the monopoly price), the results are nevertheless clear. In Schwartz's model, at least, the theory of perfect contestability is not robust (in a way that, perhaps, perfect competition is) to relatively small variations in its assumptions.

This and the other criticisms made suggest that the idea of perfect contestability may have less impact on the development of industrial economics than Baumol, Panzar and Willig initially argued. Whilst the theory produces dramatic results in the pure case, it appears that small deviations from perfect contestability can give rise to very different economic results. It is not clear, therefore, that one can rely on contestability of markets to control monopoly power when some degree of imperfect contestability exists.[20] Nevertheless the theory is a major new development and it will be interesting to see what impact it will have (on theory and on policy) in the years ahead.

## Transaction costs and the theory of the firm

In this and the next section we focus our attention on the theory of the firm. In section 2.4, we consider some of the recent work that has been done on the problem of principals and agents in the theory of the firm. In this section, in contrast, we consider the work of Oliver Williamson (1971, 1975, 1981, 1985, 1989) on the transaction cost approach to the theory of the firm.

Williamson's work takes as its starting point the pioneering work of Coase (1937). In Coase's view, the defining characteristic of a firm is that it uses 'conscious authority' in the coordination of economic resources. Coase, therefore, drew a strong distinction between the firm and the market: in the case of the firm, conscious authority (wielded by an entrepreneur) was used to coordinate factors of production, whilst in the market the 'invisible hand' of market forces achieved the appropriate coordination. The problem which Coase addressed was why should the firm supplant the market as a resource coordination mechanism in certain cases but not in others; that is, why do firms exist?

As is well known, Coase's answer to this question was that, in some situations, there are costs to using markets, and that in these cases 'firms arise voluntarily because they represent a more efficient method of organising production' (Coase, 1937, p. 335).

In modern terminology, Coase argued that the need to economise on *transaction costs* underlies the form of organisation,
in that economic transactions will be organised (at least under
competitive conditions) in the most cost-effective way. Coase
argued that traditional neoclassical economic theory, by abstract-
ing from transaction costs, was seriously incomplete since it
offered no rationale for firms to exist. In a world of costless
transactions, there is no reason why individual economic agents
cannot negotiate multilateral contracts of considerable com-
plexity with other economic agents to enable production of appropriate goods and services to take place. In Coase's view, the
presence of transaction costs can make this an inefficient way of
proceeding, and give rise to the existence of firms.

In Coase's paper, various types of transaction cost are identified: costs of discovering relevant prices; costs of negotiating
and drawing up contracts; and costs associated with the uncertainty of long-term contracts. Coase, however, did not go further
in his discussion to consider more precise circumstances under
which these costs might be important.[21] This has been an important aim in the more recent work of Williamson, however, to
which we now turn.

Williamson (1985) argues that it is necessary to adopt several
non-standard assumptions in understanding the transaction cost
approach to the theory of the firm.[22] First, following the earlier
work of Simon (1957), he argues that economic agents should be
assumed to be *boundedly rational*: that is, whilst they seek or
intend to act rationally, they can do so only to a limited extent.
This suggests that they will have limited ability to deal with
complex and/or uncertain market conditions. Second, Williamson
assumes that individuals (or at least some individuals) act *opport-
unistically*, i.e. in a self-seeking way (with guile). This assumption
implies that market contracts must be designed to take account of
possible opportunistic behaviour. Together with bounded rationality, this will create problems (transaction costs) with some
market contracts, as we discuss further below.

Williamson distinguishes three key factors which, when combined with his behavioural assumptions, lead to *internal governance* (i.e. internal organisation of transactions). First, internal
governance is more likely the greater is the *frequency* of the
relevant transaction. This is because there are set-up costs asso-

ciated with internal organisation which are only likely to be covered when large, recurrent transactions are involved. Second, the existence of *uncertainty* is important for internal governance because it creates problems in drawing up market contracts. These problems arise because of bounded rationality and the possible opportunistic behaviour of economic agents.

Third, Williamson argues that the existence of *transaction-specific assets* is likely to underlie internal governance. Transaction-specific assets are assets (such as physical capacity or human knowledge) which are used to support a transaction and which have low value in alternative use. For example, a firm may invest in specialised equipment and research in order to supply a particular component to another firm. If there are no alternative firms which it can supply and its investments have little or no value in alternative use then transaction-specific assets are involved. Williamson argues that the existence of transaction-specific assets creates hazards for market exchange and leads to the internal governance of transactions.

We can, briefly, outline Williamson's theory as follows. He argues that, because of bounded rationality and uncertainty, it is not possible to develop comprehensive long-term contracts governing recurrent transactions which cover all future contingencies. At the very least there will be a need to renegotiate and adjust market contracts as time proceeds. One solution to this problem is to employ a series of short-term contracts governing a transaction, with renegotiation at the contract renewal stage. The problem with this, however, is that, if transaction-specific investments are involved, then the parties to an exchange will be locked together in a strategic bargaining relation (i.e. bilateral monopoly) once trading has begun. This moreover, applies even if the supply (say) of a good was initially competitive, because once physical or human transaction-specific assets are used, both parties have an interest in continuing the trading relation. This may be particularly so where human capital investments (e.g. learning-by-doing, human communications) are involved.

Williamson argues, in fact, that the existence of transaction-specific assets creates a *fundamental transformation* from competitive to bilateral trade. Given the need to adapt contracts to changing economic conditions, the parties find themselves essentially locked into bilateral trade with consequent opportunities for strategic behaviour and costly haggling. In short, the use of the market (where transaction-specific assets are involved) can lead to substantial *ex post* transactions costs which may be avoided by internal rather than market organisation.

There are several reasons why internal governance can be superior to market exchange. First, internal governance may promote a more cooperative stance towards negotiations than will exist in an external bargaining environment where individuals may be more inclined to withhold or distort information. Second, internal organisation can give rise to more flexible, adaptive-sequential decision-making, thereby enabling the firm to economise on bounded rationality. And, third, decisions can ultimately be taken by fiat by top managers in place of the sometimes costly baggling which can arise in the market. For all these reasons, Williamson argues that there are sound transaction cost arguments for organising recurrent transactions involving transaction-specific assets within (rather than between) firms.[23]

Having discussed Williamson's ideas in the abstract, we now consider how they can be applied to actual firm operation. In Williamson's own work the prime example of the transaction cost argument is the case of vertical integration and we consider this case first. We also briefly mention the work by Teece (1980, 1982) on the transaction cost explanation of multiproduct firms.

Williamson notes that the traditional argument that vertical integration is linked to technological economies of integration is, at best, only part of the story. In the case of an integrated steelworks, for example, there are technological cost savings (associated with the costs of reheating steel) which dictate that a number of stages of production are (typically) carried out in a single plant. The question of internal governance, however, turns not on whether stages of production are concentrated at the same site but on the separate issue of whether it is better to organise contractual relations within a single firm. In the case of steelmaking, of course, this is likely to be the case given the need to invest in site-specific assets which bind the stages of production closely together in a bilateral relation. But just as clearly in a case with no strong technological interdependence (e.g. when a firm considers setting up its own retail distribution network) it is transaction cost considerations which matter.

Williamson's argument, of course, is that vertical integration is most likely to take place in situations of uncertainty, recurrent transactions and transaction-specific assets. In some cases (e.g. in the supply of coal to power stations), recurrent transactions are involved but economic conditions are essentially static so that long-term market contracts can usually be used (although this is perhaps less so following privatisation of the UK electricity industry). In other circumstances, however, changes in market conditions of an unpredictable type may arise leading to the possibility of *ex post* opportunistic behaviour. Thus, for example, a firm may think that a component produced using new technology is best produced in-house rather than by an outside firm in order to reduce the risks of *ex post* opportunist behaviour.

Some support for Williamson's hypotheses is given in a paper by Monteverde and Teece (1982). They show that backward integration by major automobile producers into component industries is *more likely* to take place where engineering development costs are high. Hence, we have an example in which transaction-specific investments induce, in this case, automobile firms to backward integrate. Further evidence is presented by Stuckey (1983) of backward integration by aluminium producers into the supply of the raw material, bauxite. In this case, according to Stuckey, the need to customise some aluminium plants to particular qualities of ore creates a problem of costly haggling for non-integrated firms, and thereby induces integration to take place.

Transaction cost ideas have also been applied to multiproduct firms. Teece (1980, 1982) argues that multiproduct operation can be explained in transaction cost terms through problems that can arise in exploiting *sharable* economic resources using market contracts. The basic idea here is that firms may possess a *sharable* or *quasi-public* resource (such as technical knowhow, managerial expertise, or physical capacity) which is capable of use in producing more than one product. Whilst, in principle, it may be possible to sell or lease the services of this resource to outside firms, transaction costs of various kinds may arise. Multiproduct operation can thus be seen as an attempt by a firm to exploit its sharable resources through internal organisation.

This argument is often used, in particular, in relation to technical (and managerial) knowhow. Teece argues, for example, that technical knowhow is often held in *tacit form* by a team of researchers within a firm and as such may not easily be capable of transfer to an outside firm. Technical knowhow is often more than 'a set of blueprints' and as such there can be difficulties in selling or leasing it to the market. (Similar arguments may also apply with respect to managerial knowhow.) Second, by its very nature, technical knowhow may be difficult to trade because of the problems of revealing its value to outsiders without revealing the knowhow itself (the so-called quality assurance problem). And, third, there may also be problems of protecting proprietary information from opportunistic behaviour by an outside firm. In cases such as these, in particular, the firm may see strategic advantage in multiproduct production, and this may also be the case for other sharable resources that it may have.

Transaction cost arguments have also been applied to other types of firm organisation. Williamson (1975, 1981), for example, argues that large conglomerate firms can have transaction cost advantages in allocating capital efficiently and monitoring managerial discretion. And arguments similar to those employed for multiproduct firms have also been applied to multinational firms (Teece, 1985; Casson, 1987). Whilst it is important to recognise that other factors (such as the exercise of monopoly power) can be important in analysing firms, Williamson's ideas have clearly been important in emphasising the transaction cost side of the argument. It seems likely that this will be an area of major interest in the years ahead as economists seek to develop transaction cost ideas further.

## Introduction to principals and agents

In this final section we consider a second recent development in the theory of the firm: the theory of principals and agents. Although the literature in this area is somewhat technical, we concentrate, in what follows, on an introductory account of the main ideas.[24]

It is worthwhile noting at the outset that two strands of the agency literature can be identified. On the one hand, is the more formal principal–agent theory deriving from the work of Spence and Zeckhauser (1971) which seeks to develop optimal incentive incentive contracts in situations of uncertainty or asymmetric information. Second, there is the so-called *positive* theory of agency developed by Jensen and Meckling (1976), which offers a more practical and institutional account of mechanisms designed to minimise *'agency costs'*. In this approach these costs are taken to be the costs of monitoring, bonding and the residual loss implied in an agency relationship.[25] Whilst this approach is less precise than the more formal approach, it can be seen as complementary to it, and, following Strong and Waterson (1987), we treat the two approaches as essentially one in what follows.

In general terms, an agency problem arises when one party to a contract, the principal (P), engages another party, the agent (A), to act for him in a situation of limited (and asymmetric) information. Thus, for example, a house seller (P) engages an estate agent (A) to act for him in selling a house; or an individual (P) engages a lawyer (A) to act for him in some legal matter. In the context of the firm, principal–agent problems can arise, for example, between shareholders (or debtholders) (P) and managers (A); between different levels of management; and between employers (P) and employees (A).

The key feature of a principal–agent problem is that there is *asymmetry* in the information available to principals and agents. If this were not so (or, alternatively, the principal could acquire all relevant information at zero cost), then agents would be forced to pursue policies directly in the interest of the principal.

Typically, however, asymmetric information will prevail. Principals may be unable to monitor the actions of agents, observing only the performance or outcomes associated with their actions (the so-called *hidden action*, or, in terms of the insurance literature, *moral hazard* case). Alternatively, the agent may have access to information which is not available to the principal (the *hidden information* or *adverse selection* case). In either case, the agent is assumed to use its information advantage to behave in a self-interested or opportunistic way. This creates an agency problem and the need to either monitor agents or devise incentives for them which limit the amount of opportunistic behaviour.

Much of the work on principals and agents has focused on the effort and/or risk consequences of asymmetric information and the problems of devising contracts which minimise *'agency costs'*. Consider, for example, the case where a principal is unable to monitor the level of effort of an agent (i.e. the hidden action case). The agent can put in high or low effort and the actual outcome will depend on the level of effort and various chance factors (the state of the World). If the principal can observe only the outcome of the agent's action and not the action itself, the agent may choose to put in low effort and blame any bad outcome on the state of the World. In general, therefore, it will pay the principal to offer the agent an incentive to put in high effort by linking his rewards to contract performance. An optimal contract will give the agent an expected utility from adopting a high effort which is (just) greater than his expected utility from adopting low effort. In doing this, however, the contract necessarily implies that the agent accepts some risk. If the agent is more risk averse than the principal (which he may well be (see below)) then this can lead to a sub-optimal allocation of risk.[26] In other words, the agent may be willing to undertake only lower-risk actions than the principal would be prepared to take.

Whilst somewhat abstract, these ideas have direct application to a number of relationships within the firm. First, and most obvious, they can be applied to the relationship between shareholders and top managers. It is often argued that managers (A) seek to pursue their own interests (e.g. they pursue sales or growth maximisation, or simply opt for a quiet life) rather than maximise profits in the interests of their shareholders (P).[27] Such discretion will be limited by the ability of shareholders to control managers directly (although such action is often limited) and, more importantly, by the threat of takeover by another firm. Managers will also be concerned to protect their own reputations (in relation to possible future employment) by earning a satisfactory level of profit for shareholders (Fama, 1980). Nevertheless, it is clear that a potential principal–agent problem will arise (typically of the hidden action type) because shareholders cannot monitor managers' actions directly but must just look at the overall performance of the firm.

In this context it is suggested that managers can be given incentives to follow shareholder interests (in particular, through the device of *stock options*). In contrast to shareholders, who typically have a diversified financial portfolio, managers often have significant financial and human capital tied up in the company for which they work. Stock options represent a way of encouraging managers to take more risks, since they allow managers the option of buying stock at a fixed price at some time in the future. Managers, therefore, will be keen to take more risk in order to achieve a higher expected return (and hence share price) in the future. Note, in particular, that stock options are superior to a straight allocation of shares, which also carries a downside risk; stock options offer the option of *not* taking up the shares should performance be poor, thereby encouraging greater emphasis on risk-taking. It has been shown that compensation schemes such as these can be an important factor in limiting the agency problem, although we ignore formal discussion of this point here (see Marcus, 1982).[28]

Moving down the managerial hierarchy, it is also possible to see relations between top managers and middle managers, as well as relations between managers and employees, in principal–agent terms. In the former case, top managers must devise ways of monitoring actions of divisional managers whose actions they cannot directly observe. In this case, stock options are unlikely to be an appropriate device because their incentive effects are linked to the performance of the company as a whole rather than to particular divisions. In this case firms may be expected to use remuneration linked to the accounting performance of divisions, together with close monitoring of divisional management by top management and their staff (see Thompson, 1988, for a discussion).

In the case of manager/employee relations, a mix of incentives and monitoring can be used. Under suitable conditions (e.g. where it is difficult to monitor employee effort), employees may be given performance-related payments (such as piece rates) as an incentive to put in greater effort. On the other hand, where quality as well as quantity is important, as in high-technology industries, time rates may be preferred. Other incentives can also be given. Strong and Waterson (1987), for example, note that decentralised decision-making can also be useful in allowing workers to bring local information which they have in relation to their job area to bear on production. Share ownership schemes can also be important in encouraging peer group monitoring, thereby improving the overall performance of the firm.

Clearly the problems of limited information and principals and agents are a feature at all levels of the firm's operation. As should be clear from the above, the main thrust of the agency literature concerns the use of incentives and monitoring to limit the agency problem. This work is of considerable interest in understanding how firms operate and usefully complements the transaction cost theory of the firm.

## Conclusions

In this chapter we have looked at a number of new developments in the theory of entry and the theory of the firm. These developments have produced a number of new insights and hypotheses concerning how firms and industries work. As this work continues, we expect to increase further our understanding of the operation of firms and industries in real-world markets.

In discussing predominantly theoretical developments in this chapter, we have omitted discussion of new empirical work which has also been important. Such work has shown considerable technical development in recent years, which, combined with improved data, has led to more rigorous testing of hypotheses in this field.[29] Such work is continuing at a rapid pace, and, together with new theoretical work, holds out the prospect of further important development in the industrial economics sphere.

## Notes

1 This theory was developed in the work of Bain (1956; see also Bain, 1954, 1968), Sylos-Labini (1962) and Modigliani (1958). For a recent discussion of this and other work considered in this section see Gilbert (1989).

2 According to Bain (1956), there are three basic sources of barrier to entry: absolute cost advantages, product differentiation advantages and economies of scale. In principle, any of these barriers can be incorporated in a theory of limit price, although the BSM model focuses on the last, economies of scale.

3 For a graphical treatment and further discussion of the theory, see, for example, Koutsoyiannis (1979) or Clarke (1985).

4 These terms are due to Bain. Bain also recognised that entry can be *blockaded* (such that no entry is possible) or easy (such that entry cannot be deterred).

5 In some cases, however, entrants may have a *first mover advantage* if they are able, for example, to produce new products which are superior to those of established firms.

6 For a more explicit treatment of this argument, see Dixit (1982).

7 Product proliferation and pre-emptive patent are two other possibilities. See, for example, Schmalensee (1978) on product proliferation and Gilbert and Newbery (1982) on pre-emptive patenting.

8 Spence, in fact, considers two models in his paper but we present (a simplified version of) his first one here. The analysis which follows draws on my treatment in Clarke (1985, Chapter 4).

9 Note, however, that there is some cost to the firm in holding excess capacity to deter entry. A full monopolist would set output and capacity at $Ox_m$ and charge price $Op_m$ to obtain maximum profits $p_m de(w + r)$. The incumbent, however, has to accept higher costs, $AC$, in using excess capacity to deter entry, and, thereby, earns less than full monopoly profits.

10 Spence's threat need not be empty, however, if the incumbent seeks to gain a reputation for aggressive response in this and/or other markets. For a discussion of the role of reputation in entry deterrence see Dixit (1982).

11 For simplicity, we omit the possibility (allowed by Dixit) that firm 2 can have different levels of cost from firm 1.

12 There is, in fact, a third case where $B_1 < M_1$ such that entry is blockaded and the incumbent sets the monopoly output, $OM_1$.

13 It is optimal to employ capital installed fully because, if $B_1$ is between $M_1$ and $N_1$, firm 1's marginal revenue must pass through the discontinuous section of its marginal cost curve at $B_1$. This can be shown by appropriate modification of Figure 2.2.

14 As a slight wrinkle on this analysis, Bulow, Geanakoplos and Klemperer (1985) show that Dixit's result relies on the assumption of negatively sloped reaction curves. If reaction curves are positively sloped, however, Spence's excess capacity result can still arise.

15 Stigler (1968) defines a barrier to entry in terms of asymmetries in cost and demand conditions between entrants and established firms. In his view, therefore, scale economies are not a barrier to entry if both established firms and entrants benefit from them on equal terms.

16 Maximising welfare subject to a non-negative profit constraint gives so-called *Ramsey prices*. See Baumol (1982) for a discussion.

17 The analysis of multi-output production and consideration of concepts such as economies of scope, joint products and so on is a major part of their work. See Baumol, Panzar and Willig (1982).

18 Let $w = 3$, for example. Then $k = 4/3$ and costs are constant (for one firm) for $x = x_1$ to $(4/3) x_1$; for two firms for $x = 2x_1$ to $(8/3)x_1$; and for three firms for $x = 3x_1$ to $4x_1$. Hence, with three or more firms in the market, industry costs are constant.

19 It is also possible (in the sunk cost case) that an entrant could choose

'hit and stay entry' (in the case where it could earn a present value of profits after $T$ which exceeds its recoverable costs at $T$). We ignore this possibility, for simplicity, here.

20 In their original work, Baumol, Panzar and Willig (1982) suggested that contestability ideas may apply to airline city-pair routes given the ease with which planes can be hired and switched between different routes. More recently, however, they have backed away from this idea, as factors such as space limitations at airports, quick price responses by incumbents and so on have suggested some degree of imperfection in contestability. For a discussion of this example and other recent work, see Baumol and Willig (1986).

21 Coase had often been criticised for this in that, without such further investigation, his approach can be regarded as almost tautological.

22 Williamson drops the standard neoclassical assumption of *economic man*, maximising his own welfare given full information of available opportunities. Note, however, that Williamson's view of an uncertain environment and opportunistic behaviour is consistent with much recent economic theory, including the analysis discussed in section 4 below.

23 There are also disadvantages associated with internal governance such as bureaucratic inefficiency and the loss of *high power* incentives associated with market organisation. See Williamson (1985) for a discussion.

24 A more technical and broader treatment is given by Strong and Waterson (1987); see also Thompson (1988).

25 See Jensen and Meckling (1986) for details.

26 See Strong and Waterson (1987) for a numerical example of this.

27 For a discussion of theories of managerial discretion, see, for example, Gravelle and Rees (1981).

28 Note also that, in so far as managers can influence stock prices by retaining rather than distributing profits, such schemes create a bias towards profit retentions.

29 For a sample of recent empirical work in industrial economics, see Bresnahan and Schmalensee (1987). See also Schmalensee and Willig (1989).

## References

Bain, J. S. (1954), 'Conditions of entry and the emergence of monopoly', in E. H. Chamberlin (ed.), *Monopoly and Competition and their Regulation*, London: Macmillan.

Bain, J. S. (1956), *Barriers to New Competition*, Cambridge, Mass.: Harvard University Press.

Bain J. S. (1968), *Industrial Organisation*, 2nd edn, New York: John Wiley.

Baumol, W. J. (1982), 'Contestable markets: an uprising in the theory of industry structure', *American Economic Review*, 72, pp. 1–15.

Baumol, W. J., Panzar, J. C. and Willig, R. D. (1982), *Contestable Markets and the Theory of Industry Structure*, New York: Harcourt Brace Jovanovich.

Baumol, W. J., Panzar, J. C. and Willig, R. D. (1983), 'Contestable markets: an uprising in the theory of industry structure: reply', *American Economic Review*, 73, pp. 491–6.

Baumol, W. J. and Willig, R. D. (1986), 'Contestability: developments since the book', *Oxford Economic Papers*, Supplement, 38, pp. 9–36.

Bresnahan, T. F. and Schmalensee, R. (1987), *The Empirical Renaissance in Industrial Economics*, Oxford: Basil Blackwell.

Bulow, J. I., Geanakoplos, J. D. and Klemperer, P. D. (1985), 'Holding idle capacity to deter entry', *Economic Journal*, 95, pp. 178–82.

Casson, M. (1987), 'Multinational firms', in R. Clarke, and A. J. McGuinness (eds), *The Economics of the Firm*, Oxford: Basil Blackwell.

Clarke, R. (1985), *Industrial Economics*, Oxford: Basil Blackwell.

Coase, R. H. (1937), 'The nature of the firm', *Economica*, n.s., 4, pp. 386–405. Reprinted in G. J. Stigler and K. E. Boulding (eds), *Readings in Price Theory*, London: Allen & Unwin, (1960); Page reference to latter source.

Dixit, A. K. (1980), 'The role of investment in entry deterrence', *Economic Journal*, 9, pp. 95–106.

Dixit, A. K. (1982), 'Recent developments in oligopoly theory', *American Economic Review*, Papers and Proceedings, 72, pp. 12–17.

Fama, E. F. (1980), 'Agency problems and the theory of the firm', *Journal of Political Economy*, 88, pp. 288–307.

Gaskins, D. W. Jr (1971), 'Dynamic limit pricing: optimal pricing under threat of entry', *Journal of Economic Theory*, 3, pp. 306–22.

Gilbert, R. J. (1989), 'Mobility barriers and the value of incumbency', in R. Schmalensee and R. D. Willig, (eds), *Handbook of Industrial Organisation*, vol. 1, Amsterdam: North Holland.

Gilbert, R. J. and Newbery, D. M. G. (1982), 'Pre-emptive patenting and the persistence of monopoly', *American Economic Review*, 72, pp. 514–26.

Gravelle, H. and Rees, R. (1981), *Microeconomics*, London: Longman.

Jensen, M. C. and Meckling, W. H. (1976), 'Theory of the firm: managerial behaviour, agency costs and ownership structure', *Journal of Financial Economics*, 3, pp. 305–60.

Koutsoyiannis, A. (1979), *Modern Microeconomics*, 2nd edn, London: Macmillan.

Marcus, A. J. (1982), 'Risk sharing and the theory of the firm', *Bell Journal of Economics*, 13, pp. 369–78.

Modigliani, F. (1958), 'New developments on the oligopoly front', *Journal of Political Economy*, 66, pp. 215–32.

Monteverde, K. and Teece, D. J. (1982), 'Supplier switching costs and vertical integration in the automobile industry', *Bell Journal of Economics*, 13, pp. 206–13.

Panzar, J. C. and Willig, R. D. (1975), 'Economies of scale and economies of scope in multioutput production', *Economic Discussion Paper No. 33*, Bell Laboratories.

Panzar, J. C. and Willig, R. D. (1981), 'Economies of scope', *American Economic Review*, Papers and Proceedings, 71, pp. 268–72.

Schelling, T. C. (1960), *The Strategy of Conflict*, Cambridge, Mass.: Harvard University Press.

Schmalensee, R. (1978), 'Entry deterrence in the ready-to-eat breakfast cereal industry', *Bell Journal of Economics*, 9, pp 305–27.

Schmalensee, R. and Willig, R. D. (1989), *Handbook of Industrial Organization*, Amsterdam: North Holland.

Schwartz, M. (1986), 'The nature and scope of contestability theory', *Oxford Economic Papers*, Supplement, 38, pp. 37–57.

Schwartz, M. and Reynolds, R. J. (1983), 'Contestable markets: an uprising in the theory of industry structure: comment', *American Economic Review*, 73, pp. 488–90.

Simon, H. A. (1957), *Models of Man*, London: John Wiley.

Spence, A. M. (1977), 'Entry, capacity, investment and oligopolistic pricing', *Bell Journal of Economics*, 6, pp. 163–72.

Spence, A. M. and Zeckhauser, R. (1971), 'Insurance, information and individual action', *American Economic Review*, 61, pp. 380–7.

Stigler, G. J. (1968), *The Organisation of Industry*, Homewood, Ill.: Irwin.

Strong, N. and Waterson, M. (1987), 'Principals, agents and information', in R. Clarke and A. J. McGuinness (eds), *The Economics of the Firm*, Oxford: Basil Blackwell.

Stuckey, J. A. (1983), *Vertical Integration and Joint Ventures in the Aluminium Industry*, Cambridge, Mass.: Harvard University Press.

Sylos-Labini, P. (1962), *Oligopoly and Technical Progress*, Cambridge, Mass.: Harvard University Press.

Teece, D. J. (1980), 'Economies of scope and the scope of the enterprise', *Journal of Economic Behaviour and Organisation*, 1, pp. 223–47.

Teece, D. J. (1982), 'Towards an economic theory of the multiproduct firm,' *Journal of Economic Behaviour and Organisation*, 3, pp. 39–63.

Teece, D. J. (1985), 'Multinational enterprise, internal governance and industrial organisation', *American Economic Review*, Papers and Proceedings, 75, pp. 233–8.

Thompson, S. (1988), 'Agency costs of internal organisation', in S. Thompson and M. Wright, *Internal Organisation, Efficiency and Profit*, Oxford: Philip Allan.

Weitzman, M. L. (1983), 'Contestable markets: an uprising in the theory of industry structure: comment', *American Economic Review*, 73, pp. 486–7.

Williamson, O. E. (1971), 'The vertical integration of production: market failure considerations', *American Economic Review*, Papers and Proceedings, 61, pp. 112–23.

Williamson, O. E. (1975), *Markets and Hierarchies: Analysis and Antitrust Implications*, New York: Free Press.

Williamson, O. E. (1981), 'The modern corporation: origins, evolution, attributes', *Journal of Economic Literature*, 19, pp. 1537–68.

Williamson, O. E. (1985), *The Economic Institutions of Capitalism*, New York: Free Press.

Williamson, O. E. (1989), 'Transaction cost economics', in R. Schmalensee and R. D. Willig (eds), *Handbook of Industrial Organisation*, vol. 1, Amsterdam: North Holland.

# 3 *Zafiris Tzannatos*

# Labour economics

## Introduction

One may argue that the analysis of labour, as a factor of production, lies in at the heart of all economic theories irrespective of their stylised location in the political spectrum (left or right) or time (short- or long-run). On the one hand, from Adam Smith's classical liberalism to today's neoliberalism, it is visualised that the functioning of the economy depends crucially on the labour market: if wages were determined in a competitive manner, there would be no unemployment, while the level and composition of output would be respectively maximum and optimal under the prevailing preferences and available technology. This paradigm is typically identified with the short run.[1] On the other hand, from Marx's use of the labour theory of value to the modern institutionalists, radicals, dualists, segmentalists and neo-Marxists, the outcome of the production process is historically dependent upon the way labour is 'exchanged' (or 'exploited', according to the in-house terminology) between workers and capitalists. This is more of a long-term analysis as it deals with the dynamics of the capitalist economic system.[2] Combining these two diametrically opposed views, one can get any combination of economic systems, theories and labels, all of which place due emphasis on the functioning of the labour market. One explanation for the labour-centric nature of economics is that, apart from the importance of labour as such for efficient production, most individuals' welfare depends on the income which is generated in the labour market in the form of salaries and wages. For example, employees (compared with employers, own-account and family workers) account for about

71

four in every five workers in the EEC[3] and for about nine in every ten workers in Eastern Europe.[4]

One may wonder what can be 'new' in labour Economics, the part of the discipline which studies the pricing and allocation of labour in the economy. In other words, the problem is as old as economics and has been approached from all possible perspectives. In my opinion, what can be labelled as new stems from the application of an observation made early by the founder of neoclassical economics, which has gone relatively unnoticed until very recently. In particular, one hundred years ago Alfred Marshall in his *Principles* pointed out that labour is not just another factor of production. Labour is characterised by four distinct peculiarities; that is, labour (1) cannot be stored (it perishes over time); (2) cannot be separated from the seller (it can only be rented); (3) cannot respond easily to changing market conditions (it takes a long time to alter the size and composition of the population/labour force); and (4) cannot be negotiated freely (as the seller, or worker, is at a disadvantage in the bargaining process compared with the buyer, or the employer). The neoclassical theory that followed did not or could not at the time accommodate these peculiarities in the straight-jacket of the conventional price theory: while butter, guns and other material goods may be more or less successfully analysed in a near-perfect Walrasian environment, the analysis of labour appeared in certain cases to be better understood through non-orthodox theories[5] which place due emphasis on segmented (rather than on competitive) markets. It is the broadening of neoclassical analysis to include issues which arise in a *less than perfect and less than competitive* world that can be labelled 'new'.[6]

Though this broadening has not been able to 'formalise' the claims made by the non-orthodoxy (for example, income is only a proxy for class: a plumber may earn more than a professor), it has managed to offer some explanations which conform better than ever before to the observed behaviour of the labour market(s). Among these one can mention the 'efficient bargain' model of trade union behaviour whereby unions are seen not simply as wage setters who do not care about the unemployment effects of high wages but as organisations concerned with both wages and other aspects of employment. Another development has been along the observation that individual workers (and employers) do not view the wage as the only aspect of the contractual relation; the attraction of a stable relationship between the two has been formalised in an 'implicit contract' framework. Third, if information is imperfect and acquired at some cost (the cost of search), then workers and employers will not commit themselves to any decision until they feel sufficiently informed about the implications of their actions; this could give rise to (un)employment patterns which could not be accommodated in the 'spot' labour markets postulated by the conventional approach. Finally, a recent proposal which has been met with some enthusiasm in certain quarters is that of profit-sharing: can this alternative way of wage determination solve the present problem of stagflation?

These ideas are tackled below. By the nature of this chapter, the reader is exposed only to the basic thrust of each contribution and the fine details are omitted. A comparison between the more recent models and the traditional ones is also attempted. Where appropriate, the reader is shown the way to more elaborate surveys in the particular area that is discussed. One suggestion is in order: notes have been written in a 'non-destructive' way: they refer primarily to additional reading material, though some contain explanations when a point is not immediately obvious. The majority of readers should be able to go through the text without consulting them.

## Trade unions

The traditional formulation of trade union behaviour was along the lines of monopoly theory. Trade unions were assumed to have the power to dictate the level of wages to the firm or industry within which they operate while the employer(s) were considered to have the 'right to manage', that is to adjust unilaterally the size of employment along their labour demand curve so that profits are maximised.

A formulation of trade union behaviour in this way is far from satisfactory. The interest and influence of trade unions are not usually confined to one employer, firm or industry, neither are they exhausted in wage issues only. In addition, the union's control over wages cannot be taken to be absolute, while it may not even be significant in some cases. For example, in sectors producing exportable goods the firm can be taken to be a price taker and the power of unions to impose a wage above the competitive level may be minimal, if any. Finally, don't unions care about other aspects of employment such as quality of work, holiday entitlement, hours of the normal workweek, safety at work, capital intensity/choice of production technique, other work practices (such as training and internal promotion rules), longer-term employment prospects, and so on?[7] On the labour demand side, employers do not typically have fixed production capabilities and can react to 'adversities' by changing the capital intensity of production via investment and, if this is saturated, by adopting strategic research and development which can enhance the flexibility of production. Some of these considerations were incorporated in a variety of models in the 1980s which have enlarged the terrain over which unions and firms bargain.[8] These models encompass the earlier literature as special cases and, below, a rather heroic eclecticism is adopted in this growing area of research, after a general model of union bargaining has been discussed.

In Figure 3.1, the downward-sloping curve, $D$, indicates the employer's demand for labour curve. The horizontal line at $W^c$ stands for the competitive (or reservation) wage. In the absence of any kind of friction, the firm's equilibrium would be at the intersection, $C$, of these two curves. Assume now that a union comes into play, which prescribes that workers should be paid a wage equal to $W^u$ and implicitly accepts an employment fall from $L^c$ to $L^u$. This is very much the essence of the traditional view: unions restrict employment by securing higher wages for the 'sector' (firm, industry, occupation, and so on) in which they operate. This practice can also result in unemployment, if wages in the non-unionised sector are not flexible enough downward to absorb the workers released from the unionised sector. One question remains unanswered; that is, on what criteria unions decide which level of wages they will impose. Union membership is an issue of particular interest in this respect but, as this remains one of the most contentious issues, it will not concern us further in this chapter.[9] For the time being, let us assume in rather general terms that there is a trade-off between wages and employment in the union's objective function that can be represented in the form of an indifference curve. A typical union wage–

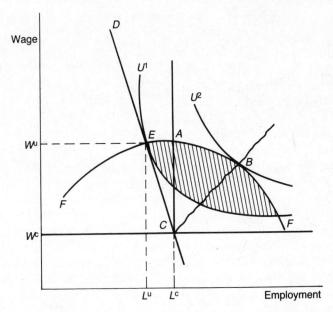

Fig 3.1 The wage–employment relationship in monopoly union and efficient bargain models

employment indifference curve ($U^1$) is depicted in Figure 3.1: the union obtains its maximum utility at point $E$, where such an indifference curve is tangential to the firm's demand for labour curve. This is in effect as far as the monopoly model of trade union behaviour can take us.

An observation made by McDonald and Solow (1981) is that the previous equilibrium is not an efficient one, in that there is room for at least one of the parties (unions and/or employers) to attain a higher level of welfare (utility and/or profits respectively) compared with point $E$. This improvement can be shown in the following way. The firm has a certain level of profit at point $E$. If employment were to increase *at that wage level*, then profits would fall as the value added to the firm's total product by the marginal worker would be lower than the wage. However, if wages were reduced sufficiently, there is bound to be another combination of (lower) wages and (higher) employment which would result in the same level of profits as those attained at point $E$. If one were to trace all the possible combinations of wages and employment which fetch the same profits as those at point $E$, one would get an inverted-U curve like the $FF$ curve in Figure 3.1 ($FF$ stands for the firm's 'iso-profit' curve which can be thought as the firm's indifference curve). For completeness one should add that (1) the typical shape of the iso-profit curves resembles that of curve $FF$; that is, initially all iso-profit curves increase, but they turn downward as soon as they cross the labour demand curve; and (2) the lower an iso-profit curve is positioned in the wage–employment space, the higher the profit level it represents.[10]

The reader may have already guessed the obvious. Given that the union's indifference curves are convex and the firm's iso-profit curves are concave, there is bound to be an area which represents higher welfare for at least one of the two parties compared with any point on the labour demand curve (such as point $E$). This area is shown in the figure as the lens-type shaded area. Consider the union indifference curve $U^2$ and point $B$. Now, the firm is at the same profit level as at point $E$ but the utility of the union has increased. Point $B$ indicates an efficient outcome compared with the traditional equilibrium at $E$; hence, this approach is called the 'efficient bargain model'. Obviously, efficient bargain models are superior to the 'right-to-manage' models because the former (1) are more realistic in that they allow bargaining to be over both wage *and* employment levels compared with the right-to-manage models which assume that unions are single minded over wages only; and (2) are efficient, that is, a solution off the demand is preferable to at least one of the parties compared with the conventional marginal productivity prediction.

The implications of the efficient bargain model can be seen more clearly if one plots the contract curve, that is the loci of points which represent gains for at least one party compared with points along the labour demand curve. The contract curve can be traced as follows. The competitive equilibrium in the absence of trade union influence would be at point $C$. Now assuming that unions either do not care about employment (risk neutrality) or they do (risk aversion), let us examine how the two parties would view their welfare if the wage were set above the competitive level.[11] Under union risk neutrality, the union does not enhance the opportunities for employment but would like to increase the wage for those workers/members who are employed in the firm. This implies that the union would prefer any point along a vertical line above point $C$, the competitive outcome. At the same time, the firm would prefer some points to the south-east of $E$, such as any point at or below $A$. Thus, the contract curve in this case would be a straight line vertically above the competitive outcome (line $CA$; the firm will not accept a wage level above its original iso-profit curve). If unions are risk averse, they would negotiate a wage that is higher than the competitive one, as long as this does not result in higher costs to their members. This amounts to postulating a positive relationship between wages and the level of employment as far as the union's preferences are concerned: the higher the wage, the greater the opportunity cost to those members who do not get employed by the firm, the greater the willingness of the union to increase employment in order to compensate for this. In this case, higher wages are compromised by concern for greater employment and the contract curve is positively sloped (such as the line $CB$).

Let us examine the basic properties of the efficient bargain model. Recall that bargaining takes place over which part of the firm's surplus (excess profits) would be apportioned by the union and, in the general case, the union is concerned over employment as well as wages (risk aversion). In this environment (1) if surplus increases, then wages as well as employment will increase; (2) if the competitive wage increases, the starting point of the contract curve moves to the left along the labour demand curve, wages increase and employment falls; and (3) if the demand curve shifts, say, to the right (for example, because of higher prices for the product), employment will definitely increase (the new competitive equilibrium will be to right of point $C$) but the effect on wages is indeterminate.

In conclusion, comparing the right-to-manage and efficient bargain models, they both assume that unions are concerned about wage levels and, in fact, both predict that wages in the presence of unions would be higher than those which would have prevailed in their absence. However, the efficient bargain model, even in its simplest form presented here, incorporates an additional union concern, that is, employment. While this difference results in lower wages compared with the rig... to manage model, it implies that in general there will be no adverse effect on employment, while, under conditions of risk aversion, the employment effect would be positive. It is this result which spurred the comment that 'given the recent legislative changes in the UK designed to alter the power of the unions, this difference could be very important in predicting the employment consequences'.[12] Consequently, though the present state of labour economics is still short of offering a general theory of trade union behaviour, some progress was made in the 1980s away from the traditional monopoly theory which views unions as single-minded organisations with no respect for employment matters.

## Implicit contracts

The theory of implicit contracts attempts to explain some of the questions that cannot be answered by, what one may call, the naive version of the neoclassical labour market theory. For example, conventional marginal productivity analysis has considerable difficulty in accommodating the fact that wages are rigid over the cycle and adjustment takes place usually though employment: this gives rise to short-run increasing returns to labour – a theoretical impossibility, as wages paid to workers cannot exceed the total revenue of the firm.[13] Another uncomfortable empirical observation relates to the existence of involuntary unemployment: why wouldn't workers accept a wage slightly lower than the prevailing one, if such a wage cut would secure them a job today? The answer to these questions is attempted by the theory of implicit contracts. To outline this theory one has to emplain, first, what such a contract is; second, how it arises; third, why it is undertaken between the worker and the employer instead of between the worker and a third party (it will soon become obvious that an implicit contract is in effect an insurance policy, hence it could be offered by an insurance company); fourth, and finally, how it is enforced. After this is done, the implications for the labour market and, in particular, the macro-economy are examined.

What is, then, an implicit contract? In modern economics an implicit contract is typically viewed as an insurance policy between a worker and his employer in the form of some security offered by the employer against the worker's employment status (hence labour income) in the uncertain economic environment within which the firm operates. Though such an arrangement is rarely observed in practice, it can be justified (or suspected to exist) on theoretical grounds.

This observation brings us in effect to the second question: how such a contract arises; the answer lies in the supposition that a worker may be more risk averse than the employer. The asymmetry in the perception of risk can arise as follows. On the one hand, a worker has usually just one type of (human) capital and his income is either the wage, if he is employed, or nothing, if he loses his job (omitting for simplicity social insurance benefits and non-labour income). Consequently, it is not easy for the worker to 'spread the risks' and, if adverse economic conditions prevail, the implications for the worker's welfare are severe (loss of income, at least in the short run, and subsequent loss of experience, with adverse consequences for re-employment in the longer run). On the other hand, employers or owners of capital can be less risk averse because (1) they can diversify between different assets or activities; (2) the loss from a worker separation is not that severe for them as there is usually some degree of substitution between different types of labour and, in theory, employers should be able to replace the worker even at a somewhat higher wage than the one previously paid. Hence, the worker may have a higher probability of an adversity happening to him (more workers become unemployed than firms go bankrupt) and the implications may also be more severe for him compared with the employer.

This brings us to the third point: why this insurance is not undertaken by a third party. The answer is information. A third party, such as an insurance company, can hardly know whether a worker's services are no longer demanded because his skills are no longer relevant or his work effort is below par. In contrast, such information is available to the employer.

The final question – how implicit contracts are enforced – can be answered only in an indirect way as by their very nature such contracts are difficult to detect by outsiders and even more difficult to enforce by a court or an industrial tribunal. In short, the problem of enforcement arises from two different considerations (recall that an implicit contract amounts to workers paying an insurance premium to their employers during good times and the firm having to secure the worker's status during bad times). First, if wages elsewhere rise above those paid by the firm, the worker can quit, leaving the employer with a cost (that is, the cost of retaining the worker when the firm was facing adverse conditions). Second, if wages elsewhere are lower than those currently received by the worker, the firm can replace the worker with another worker from the open market and the worker would have to bear the cost of a protection which did not materialise (lower wage in the previous period). The theory attempts to answer this dilemma in three different ways. First, and least successfully, if adjustment is not costless for the worker and the firm (for example, if a separation involves costs of moving house, costs of hiring/training, and so on), the contract wage would be enforced as long as such costs are sufficiently high to make a separation undesirable.[14] (However, the firm can still lay off the worker if the marginal product of the worker falls sufficiently below the wage, while one may alternatively argue that in the presence of workers' adjustment costs the under-payment of the worker in the first instance is not really the result of an implicit undertaking on behalf of the firm to insure the worker's employment status but a wage policy which pays the worker the minimum he would accept to stay in his present job, given his constrained mobility.) A second way of enforcing an implicit contract is by asking the worker to accept a low wage initially (in the first contract) on the understanding that his wage will increase in future contracts: this ensures that the worker will not leave in the second (or successive) period(s) and the theory goes through as long as the firm has committed itself to honour the contract. Finally, one can appeal to reputation effects: which-ever party acquires the reputation of dishonouring the contract would find it difficult to contract elsewhere in the future.[15]

Let us now introduce a stylised presentation of implicit contracts. Recall that risk is a crucial ingredient of the model. Workers are assumed to be risk averse in that they do not like fluctuation in their wages/employment status, while employers are risk neutral in that they care only about the average wage bill. One can show that both parties can be made better off (compared with an 'always on the demand curve' spot equilibrium), if the wage is lower than that in the conventional marginal productivity framework *and* does not vary over time. Assume that uncertainty exists about the price of the product the firm supplies.[16] For simplicity assume that the future price of the product can be either low or high with a probability of the former occurring known to all parties to be equal to $p^1$ and the probability of the latter to be equal to $p^2 = 1 - p^1$. Under the conventional marginal productivity analysis and other things being constant, these two prices would result in either a low wage or a high wage ($W^1$ or $W^2$ respectively). Now suppose that the employer has decided to employ the worker, so uncertainty relates only to the level of wage that will be paid to the worker in the two different price outcomes ('states'). The expected utility, $V$, of the worker is

$$V = p^1 U(W^1) + p^2 U(W^2), \qquad (3.1)$$

Where $U(W^i)$, $i = 1$ or 2, is the utility the worker derives from a particular wage level. Equation (3.1) can be thought of as an indifference curve representing the trade-off between different levels of wages for given probabilities.

Assume that the employer wants to minimise the expected average wage bill, $C$, of employing the worker, which is given by

$$C = p^1 W^1 + (1 - p^1)W^2, \qquad (3.2)$$

which gives rise to a family of iso-cost curves. Equations (3.1) and (3.2) provide the basics for the determination of an optimal contract between the worker and the employer, that is, a solution that leaves the worker at his original utility level while it minimises the costs to the employer (alternatively the gains can be shared between the two parties or the worker's utility can increase for given costs to the employer). It is easy to show that under these conditions the optimal contract would be one which specifies that the worker's wage would be the same ($W^1 = W^2$) irrespective of which of the two prices is realised. This is so because the slope of the indifference curve is:

$$[-p^1/(1 - p^1)][(U'(W^1)/(U'(W^2)], \qquad (3.3)$$

where $U'$ stands for the change in utility of the worker due to a change in the wage (marginal utility). The slope of the iso-cost curve(s) is

$$-p^1/(1 - p^1). \tag{3.4}$$

The equilibrium condition requires that the indifference curve is tangential to the highest iso-cost curve in the wage space, which amounts to saying that the slope of the worker's indifference curve should be equal to the slope of the employer's iso-cost curve. This requires that the second term in equation (3.4) is equal to one ($U'(W^1) = U'(W^2)$) which is possible only if $W^1 = W^2$.

This analysis shows that combining uncertainty in the (risk-neutral) employer's and the (risk-averse) worker's maximisation problems, the optimal contract would be one which provides for wages which do not vary with the output price.[17] Therefore, the observed wage stickiness has been explained. In terms of employment, one can show that employment will always be greater in an implicit contract framework than it would be in the conventional competitive labour market.[18] The intuition behind this proposition rests on two observations. On the one hand, the firm is interested in profits. Under marginal productivity conditions, profits are maximised on the negatively sloped firm's demand for labour curve. However, the level of profits which corresponds to any point on the labour demand curve (that is, for a given wage) can be achieved also with more employment if the wage drops sufficiently (this is in effect the same line of reasoning as in the case of the efficient bargain model described earlier). On the other hand, the worker is assumed to be concerned not only about the wage but also about his employment prospects. Hence, he would be prepared to trade off some of his wage for more (or more secure) employment. Consequently, the firm would not resist a combination of lower wages and higher employment (as long as profits are the same) while this would make the worker better off. The theory therefore predicts that in an implicit contract framework there would be, first, overemployment and, second, lower but rigid wages compared with the conventional marginal productivity equilibrium. One should also mention that this outcome is efficient and the popular belief that wage rigidity leads to inefficiencies is no longer necessarily justified.

The model presented in this section was a basic one and can be extended in a number of ways. For example, one can incorporate variable hours or even allow for employers to pay unemployment compensation.[19] Nevertheless, the basic message of the theory of implicit contracts has come through in that wage rigidity and, even, unemployment may be efficient given, on the one hand, the desire of workers to get some form of insurance against future variability of their work status/conditions and, on the other hand, the existence of less than perfect information and the inappropriateness of insurance markets offering such security to workers. Though the theory cannot explain fully the existence or severity of involuntary unemployment, it has provided some explanation in the right direction.

## The theory of search

The theory of search became a standard entry in the textbooks of labour economics in the 1980s but was hardly mentioned before. What spurred this direction of research was the fact that unemployment had risen significantly since the late 1960s and had stayed high ever since. An increase in the unemployment rate can be due to (1) an increase in the number of persons who join the unemployment pool (such as employees who were made redundant or school leavers who cannot find a job) and/or (2) an increase in the time that those who have become unemployed remain unemployed (for example, it may take two months rather than one week to find alternative employment). The relevant observation here is that in practice the *stock* of unemployed workers has increased primarily because of changes in the *duration* of unemployment rather than the *flow* into unemployment. The relationship between these three variables can be seen from the following formula, assuming that the inflow to and the outflow from the stock of the unemployed are the same:

Stock of unemployed
= (inflow) × (average completed duration of unemployment).

For example, if 1,000 workers become unemployed per month and they stay unemployed for 3 months, then the economy would have 3,000 unemployed workers in any given month. If the duration of unemployment increases to 6 months, then the number of unemployed workers will double and so on. One should not worry about the assumption that inflows and outflows are the same, an assumption which implies a steady state: in recent years the unemployment situation in many European countries has been stabilised and this is broadly consistent with this type of assumption.[20] Another reservation may refer to the fact that the average completed duration of unemployment would be different if estimated from *current* duration compared with *completed* duration. The former refers to time spent unemployed by those currently unemployed while the latter refers to the completed spell of unemployment of those who are back to employment. The relationship between the two is a complex one[21] but it can be assumed that the unemployed is surveyed half-way through his unemployment spell and the average duration of a completed spell is therefore approximately double the measured average current duration.

Consequently, the question becomes: what determines how long an unemployed person remains unemployed? An answer to this is attempted by the theory of search, which can be presented in a simple form as follows. Let us consider a worker who is currently unemployed but would like to get a job. The reason for wanting a job can be taken to be his desire for additional income (on top of his other income, which can include unemployment compensation, spouse's income and so on). If, given his skills, he could find employment at one wage only, then he could instantaneously decide whether he would be better off by accepting employment at that wage or not. In this case the choice is simply between that particular wage and the value he attaches to his leisure, and the duration of unemployment depends on how long it takes for the first offer to be made. The complication arises when there are a number of potential wage offers and information is less than perfect, that is, when offers can be identified only after 'searching' in the labour market. In this context, search becomes a balancing exercise between expected costs and expected benefits. On the one hand, the more he searches, the higher wages he can discover. On the other hand, the more he searches, the later he starts getting paid while the direct cost of search increases, too. What is the optimal strategy that the worker should adopt? One way of answering this is through the concept of the 'reservation' wage explained below.[22]

Suppose that jobs are identical in all respects other than the wage they offer and the unemployed worker has an infinite time horizon, his subjective rate of discount (time preference) is $r$ per period (say, 10 per cent), he contacts one employer per period receiving a wage offer equal to $W$, and the objective is to maximise his expected discounted income. An important additional assumption is that the distribution of all possible wage offers is known to the worker; that is, $W$ can be thought as a random drawing from this particular distribution. If the worker accepts the offer, he starts work at the beginning of the next period and stays in that job for ever; consequently, his expected discounted income is $W/r$. If the worker rejects the offer, his expected discounted income is $(W'/r)/(1 + r)$, where $W'$ is the expected value of future wage offers (calculated from the known wage offer distribution) before next period's offer is known.[23] Whether the worker would accept the offer or not depends on which of the two options yields a higher expected discounted income. The level of the wage offer which makes the unemployed worker just indifferent between acceptance and rejection is the reservation wage $(W^r)$ and can be shown from the above two expressions to be equal to

$$W/r = (W'/r)/(1 + r) \Rightarrow W^r = W'/(1 + r). \qquad (3.5)$$

The optimal strategy is to accept the offer if $W > W^r$ or reject the offer if $W < W^r$. This observation brings us to the comparative statics of the search theory. First, if $r$ decreases (which amounts to saying that the searcher is less concerned about present income), then the denominator of equation (3.5) decreases. As a result, the reservation wage increases and the probability of accepting a wage offer decreases; hence, the duration of unemployment increases. Second, if the wage offer distribution becomes more favourable, then the expected benefit $(W')$ from rejecting the present wage offer increases and the reservation wage increases, too; the duration of unemployment increases again.

Two additional observations can be made, though they are not explicitly incorporated in the above formulation. First, the introduction of or an increase in unemployment compensation (or other benefits) increases both the reservation wage as well as the optimal duration of search (and unemployment). In fact, there is bound to be a critical level of benefits which makes search unprofitable and the unemployed would stay indefinitely on the dole. Second, if wage offers become more frequent (that is, if the unemployed person intensifies his search effort or macro-economic conditions improve and there are more vacancies than before), then the reservation wage increases but the effect on duration is ambiguous. The reason why the reservation wage increases is obvious: waiting for other offers within the same period does not incur the penalty of forgone income if a better offer arises. The ambiguous effect on duration stems from the fact that leaving unemployment depends on the probability of receiving a wage offer which is higher than the reservation wage *and* on the number of wage offers per period: as the reservation wage has increased, the probability of receiving an acceptable offer has decreased but, as wage offers have become more frequent, it is more likely that a higher offer will be made.

The fact that our simple model assumed infinite time horizons is not damaging: the analysis goes through even if one realistically assumes a finite working life. The difference in the second case is that the reservation wage will not be constant over time: for example, if the searcher eventually reaches the last working period of his life, he would accept any wage offer that is greater than the unemployment benefit level. Equally, one does not have to assume that the wage offer distribution is known at the beginning of unemployment: the unemployed worker should be able to form an idea about the shape of the distribution as he searches and receives new offers. Obviously, in the latter case (adaptive search) the reservation wage need not fall continuously over time: the searcher may realise that his early estimates about the wage offer distribution were too pessimistic compared with what the actual offers turned out to be.

Before we return to the empirical observation which spurred the interest in search theory and examine whether the theory provides an explanation for the rise in unemployment due to increases in the duration of unemployment in recent years, let us trace some implications of search theory. First, the theory suggests that the rational strategy in the absence of perfect information is not to accept the first offer that is made unless it is greater than some minimum wage; hence, some kind of voluntary search unemployment is bound to exist. Second, since the criterion for acceptance is not the maximum wage one can get but a wage that is simply higher than the reservation wage, practically all workers should be underemployed. Third, wage differentials are bound to exist even among identical individuals in the same labour market (industry, occupation, location) because of the probabilistic (pure luck) nature of how wage offers are made. Fourth, given that the poor have a higher preference for present rather than future income (higher discount rates), they should also have a lower reservation wage and, as a result, they should settle for low-pay jobs more often than richer but otherwise comparable unemployed individuals (hence, an indirect finding of search theory is that income inequalities would tend to persist). Fifth, and finally, the shorter the working horizon of an individual, the lower the benefit from search and also the smaller the reservation wage will be: for example, the duration of unemployment and the level of post-unemployment wages would be smaller among older workers or workers in sectors characterised by severe seasonal or cyclical variation.

How well does the theory of search explain the increase in unemployment duration? The answer should be sought in empirical evidence which examines (1) the introduction of more generous or more widespread benefit provisions; (2) the effects of changes in unemployment insurance upon the searcher's behaviour. The measurement of the former is not an easy task. Economists have typically utilised the 'replacement ratio' (RR) as an indicator of the relationship between income from employment and income on the dole. In theory, RR is defined as the ratio of income when unemployed to income when employed. Both the numerator and the denominator are elusive. For example, one can use the average level of benefits divided by the average level of earnings, both net of taxes and other contributions. However, the incidence of unemployment is skewed among workers of different age, skills, family characteristics, location and so on, and the use of 'average' is inappropriate, if not misleading. Also, should one compare benefits with pre-unemployment earnings or with expected post-unemployment earnings? If the latter, information is scarce. For present purposes one can skip a detailed discussion of the issue, mentioning three points.[24] First, some authors have argued that RRs were lower in Britain during the inter-war years, when the country experienced its highest historic unemployment rates, especially when compared with the low unemployment rates in the immediate post-war era.[25] Second, RRs were 'untrended' from the late 1960s till the mid-1980s, and it was during this period that unemployment rose substantially in Britain.[26] Third, evidence from both sides of the Atlantic and especially Britain suggests that: (1) only a minority of unemployed workers have quitted (around one in ten) while the vast majority of the rest were made redundant;[27] (2) many unemployed workers never reject any wage offer;[28] (3) the elasticity of unemployment duration with respect to unemployment benefits is low – substantially less than unity (in the region of around 0.35 to 0.70 though most estimates are closer to the former);[29] (4) unemployment insurance has a declining effect over time and the probability of accepting an offer by the longer-term unemployed (more than 6 months) tends to unity. Consequently, the rise in unemployment in the 1970s and 1980s cannot really be attributed to workers becoming more reluctant to accept what was on offer – rather, too little was on offer.

In this respect, the initial objective of the theory of search (that some considerable part of the rise in unemployment could be attributed to workers' search activities) has not materialised fully. First, search unemployment is but one type of voluntary frictional unemployment, which itself is but one type of overall unemployment. Consequently, search theory deals with only a small portion of the total unemployment problem. Second, search theory may not even explain frictional unemployment, if workers search on the job and quit only after they have secured a better offer. In this case, what the theory tells us is about the behaviour of unemployed searchers, not increases in unemployment. Third, the theory of search is not incompatible with involuntary unemployment, if market wages are greater than reservation wages (hence, any offer would have been accepted) but there are no job offers (vacancies).[30] In this case, search intensity is of little relevance. Fourth, it is obvious that search theory is primarily a supply-side explanation because it explains rejection–acceptance of offers. As a result, the other (and, perhaps, more important) side of the market scissors (labour demand) is not taken into account.[31] Yet, the fact that the theory offers only a partial explanation of unemployment should not be taken in a negative way: search theory should be evaluated as an early attempt to understand (un)employment dynamics when information is less than perfect, an issue which is still under-researched.

## Profit-sharing

Though the theory of profit-sharing was developed and proposed by economic theorists and macroeconomists rather than labour economists and has still to secure a place in the standard textbooks, it is too important to be omitted from the present review. After all, labour economics is about the pricing of labour, and profit-sharing purports to change the way labour is priced away from the conventional wage system. This change is perceived to be a fundamental one because, if implemented, it may have far-reaching implications for the structure and performance of the capitalist system. The decision of the British government to encourage profit-sharing (through the subsidisation of profit-related pay schemes in the Finance Act of 1987) is indicative of the apparent attraction of profit-sharing compared with more traditional methods of determination of labour earnings.

The recent interest in the subject was sparked by a series of publications by Martin Weitzman (1984, 1985, 1987). In a simplified way, the characteristics and properties of the Weitzman model can be shown as follows. In line with the theory of labour demand outlined in the preceding sections, a firm employs labour up to the point where the revenue the last worker to be employed generates for the firm is equal to the wage. However, the *average* product of the firm's workforce exceeds the value added to production by the last worker to be employed – otherwise there would be no profits, even if there were no fixed costs of production.[32] Under these conditions let us assume, first, that the value added by the last worker, which is equal to the wage paid by the firm to all workers in the firm, is £100 and, second, that the average revenue per worker is £150 (or the gross operating profit per worker is £50). What would happen if workers were paid £90 as a *basic* wage plus a *profit-related* supplement? If the supplement were equal to £10 (that is 10/60 or 16.7 per cent of the gross profits per worker, which are now £60 = £150 − £90), existing workers would be indifferent between the traditional wage determination and the profit-sharing arrangement. However, the firm can now increase its profits by hiring additional workers, if they were to be paid along this profit-sharing scheme: an extra worker will increase the firm's revenue by £100 while the cost to the firm increases by £90 plus 16.7 per cent of the additional gross profit (£10 = £100 − £90) or £1.67. Hence, if the firm employs an additional worker *at that cost*, it can increase its profits by another £8.33.

From this microeconomic foundation one can examine the macro effects. First, employment will increase. Second, production will expand. Third, prices for the firm's product will come down as, by the law of demand, additional amounts of a good can be bought (= sold) only if the price is lowered. Finally, there would be external effects to other firms and, if profit-sharing is adopted widely, the economy will produce more at lower prices while unemployment will be reduced. In fact, it can be shown that an economy characterised by profit-sharing arrangements along the lines assumed earlier is closer to the classical theory (compared with the Keynesian theory) in that output is 'locked' at the full employment level and the economy and prices respond directly to government policies.[33] Thus, monetary policies can be singularly targeted at inflation alone while the wedge that profit-sharing drives between the marginal and average cost of labour creates an unsaturated demand for labour: a treatment has been found for the so common disease in recent years, namely stagflation. There can also be other beneficial effects. For example, the functioning of the labour market can be enhanced if linking pay to performance stimulates the work effort of the labour force. Also, if pay varies with profits and profits vary with the trade cycle, profit-sharing will provide some flexibility in wages (hence, profits) and unemployment will ease during recessions, which will not be as severe as before (because profits will not be reduced as much).

All this sounds too good and, perhaps, it is. Starting with the easier first, what profit-related pay means is that the *workers' pay* is determined by the *firm's performance*. If expressed in negative terms, the worker is expected to bear costs of entrepreneurial failure. In fact, failure may have little to do with bad management: unanticipated changes in raw material prices, in interest rates, in exchange rates, adverse weather and so on can all affect profits while they are all independent of the workers' effort. In the discussion of implicit contracts it was shown that workers would prefer a stable, albeit lower, wage rather than a variable one depending on market conditions. Recall that the model of profit-sharing outlined earlier is *neither* a model of labour management *nor* a model of a participatory economy. In fact, in Weitzman's view of the world employee involvement in decision-making or ownership of the firm is explicitly ruled out: the model goes through assuming that firms are pursuing conventional profit-maximisation objectives and some of the profits are used to pay labour according to some rule.

In this context, one can mention the case of 'creative' accounting on behalf of the firm. Profit is simply the difference between revenue and costs. Costs may well include dining expenses, company cars and the acquisition of holiday resorts, which can be justified as public relations exercises for the firm in which the managers, who may also be the owners of the company, usually participate. If this happens, then profit-sharing may amount to little more than management consumption being subsidised out of a reduction in workers' consumption via lower wages because of lower 'profits'. This can increase the conflict between the firm and its labour force and may also work against the view taken by the Green Paper of 1986 (Consultative Document on Profit Related Pay) that under profit-sharing there would be greater identification between the workers and the firm, which would result in a collusion between the two parties with the view to maximising the 'joint wealth'.

The link between profit-sharing and greater work effort is also unclear. On the one hand, profit-sharing enhances the collective work effort (improves productivity) while less monitoring would be required on behalf of the firm as there would be peer group pressure (reduction in costs). On the other hand, if profit-sharing replaces an individual incentive scheme, then it can easily increase shirking: the reward to additional effort is shared by everyone rather than accruing to the worker responsible for it. Having said this, there may be some cases (more precisely, types of production processes) where individual incentive schemes cannot apply while profit-sharing could make the workers raise their work effort. The former would be more appropriate for a door-to-door salesman: the incentive to sell more would not be there if the clerical worker back in the office has a share in the commission he makes out of his sales. The latter would be more appropriate on assembly lines: anyone who shirks will be easily detected (the product will pile up in front of him) while a faster pace of work will increase the size of the pie for all. Hence, the general case for profit-sharing is still to be made.

Another criticism relates to the short-run implications of profit-sharing. The attraction of the model derives in effect from the fact that the total remuneration paid to workers would be less compared with a conventional wage economy. However, if this happens, then the existing workers in the firm would be worse off. In fact, there can also be resistance from the firm's side along the lines of the efficiency wage hypothesis. According to this hypothesis, a cut in wages may increase the firm's costs: the average quality of the workforce may deteriorate as the better workers usually leave first and turnover costs (such as costs of recruitment and training) may also increase. Consequently, if profit-sharing amounts to leaving both parties in the same position as in a regime of pure wage employment, then there will be no short-run difference in the properties of the two systems of pay determination and the macroeconomic effects of profit-sharing would be unwarranted. If, however, profit-sharing were adopted on an economywide basis, then these reservations may no longer hold as there will be no antagonism between firms and their workers with other firms and other workers. It is in the spirit of this externality – that is, the failure of individual behaviour to produce a generally desirable outcome – that the UK government introduced successive legislation which provides for tax incentives conditional upon the adoption of profit-sharing schemes. In this way the centre of gravity of the allocative mechanism moves away from individual workers and individual firms (or their respective representatives) toward arrangements agreed between the society and its elected representatives, that is the government. However, the effectiveness of such schemes has already been questioned on the grounds that firms and workers can agree upon a cosmetic agreement which makes them better off in terms of tax treatment but leaves their original arrangements intact.

What is then left of Weitzman's proposal? One interpretation of the model is that the economy will be pushed to a permanent equilibrium position characterised by excess demand for labour, which amounts to saying that there will be no employment variability, given the full employment constraint. In this spirit, Weitzman's model can be seen as a more stable system over time compared with the intensity of trade cycles experienced in an otherwise comparable wage economy. In fact, this case has been made for the United States, where Weitzman resides. There contracts are typically renewed every three years and unanticipated developments are absorbed through changes in quantities (employment) as prices (wages) are fixed throughout the contract period. In this context, a profit-sharing scheme calculated on annual profit figures has the advantages that, on the one hand, it allows for wage adjustments without the negotiating costs and frictions associated with a wage system and, on the other hand, it stabilises employment. However, the practice of three-year contracts is not prevalent outside the United States; for example, the vast majority (95 per cent) of all private sector settlements in the Britain are negotiated annually. Hence, one could argue that the issue is not only over profit-sharing but also about the general framework and provisions within which collective/individual pay determination takes place.

This discussion suggests that profit-sharing is neither a panacea in theoretical terms nor easily implemented. The transition between the short run and long run is not easily established within a profit-sharing framework and, at the very end, the long-run properties of a profit-sharing system are identical to those of a wage economy. In practice, there are many reasons why profit-sharing would not be accepted by either the firm or its workforce or both while there are certain individual arrangements in a the traditional wage environment which can be superior to the collectivised nature of the share economy.

## Concluding remarks

New analyses emerge from new issues. The classical analysis could not explain the stagnation and unemployment which followed World War I. As an alternative Keynes put forward the ideas that, first, labour supply may be inappropriate (workers suffer from money illusion) and, second, aggregate demand may be inadequate (deficient). The Keynesian analysis was subsequently considered to be an adequate description of the economy in the post-World War II era up until the mid-1960s. The few labour economics textbooks at the time dealt more with industrial relations and the overall institutional framework within which labour operated: the belief at the time was that the state can tune the economy towards a desired objective, bypassing market failures. As times changed, it was deemed that political externalities and policy failures contributed in part to a rising phenomenon, namely stagflation. Thus, macro-economic intervention became simpler and the emphasis of analysis shifted to how the labour market works at the individual level – something which gave rise to the micro-foundations of macroeconomics. Micro-analysis is, of course, the stronghold of neoclassical economics and in recent years our understanding of the labour market has improved by moving away from instantaneously clearing markets: incorporating frictions arising from imperfect markets (adjustment costs and incomplete information) and non-competitive practices (such as union behaviour and, more precisely, 'insiders' and 'outsiders' in the labour market) has been the 'new thing' in labour economics. If these imperfections in the labour market are better understood, inflation could be controlled by relatively simple monetary policy and corrective policies could be targeted. This is the message of the present survey. However, we are still short of a general theory of the labour market and, when our skills develop beyond the present analytical limitations and stagflation is successfully tackled, new problems may arise which would require fresh analyses: labour is attached to humans and humanity has never been the same at two different points in time.

## Notes

1 For an exposition see Parkin and Bade (1983), Part III, especially Chapter 9.
2 See Gregory and Stuart (1985), chapter on Marxian Economics, or Catephores (1989), Chapter 4.
3 *Basic Statistics of the Community*, Table 3.16, Luxembourg: EUROSTAT, 1990 (27th edition).
4 Schultz (1990), Table A1.
5 The description 'non-orthodox' has conventionally been applied to theories which challenge neoclassical economics from a 'left' perspective. See Cain (1976).

6 For an excellent picture of the state of labour economics at the end of the 1970s see Addison and Siebert (1979). For developments since then, see Fallon and Verry (1988) and Sapsford and Tzannatos (1989).

7 For an exposition and evaluation of traditional trade union theory, see Hamermesh and Rees (1988), Part IV.

8 For a comprehensive survey of union behaviour, see Ulph and Ulph (1989).

9 For trade union membership models, see Osborne (1984), Booth (1985), Carruth and Oswald (1985), Kidd and Oswald (1987), Booth and Ulph (1988).

10 This follows easily from the fact that lower wages allow higher levels of profit at the same level of employment.

11 In the present exposition, the new wage can be thought of as the maximum level which the unions can impose and the firm could afford to pay. In other words, it is at the point where all surplus (super-normal profits) accrues to unions.

12 Ulph and Ulph (1989), p. 101.

13 Output per worker varies procyclically in practice. Hence, in a recession average productivity falls. This implies that labour is employed at the *convex* part of the production function, assuming fixed capital stock (=capital utilisation). In theory, labour is paid its marginal product, which is represented by the tangent to the production function at the appropriate level of employment. The convexity implies that the tangent 'cuts' the output axis below zero; that is, the total remuneration to labour exceeds total output. Such a conclusion cannot be sustained by the assumptions of the model. Two explanations (alternative to the implicit contract theory) which attempt to solve this apparent contradiction are, first, variations in capital utilisation (Nadiri and Rosen, 1969) and, second, labour fixity (Oi, 1962; Becker, 1975). Representative empirical evidence for these propositions can be found respectively in Solow (1972) and Nissim (1984).

14 Baily (1974).

15 Holmstrom (1981).

16 Alternatively, one can consider any reason which causes a change in the firm's demand for labour via a change in the value of production or in the production function as such. For example, the demand for agricultural labour can be affected by adverse weather while workers in the hospitality industry may be affected by a change in the exchange rate or events abroad.

17 If employers are also risk averse, then wages will vary with the firm's output price as in the conventional marginal productivity model.

**18** Akerlof (1980); Pissarides (1981). For a proof of this proposition, see Manning (1989), pp. 82–3.

**19** Oswald (1986).

**20** For a verification of these propositions across Europe, see Sexton (1988).

**21** Assuming a steady state (inflow and outflow constant over time and equal to each other), one can show that the average length of complete spells in outflow can be greater than, equal to or less than the average length of incomplete spells in the stock of the unemployed. For example, (1) if all unemployed workers stayed unemployed for 10 weeks, then the complete spells would be equal to 10 weeks while the duration of unemployment calculated from those in the stock would be on average 5 weeks; (2) if all unemployed workers had the same probability of being re-employed, then the duration of unemployment would be equal irrespective of whether it was calculated from the stock or outflow, as the outflow is simply a random sample of the stock; and (3) if (2) holds but the probability of re-employment decreases the longer one stays unemployed (state dependence), those with long duration would form a higher proportion of the stock than they do of the outflow, so the duration of unemployment would be smaller if estimated by complete spells rather than by incomplete spells. In practice, the third case is the most common one. For example, in Britain around the mid-1980s the duration of unemployment calculated from incomplete spells had a mean (median) of 72 (39) weeks, while the duration of complete spells was only 36 (16). See *Employment Gazette*, October 1985.

**22** The reservation wage is alternatively called the 'minimum acceptance' wage, more often in the American literature (see Ehrenberg and Smith, 1982, p. 447).

**23** The present value of the current wage offer, $W$, which is to be paid for ever at the beginning of next period, is

$$W/(1 + r) + W/(1 + r)^2 + W/(1 + r)^3 + \ldots = W/r,$$

and the same formula applies to the expected discounted income (that is, $W'/r$) if the searcher rejects the offer, but the latter should be divided by $(1 + r)$ because the searcher has rejected the present offer and has to wait for an additional period before work starts.

**24** For additional reading, see the collections of papers in Creedy (1981), especially Atkinson (1981).

**25** Metcalf, Nickell and Floros (1982).

**26** Fallon and Verry (1988), p. 270.

**27** Fleisher and Kniesner (1980).

**28** US Bureau of Labor Statistics, Bulletin 1886, *Job Seeking Methods Used by American Workers*, Washington DC: US Government Printing Office, 1975.

**29** Nickell (1979); Lancaster and Nickell (1980); Layard and Nickell (1985); Atkinson and Micklewright (1985); Narendranathan, Nickell and Stern (1985). An exceptionally high estimate (4.0) is reported in Minford (1985).

**30** Hahn (1987).

**31** For a survey and evaluation of the (less successful) extension of the theory along the lines of employer search, see Pissarides (1985).

**32** A straightforward proposition of the marginal productivity theory is that the firm cannot be at equilibrium at any level of employment where the marginal product of labour exceeds the average product of labour. This is so because if marginal product $= W/P > Q/L =$ average product, then $WL > PQ$, thus labour costs (wages times employment) exceed total revenue (prices times product) and the firm cannot be in a long-run equilibrium position. In fact, the firm cannot be in a short-run equilibrium position either, because it does not cover its variable costs – assuming that labour is a variable factor of production.

**33** Estrin and Wadhwani (1989).

# References

Addison, J. T. and Siebert, W. S. (1979), *The Market for Labor: An Analytical Treatment*, Santa Monica, Calif.: Goodyear.

Akerlof, G. A. (1980), 'The theory of social custom of which unemployment may be one consequence', *Quarterly Journal of Economics*, 94, June, pp. 749–75.

Atkinson, A. B. (1981), 'Unemployment benefits and incentives', in J. Creedy (ed.), *The Economics of Unemployment in Britain*, London: Butterworths.

Atkinson, A. B. and Micklewright, J. (1985), 'Unemployment benefits and unemployment duration', Suntory-Toyota International Centre for Economics and Related Disciplines, London School of Economics.

Baily, M. N. (1974), 'Wages and employment under uncertain demand', *Review of Economic Studies*, 41, pp. 37–50.

Becker, G. S. (1975), *Human Capital*, 2nd edn, New York: Columbia University Press.

Booth, A. (1985), 'The free rider problem and a social custom theory of trade union membership', *Quarterly Journal of Economics*, 100, pp. 253–61.

Booth A. and Ulph, D. (1988), 'Union wages and employment with endogenous membership', mimeo, Bristol University.

Cain, G. G. (1976), 'The challenge of segmented labor market theories to orthodox theory: a survey', *Journal of Economic Literature*, 14(4), December, pp. 1215–57.

Carruth, A. A. and Oswald, A. J. (1985), 'Miners' wages in post-war Britain: An application of a model of trade union behaviour', *Economic Journal*, 95(380), December, pp. 1003–20.

Catephores, G. (1989), *An Introduction to Marxist Economics*, Basingstoke: Macmillan.

Creedy, J. (ed.) (1981), *The Economics of Unemployment in Britain*, London: Butterworths.

Ehrenberg, R. G. and Smith, R. S. (1982), *Modern Labor Economics: Theory and Public Policy*, Glenview, Ill.: Scott, Foresman.

Estrin, S. and Wadhwani, S. (1989), 'Profit-sharing', in D. Sapsford and Z. Tzannatos (eds), *Current Issues in Labour Economics*, Basingstoke: Macmillan, pp. 227–58.

Fallon, P. and Verry, D. (1988), *The Economics of Labour Markets*, Oxford: Philip Allan.

Fleisher, B. M. and Kniesner, T. J. (1980), *Labor Economics*, Englewood Cliffs, NJ: Prentice-Hall.

Gregory, P. and Stuart, P. (1985), *Comparative Economic Systems*, 2nd edn, New York: Houghton Mifflin.

Hahn, F. H. (1987), 'On involuntary unemployment', *Economic Journal*, 97 (Supplement), pp. 1–16.

Hamermesh, D. S. and Rees, A. (1988), *The Economics of Work and Pay*, 4th edn, New York: Harper & Row.

Holmstrom, B. (1981), 'Contractual models of the labor market', *American Economic Review, Papers and Proceedings*, 71, pp. 308–13.

Kidd, D. and Oswald, A. (1987), 'A dynamic model of trade union behaviour', *Economica*, 54(215), August, pp. 355–65.

Lancaster, T. and Nickell, S. J. (1980), 'The analysis of re-employment probabilities for the unemployed', *Journal of the Royal Statistical Society*, Series A, 143, pp. 141–65.

Layard, R. P. G. and Nickell, S. J. (1985), 'Unemployment, real wages and aggregate demand in Europe, Japan and the USA', Centre for Labour Economics, London School of Economics, Discussion Paper No. 214.

McDonald, I. M. and Solow, R. M. (1981), 'Wage bargaining and employment', *American Economic Review*, 71(4), September, pp. 896–908.

Manning, A. (1989), 'Implicit contract theory', in D. Sapsford and Z.

Tzannatos (eds), *Current Issues in Labour Economics*, Basingstoke: Macmillan, pp. 63–85.

Metcalf, D., Nickell, S. and Floros, N. (1982), 'Still searching for an explanation of unemployment in interwar Britain', *Journal of Political Economy*, 90(2), April, pp. 386–99.

Minford, P. (1985), *Unemployment: Cause and Cure*, Oxford: Blackwell.

Nadiri, M. I. and Rosen, S. (1969), 'Interrelated factor demand functions', *American Economic Review*, 59(4), September, pp. 457–71.

Narendranathan, W., Nickell, S.J. and Stern, J. (1985), 'Unemployment benefits revisited', *Economic Journal*, 95(378), June, pp. 307–29.

Nickell, S. J. (1979), 'Education and lifetime patterns of unemployment', *Journal of Political Economy*, 87(5), Part 2, pp. S117–S131.

Nissim, J. (1984), 'The price responsiveness of the demand for labour by skill: British mechanical engineering, 1963–1978', *Economic Journal*, 94(376), December, pp. 812–25.

Oi, W. (1962), 'Labor as a quasi-fixed factor', *Journal of Political Economy*, 70, pp. 538–55.

Osborne, M. J. (1984), 'Capitalist–worker conflict and involuntary unemployment', *Review of Economic Studies*, 51, pp. 111–27.

Oswald, A. J. (1986), 'Unemployment insurance and labor contracts under asymmetrical information: theory and facts', *American Economic Review*, 76(3), June, pp. 365–77.

Parkin, M. and Bade, R. (1983), *Modern Macroeconomics*, Oxford: Philip Allan.

Pissarides, C. A. (1981), 'Contract theory, temporary lay-offs and unemployment: a critical assessment', in D. Currie *et al.* (eds), *Microeconomic Analysis*, London: Croom Helm.

Pissarides, C. A. (1985), 'Job search and the functioning of labour markets', in D. Carline, C. A. Pissarides, W. S. Siebert and P. J. Sloane, *Surveys in Economics: Labour Economics*, London: Longman.

Sapsford, D. and Tzannatos, Z. (eds) (1989), *Current Issues in Labour Economics*, Basingstoke: Macmillan.

Schultz, T. P. (1990), 'Women changing participation in the labor force: a world perspective', *Economic Development and Cultural Change*, 38, pp. 457–88.

Sexton, J. J. (1988), *Long-Term Unemployment: Its Wider Labour Market Effects in the Countries of the European Community*, Luxembourg: EUROSTAT, Theme 3 (Population and Social Conditions), Series D (Studies and Analyses).

Solow, R. M. (1972), 'Some evidence on the short-run productivity puzzle', in J. Bhagwati and R. S. Eckaus (eds), *Development and Planning: Essays in Honour of Paul Rosenstein-Rodan*, London: Allen & Unwin.

Ulph, A. and Ulph, D. (1989), 'Union bargaining: a survey of recent work', in D. Sapsford and Z. Tzannatos (eds), *Current Issues in Labour Economics*, Basingstoke: Macmillan, pp. 86–125.

Weitzman, M. (1984), *The Share Economy*, Cambridge, Mass.: Harvard University Press.

Weitzman, M. (1985), 'The simple macroeconomics of profit sharing', *American Economic Review*, 75(5), December, pp. 937–53.

Weitzman, M. (1987), 'Steady state unemployment under profit sharing', *Economic Journal*, 97(385), March, pp. 86–105.

# Welfare economics

## Introduction

Welfare economics is the normative branch of modern micro-economics. It addresses the basic question, 'how *ought* resources to be allocated' in an economy? The purpose of much of welfare economics is, therefore, a search for the criteria or a set of guiding principles which will inform the economist about what constitutes a 'good' or a 'bad' society judged in terms of its allocation of scarce resources. Thus welfare economics differs in substance from positive microeconomics, which is concerned with predicting the outcomes of alternative allocative mechanisms and decisions.

Welfare economics has always been the focus of much controversy. This is to be expected when the subject matter is judgement about what might be regarded as 'good' or 'bad' – one man's meat is another's poison. Unless one holds the strong belief that judgements about good and bad and hence what constitutes the 'good life' are codified in absolute rules given by God, then views about good and bad will be relative to the time and the place within which the individual finds him/herself. Economists have, however, sought to establish some fundamental principles regarding resource allocation. Good and bad in this case are defined relative to whether or not the allocation of resources is efficient or inefficient. Controversy, however, arises when the distribution of resources (no matter whether the allocation is efficient) is judged in terms of 'fairness'. Indeed, other subjects such as moral or political philosophy regard the economist's approach when judging a good society to be too narrow in its conception.

Many of the principal architects of the early welfare economics have since denounced its claims and have gone so far as to regard welfare economics as being a failure because it is based upon value judgements which are ethically unacceptable. Sir John Hicks (1969), one of the founding fathers of the modern welfare economics of the 1930s, repudiates what he calls 'Economic Welfarism' on the grounds that the postulates of modern welfare economics do not reflect a sufficient concern for the non-pecuniary values of freedom and justice. Kenneth Boulding (1969), in his presidential address to the American Economics Association, described welfare economics as 'a failure, though a reasonably glorious one'. The reason for the failure in the subject was that its ethical foundations are 'extremely shaky'. Howard Bowen (1972) attacks welfare economics because it takes market price as a measure of welfare and then assumes that more is always better than less. Thus, Bowen argues, welfare economics is 'based upon values that are patently naive and crass'. Mishan (1984) has argued, 'I consider the conventional economic framework to be inadequate and misleading – at least for determining the direction of human well-being over time within a modern or post industrial society under continuing institutional compulsion to innovate and expand . . . the factors that can be identified and (in principle at least) measured by the economist seem to me to be manifestly of less importance than those considerations that do not lend themselves easily, if at all, to measurement.'

Partly in response to these criticisms, modern microeconomics has reconsidered the foundations of welfare economics. In this chapter a selective review of modern developments in the subject will be presented. It should, however, be emphasised that the review is selective. Nowadays what is regarded as welfare economics covers a wide and diverse territory with its boundaries encompassing public and social choice theory and applied public policy.[1] This chapter will concentrate upon principles rather than applications.

After reviewing the basic theorems of traditional welfare economics, the problems caused by uncertainty and asymmetric information will be examined. This is followed by an examination of potential competition, the issues of distributive justice and welfare criteria, and the role of the state. The chapter concludes with a brief consideration of where the subject is leading.

## Traditional welfare economics

The origins of welfare economics could be traced back as far as Aristotle, but it is usual to take the publication of Pigou's (1920) *The Economics of Welfare* as the starting point for the systematic treatment of welfare economics as a distinctive branch of economics.[2] Adam Smith of course had established a basic welfare economics in his criticism of the mercantilist system by advocating the superiority of free market exchange as a means of establishing the 'common good'. Moreover, Smith in the *Wealth of Nations* (1776) built upon his earlier work in the *Theory of Moral Sentiments* (1759) and the *Lectures on Jurisprudence* (1766), which formed the institutional basis of a good society. It was, however, the publication of Robbins' (1932) *Essay on the Nature and Significance of Economic Science* which brought about the quantum leap in the subject and spawned a new research agenda for micro economists which is traditionally labelled the 'New Welfare Economics'.[3] Robbins emphasises the arbitrary character of interpersonal comparisons of utility. It was Robbins who reminded economists of Kant's propositions that there is a fundamental distinction to be drawn between 'ought' and 'is' statements (i.e. between the normative and the positive) and that it is a logical fallacy to progress from 'is' to 'ought' statements. The reason for the need for this reminder was that much of economics at that time had been taken over by a form of logical positivism.[4] A feature of the new welfare economics was that value judgements could not achieve a status comparable to factual propositions. Hicks (1939) draws the distinction between the 'scientific' procedure of the economist and the unscientific method which characterises the 'prophet and social reformer'. Value judgements which involved interpersonal comparisons of utility were, therefore, to be kept to a minimum and if possible totally eliminated. If they had to be made, then they must be made explicit rather than concealed.[5]

## The fundamental theorems of welfare economics

When comparing different social states and judging them in terms of whether or not they are 'good' or 'bad', economists rely upon the fundamental theorems of welfare economics which have been developed over the past fifty years. These theorems are based upon two basic assumptions: first, the assumption of methodological individualism – that is, the individual is the best judge of his/her own welfare; second, the welfare of society depends only upon the welfare of the individuals who comprise it. Taken together these two assumptions reject any anthropo-morphisms such as the 'state' being something other than the individuals who make it up or that individuals exist to further the goals of the state. The converse is considered to be true – any economic system exists to serve the needs of individuals. This approach was established early on by Samuelson (1947, p. 233), who argued that states of an economy are to be judged as good or bad according to individual preferences and not ac-cording to some external higher order or standard.

The first and second fundamental theorems of welfare econ-omics existed in essence in the literature of the 1950s. However, it was Arrow (1963a) who codified them and set them down formally. Their lineage goes back to Pareto, who had developed the optimality conditions for production in his two volumes of *Cours* (1896 and 1897) and the optimality conditions for ex-change in his *Manuel* (1909). Combined, the first and second theorems are often referred to as 'first-best Paretian welfare economics'.

Does the interaction of buyers and sellers in a competitive economy promote the common good? Adam Smith in the *Wealth of Nations* (1776, Book IV) asserted that the answer was yes. Lange and Lerner in the 1930s claimed that it was so, but did not produce a formal proof. This awaited the formal analysis of Arrow and Debreu.[6]

The first theorem of welfare economics states that:

> *A private property competitive equilibrium (if it exists) is a Pareto optimum*

Proof of the existence of a competitive equilibrium requires a strong set of assumptions; i.e. atomised competition, price taking, prices signal all of the necessary information, and price adjustment towards equilibrium. The efficiency (first-best) pro-perty of the competitive equilibrium is easy to understand. Price signals are sufficient to coordinate economic activities in a satis-factory way. Each economic agent (consumer or producer) at-tempts to maximise an objective function (utility or profit) by equating marginal rates of substitution, as in the case of consumers, and marginal rates of transformation in the case of firms. Since everyone faces the same set of prices, all the marginal rates of substitution between any two commodities will be equal over all individuals. In a convex world (i.e. non-increasing returns to scale; convex preferences for consumers; and no externalities), equilibrium prices combined with equality of the marginal rates of substitution characterise Pareto-efficient allocations.

A Pareto-efficient allocation is one for which no reallocation of either commodities between consumers or factors of production between producers can make someone better off without making someone else worse off. This can also be interpreted as a state of the world in which it is not possible to reallocate resources and thereby produce more output. This is not, however, to say that a Pareto-efficient allocation maximises GNP or that it is best in a unique sense.[7]

The proof that a competitive equilibrium is Pareto efficient is a powerful result. It has often been used to justify capitalism and laissez-faire over other forms of economic organisation.

The second fundamental theorem of welfare economics states that:

> *If all individuals and producers are selfish price takers, then any Pareto-optimal equilibrium can be achieved via the competitive mechanism, provided appropriate lump sum taxes and transfers are imposed on individuals and firms.*

These two theorems gave rise to a tortuous debate in the 1930s which centred upon the use of 'compensation tests' to judge whether or not a policy intervention or any change in the state of the economy resulted in a welfare improvement. The issue centred round the question, how is it possible to say that there has been a welfare improvement without making interpersonal comparisons of utility (see Robbins, 1938; and Harrod, 1938)?[8] This question was answered by Kaldor (1939) and Hicks (1939), who argued that any change could be regarded as being an improvement if those who gain from the change can *potentially* compensate those who lose, thereby making everyone better off. Whether or not the compensation should actually be paid was regarded by Kaldor to be a political question. What he had proposed was a test for a potential Pareto improvement in welfare. Hicks argued that if compensation was to be paid

The South East Essex College of Arts & Technology
Carnarvon Road, Southend on Sea, Essex SS2 6LS
Tel: Southend (0702) 220400   Fax: Southend (0702) 432320

in practice then the economist must point out the efficiency losses derived from the means of compensation (i.e. grants, subsidies, taxation, etc.) However, Hicks took the analysis a stage further, arguing that there would be a social improvement if the losers cannot profitably bribe the gainers not to make the change.

The Kaldor/Hicks papers generated a great debate which centred around the robustness and reasonableness of their compensation tests. Scitovsky (1941) argued that the gainers might be able to compensate the losers and be better off but that the losers might try to bribe the gainers to return to the original position. This gave rise to Scitovsky's 'reversal test'; that is, a welfare improvement required that, whilst the gainers can bribe the losers to make the change, the losers cannot bribe the gainers to return to the *status quo*. Little (1950) added the requirement that for one state to be regarded as better than another then the Scitovsky reversal text was required, plus the distribution of income in the superior state should be no worse than in the inferior state. Mishan (1969) developed this.

It is crucial for the compensation tests to assume that each person's utility depends upon their own consumption of goods and services (i.e. no externalities). However, despite attempts to make comparisons value free and to link plausible distributional value judgements with compensation criteria, this literature has not given the policy-maker or the cost–benefit analyst a clear set of rules to judge the desirability of economic changes. What it has done, however, is to make the problem clearer if not entirely tractable.

A third fundamental theorem can be added to the first two. It states that:

> There is no Arrow social welfare function that satisfies the conditions of universality, Pareto consistency and non-dictatorship.

The first theorem of welfare economics concluded that a perfectly functioning competitive market economy will generate a Pareto-efficient allocation of resources. When it comes to the issue of equity in the distribution of resources, the first theorem is neutural. The problem is how to choose a single Pareto-efficient allocation from an infinite set of income distributions. Equity objectives are summarised in a 'social welfare function', which can be thought of as a device to bring distributional considerations back into the analysis.

This problem was tackled by Bergson (1938), who attempted to integrate efficiency and equity into a single welfare criterion – the social welfare function.[9] The social welfare function embodies some of the ideas of the compensation tests but goes further as an attempt to order social states. A Bergson welfare function is a weighted sum of individual utilities and assumes that, if the welfare of one person increases, then there is a social welfare increase; that if one person's welfare is decreased then, to keep social welfare constant, another person's utility must increase by an equal amount; if one person has a very high level of utility and another a very low, then society will be willing to sacrifice some of the high person's utility to get a slight improvement in the low person's utility; each person's utility function is assigned a weight and the objective is to maximise the weighted sum of individual utilities. The maximisation of this social welfare function secures Pareto efficiency whilst achieving society's distributional objectives. This exercise is, however, based on cardinal measures and requires interpersonal comparisons in order to assign the welfare weights.

The Bergson social welfare function is individualistic, being defined in terms of individuals' utility functions as follows:

$$W = W[U^1(X_1 \ldots X_N), \ldots, U^H(X^1 \ldots X_N)],$$

where $U^H$ is the ordinal utility function of individual H and is defined over the set of $N$ commodities. This welfare function is graphed as a set of social indifference curves in utility space. It enables society to choose the distributionally best allocation from the set of an infinite number of Pareto-efficient allocations. This best Pareto allocation was defined by Bator (1957) to be the 'bliss point' for society as shown in Figure 4.1, where $U_1$ and $U_2$ refer to the ordinal utility indices of individuals 1 and 2 respectively. The social welfare function gives an ordinal ranking of social preferences over alternative combinations of individuals' utilities. It enables the economist to compare two allocations and to choose one, even it involves an increase in one person's utility whilst the other's falls.

In more applied welfare economics it is usually necessary to be more specific than the Bergson approach allows and to evaluate

107

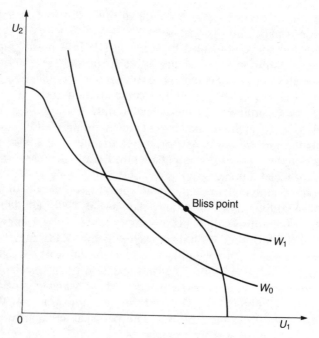

Fig. 4.1

how sensitive policy rules are to society's welfare rankings. For this reason a specific functional form is required. The form which is frequently used (see Atkinson, 1973, and Feldstein, 1973) is:

$$W[U_i(.)] = \left( \sum_{i=1}^{H} U_i^{\nu} \right)^{1/\nu} \quad \nu \leq 1$$

where $\nu$ is a constant reflecting society's aversion to inequality; $\nu = 1$ implies equal social marginal utilities (indifference to inequality). This is the utilitarian perspective (see below) in which utilitarians totally ignore distributional rankings. Public policy decisions are then based upon the simple rule of summing individual gains and losses arising from the policy. This view is strongly advocated by Harberger (1971).

If $v$ tends to $-\infty$ then this implies maximising the utility of the worse-off individual; i.e. it is the Rawlsian 'maximin' criterion. Thus, $v = 1$ and $v = -\infty$ are the limits. If $v$ tends to a large negative number, this reflects an increasing aversion to extremes in the distribution of individual utilities: $\delta W/\delta U_i$ increases as $v$ tends to minus infinity.

Bergson's approach generated much debate. Graff (1957) argued that the members of society need to agree the ethical postulates which lie behind the social welfare function. This requires agreement on the appropriate distribution of wealth. But how is this to be done? The social welfare function approach introduced ethical considerations explicitly into the analysis. Some individuals' welfare could be made to count more than others. This went beyond the Pareto criterion, which required that collective utility would increase if all component utilities increased, or if some increased but none diminished. The problem of the Bergson social welfare function approach is that the ethical postulates, which it embodies, need to be evaluated whilst at the same time the possible ways of aggregating a set of individual orderings into a social or collective ordering need to be evaluated also. In other words, where do the social welfare functions come from?

Arrow (1963b) addressed these issues, producing his famous 'possibility theorem'. If society is to judge between welfare distributions, it has to know when one alternative is as good as or better than another, even if both are Pareto optimal. Arrow imposed a number of conditions on a welfare function. First, the social ranking between two social states, $x$ and $y$, has to be complete, in the sense that society either prefers $x$ to $y$ or $y$ to $x$ or is indifferent between the two. Second, the social preference ordering has to be transitive; i.e. if there are three alternative economic states $x$, $y$ and $z$, then if $x$ is preferred to $y$ and $y$ is preferred to $z$ then $x$ must be preferred to $z$. An Arrow social welfare function has been defined by Sen (1970) as one which is complete and transitive.

Just as there are any number of Bergson social welfare functions, so too there exist an infinite number of Arrow welfare functions. Arrow attempted to narrow the number down to those which conformed to a set of reasonable requirements. These conditions are:

(1) unrestricted domain (or universality); that is, no matter what the individual preference orderings are, the social welfare function (i.e. collective preference ordering) should produce a rational ordering;

(2) Pareto consistency: if everyone prefers $x$ to $y$, then the social welfare function should 'prefer' $x$ to $y$;

(3) independence of irrelevant alternatives; if new feasible states, such as $w$, become feasible, then that should not affect the social ranking of original states $x$ and $y$;

(4) non-dictatorship; that is, no single person's preferences should dominate all others.

The power of Arrow's analysis was to demonstrate that an Arrow social welfare function which satisfies the four requirements set out above does not exist. Despite an extensive literature which has sought to find ways around the Arrow barrier, the result remains valid today. Some (see Hildreth, 1953) attempt to introduce intensity of preferences to influence the social ordering. This changes the ordinal nature of the welfare function by introducing cardinality. The public choice literature has incorporated various alternative voting rules and logrolling games (see Mueller, 1989, and Inman, 1987). The problem, however, remains – there is no way to solve the problem of income distribution. There does not exist a universal ranking rule consistent with a set of reasonable individualistic ethical restrictions on the social welfare function.

Is it possible simply to dictatorially impose a set of distributional rankings by some social policy committee? Apart from the undesirable loss to individual freedom, a dictatorial rule runs into severe analytical problems. Kemp and Ng (1977) demonstrated that an imposed real valued welfare function does not exist, even under the mild assumptions of ordinal individual utility functions. Decision rules for ranking various resource allocations by a set of equity norms will require cardinality of individuals' preferences and direct interpersonal utility comparisons.

Do estimates of real social welfare functions exist? Is it possible to finesse a welfare function from the revealed preferences exposed in policy decisions? Attempts have been made (see Wiesbrod, 1968, and Christianson and Jansen, 1978) but these studies are fraught with both analytical and empirical problems. The role of the social welfare function is, therefore, essentially as an analytical device which enables the policy analyst to sort out the distributional consequences of policy instruments and policy rules. The social welfare function does not tell the analyst what the distributional judgements should be.

## First- and second-best welfare analysis

In a first-best world, all markets are assumed to be perfectly competitive, or, if not, by the use of suitably designed policy instruments the government can intervene to replicate the perfectly competitive result. This is generally done, analytically, by means of lump sum transfers between individuals, i.e. transfers which are invariant to economic decisions. Lump sum transfers, since they are pure income effects, do not influence relative prices *ex ante*. This does not, however, imply that they do not have an *ex post* effect upon prices and hence economic activity. For example, the changes in demand brought about by the lump sum transfer will result in changes in marginal rates of substitution and marginal rates of transformation. A movement along the utility possibility curve caused by the lump sum transfer will also cause a movement along the production possibility curve and hence a change in the marginal rate of transfer will also cause a movement along the production possibility curve and hence a change in the marginal rate of transformation and changes in the marginal rates of substitution as the economy adjusts to the new Pareto-efficient conditions.

In a first-best world, allocative efficiency and distributional issues can be separated out. This means that, if there is some market imperfection which results in a misallocation of resources, then policies can be designed to correct the misallocation without worrying about the distribution of income, which can be corrected by another set of policies such as lump sum transfers. Now strictly speaking this is a gross over-simplification because, as Samuelson has pointed out, it is necessary to solve for the efficiency and distributional conditions simultaneously. However, in the first-best analysis distributional issues are ignored and attention is concentrated upon the Pareto-efficient allocation of resources.

If lump sum transfers are not feasible then the whole analysis changes dramatically. Suppose the government has at its disposal non-lump sum taxes and that markets are imperfect. This means that not all consumers face the same prices (i.e. MRS = MRT for all consumers), there are a series of differential wedges driven between producer and consumer prices and the economy will be forced beneath its first-best utility possibility frontier. This is illustrated in Figure 4.2. The shaded area indicates the feasible allocations given the imperfections which exist in markets and given that the government cannot use lump sum transfers. This feasible set may or may not include any of the first-best Pareto allocations given by the utility possibility frontier, but only by accident would it include the 'bliss point'. In Figure 4.2 the bliss point is not an element of the feasible set. This is the essence of *second-best analysis*, which is the analysis of optimal public sector policy when the bliss point of first-best analysis is unattainable.

The principal and striking result of second-best analysis is that government policy should not necessarily aim to keep society on its first-best utility possibility frontier. To do so can reduce welfare. This is illustrated in Figure 4.3. Assume society is at point

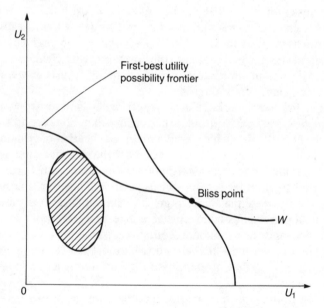

Fig. 4.2

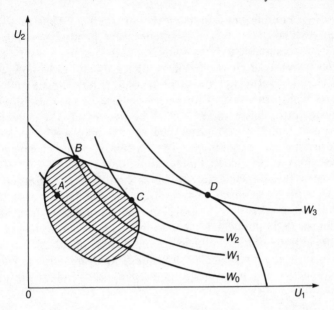

Fig. 4.3

*A* and welfare is given at that point by reference to $W_0$. If lump sum transfers were available and there were perfect markets, then the government could shift the economy to *D*. That option is not feasible in a second-best world. If the government were to take the economy to the only feasible Pareto-efficient allocation, then it would move from *A* to *B*. This is welfare improving since welfare has increased from $W_0$ to $W_1$. If, however, the objective is to do the best in welfare terms, then the Pareto-efficient outcome, *B*, is inferior to *C*, which is the maximum feasible level of social welfare. *B* is Pareto efficient compared to with *C* but *C* is better than *B* on distributional grounds. Thus, chasing first-best Pareto-efficient allocations in a world which is constrained to a set of allocations mostly below the first-best frontier can result in society being made worse off.

The first two theorems of welfare economics form the basis of liberal economics. But there are problems, such as that of the second best, which have to be confronted as soon as the idealised assumptions of competition are departed from. Preferences are in practice not given and can be influenced by advertising; equilibrium seldom exists – markets are slow to adjust in prices and many agents find themselves quantity constrained; perfectly competitive behaviour is not prevalent – real economies are instead characterised by oligopoly and monopoly; and externalities and other forms of market failure are ubiquitous. Thus, whilst the first theorem of welfare economics is often used to justify laissez-faire, it must be remembered that the first theorem applies to an ideal type of economy and completely ignores income distribution. The existence of significant non-convexities (externalities, increasing returns to scale, etc.) invalidates the fundamental theorems and gives justification to instruments of public intervention to restore Pareto efficiency either via market interventions or via planning. As has been demonstrated, public intervention aimed at securing improvements in both allocative efficiency and income distribution comes up against the problems of how best to aggregate individual preferences and how to design policies in a second-best world.

## The performance of economics with imperfect information and incomplete markets

In particular, the mathematical structure which underlies competitive analysis, such as assumptions about convexity of preferences and technology, is violated by the existence of increasing returns to scale (decreasing costs), externalities, imperfect information, uncertainty and the need for long-term planning horizons. Moreover, the results of the welfare theorems depend upon the existence of an enormous number of markets all of which are expensive to operate in terms of transactions costs. Extension of the Arrow–Debreu general equilibrium model (which is static) to the case of dynamic economies characterised by uncertainty was done by associating a commodity with every conceivable date and contingency. This approach, however, is faced with the problem that far too many markets, including future markets, are required. It also requires that each decision-maker's information set be complete. Information is expensive to acquire.

The assumptions required for full Pareto efficiency are very demanding. Some have responded to this by suggesting a weaker set of requirements that recognise the constraints imposed by incomplete markets and imperfect information. This approach produces the concept of 'constrained Pareto efficiency'. Hart (1975) has defined the concept in the following way. A competitive equilibrium, when markets are incomplete, is constrained Pareto efficient if there is no other competitive equilibrium based on the same initial endowments which Pareto-dominates it. When information is imperfect or risk markets are incomplete, the theorems of welfare economics break down. With imperfect information, a free market equilibrium is never Pareto efficient. An incomplete market equilibrium is not a full Pareto optimum. The question then becomes, 'is it a constrained Pareto optimum'? To answer this it is necessary to know the relevant constraint set.

Does all of this mean that we abandon the welfare theorems? Not entirely, but it does mean that they need to be handled with care. Malinvaud (1973) has shown that if individual risks are independent then simple insurance institutions perform as well as a complete set of contingent markets. Rational expectations have also been used to rescue some of the power of the theorems. If agents have the same project information set and form rational expectations about prices that will be set in future markets, then the system will perform as if there were complete markets. There remains the issue of whether or not rational expectations is a reasonable approximation of behaviour. Incomplete information on which to base expectations will produce the results of incomplete markets. The problem which is currently on the research agenda is – what is the performance of incomplete markets in which agents form rational expectations? How inefficient are the anonymous competitive equilibria of incomplete markets?

A number of causes give rise to incomplete markets. Future events cannot always be forecast. Many future events are not even thought of; this is expecially true of catastrophic events. In these cases insurance markets will be missing. In reality there are too many events. Pairwise comparisons carried out in an optimisation exercise would be too complex, too time consuming and, therefore, too costly. Hence, rather than thinking in terms of full rationality (i.e. searching for a global optimum), economists tend to formulate these problems in terms of 'bounded rationality' (i.e. searching for a local optimum).

It is costly to organise a complete set of contingent markets.

Each future transaction would need to be recorded and then a complex set of organisations would be needed to check that promises to demand and supply, in the future, had been fulfilled. Courts would need to be established to arbitrate disputes; Telser (1980) has advocated the use of self-enforcing contracts when courts are costly to use. The problem is magnified if international transactions are considered, in which case an expensive international court is required to deal with cases that extend across custom and language boundaries.

Knowledge about whether a particular state of nature has occurred (and hence which contingency is to be traded) is information which is not equally shared throughout the community. Thus, knowledge is frequently non-verifiable by third parties or information is asymmetric (i.e. impacted). In an extreme case, only one party to a transaction has information about, for example, the quality of the commodity. This is referred to as the problem of *adverse selection* (Arrow, 1971). It is 'hidden information'. A market contingent upon the information of the commodity (its quality) cannot be set up because the buyer cannot confirm the quality at the time of purchase.

Another problem which arises is that of *moral hazard*. This idea was first used by Knight (1921) but was not picked up and developed until Arrow (1963a). Moral hazard exists when agents can affect the probabilities of some random event they face through actions which are unobservable to others; i.e. they can cheat to their own advantage. This problem can arise in insurance markets. If A is insured against fire damage, then she might engage in careless behaviour which she would avoid if uninsured. This is not a problem if the insurance company can monitor the insured's behaviour. Next time round a higher premium is charged which reflects the assessment of the careless behaviour. However, not only is monitoring (information) expensive, it is often not possible to obtain such information at all.

One way of modelling the general problem of incomplete markets is to do so in terms of Radner equilibria (Radner, 1979). Assume a set of sequence markets in which individuals forecast future prices perfectly. If there are multiple equilibria, agents agree upon a single price for planning. This system produces Radner equilibria. But what is the welfare performance of Radner equilibria? Are they constrained Pareto efficient in the sense that it is not possible to find allocations which use the same limited set of markets and which realise Pareto improvements over these equilibria? Stiglitz (1982) and Geanakoplos and Polemarchakis (1986) show that Radner equilibria are not constrained efficient. Pareto improvements could be brought about by excise taxes, but the government would need to know a great deal about individual preferences to carry out a successful taxation policy. If it is difficult (costly) to design suitable tax policies and if it is costly to create additional markets, then how serious a problem is constrained Pareto optimality? This question remains to be answered.

The problem of adverse selection was formally analysed by Akerlof (1970). In that paper Akerlof shows that when the quality of a commodity is unknown to the purchaser then the outcome of competitive exchange depends upon the quality expected by the purchaser. Prices transmit information about the average level of quality and consumers have rational expectations conditional upon equilibrium prices. Akerlof demonstrates that this rational expectations equilibrium is a bad outcome and can in the limit correspond to a complete breakdown of the market with no exchange taking place (see also Laffont, 1975). Is the Akerlof rational expectations equilibrium constrained Pareto optimal? Do there exist allocations which use the same markets, which recognise the asymmetry of information and which do better? This question has been addressed by Belloc (1986) and Greenwald and Stiglitz (1986). When a purchaser increases consumption of a commodity, this signals to other purchasers that there is a confidence in the quality of the product being purchased. Other purchasers benefit from this signal (i.e. there is a public good element in the signal). Purchasers do not internalise this externality – a benevolent government could do better than the Akerlof rational expectations by subsidising the commodity. On balance, then, competitive equilibria with incomplete markets due to adverse selection perform poorly.

## Potential competition, contestability, and welfare economics

A paradox exists in applied industrial economics. Anti-trust and monopoly legislation is based upon ideas of what is regarded to be good economic performance, which is derived from the basic theorems of welfare economics. Such legislation is appraised in terms of how closely it conforms to the theorems. It has, however, been demonstrated already that the basic theorems of welfare economics are not well suited to deal with issues such as the market imperfections with which anti-monopoly legislation is supposed to deal.

One proposed way out of this paradox was to use the notion of potential competition. Demsetz (1968), Grossman (1981) and Baumol, Panzer and Willig (1982) argued that it was not actual competition which was important for economic performance but rather it was potential competition which ensured Pareto efficiency by driving profits to zero. The idea of potential competition along with Schumpeterian notions of dynamic efficiency (compared to the static efficiency of standard welfare economics) could be used to justify the performance of monopolies.

Those who believed in potential competition argued that a large market share was not sufficient to justify government intervention via monopoly legislation. The fear of potential entrants into contestable markets plus the assumption of zero exit costs would result in monopolists pricing at the Pareto-efficient level. If this result is true, then it is powerful.

Stiglitz (1981) and Dixit and Stiglitz (1979), however, showed that potential competition could be Pareto inefficient. Free entry was not sufficient to guarantee economic efficiency if non-convexities existed. Firms could undertake strategic responses to the threat of entry by over-expanding capacity, investing in more durable machines, and other entry-deterrent activities. In other words, the level of welfare would be lower than it might otherwise have been if there was no competition! Potential competition was, therefore, not necessarily welfare enhancing. Entry-deterrent responses by incumbent firms fearing the threats from potential competition meant that potential entrants would be no better off whilst incumbents' profits would be lower than they might otherwise have been.

The power of the Baumol, Panzer and Willig theory of contestable markets and potential competition and hence its welfare implications depends crucially upon their assumption of zero sunk costs; i.e. exit is assumed to be inexpensive. It was, however, thought that even if sunk costs were not too great (slightly greater than zero) then the result of zero profits arising from potential competition would still hold good. Stiglitz (1988) demonstrated that this is not the case. Even if there are small sunk costs, potential competition may not be effective in driving profits to zero.

What is meant by small sunk costs? Generally, sunk costs are small relative to variable costs of production. Why might even small sunk costs render potential competition ineffective? This is the problem that Stiglitz set out to solve. Suppose there is a large number of firms and that one firm differs from the rest in the sense that it alone has entered the market. Once a firm invests $E$ in sunk costs it faces a constant return to scale technology. Furthermore, each firm believes that if there is more than one firm in the industry Bertrand competition will exist and price will be equal to the marginal cost of production, $C$. The firms outside the industry will not enter because they know that at the Bertrand price they will not be able to recover their sunk costs however small they might be. Thus, the incumbent firm can charge the monopoly price. Potential competition when sunk costs are significant is ineffective. Even small sunk costs can result in large degrees of monopoly power.

Another example will illustrate the problem. Potential competition might force *profits* to zero but nevertheless the firm will charge a monopoly price. Consumers, therefore, do not benefit from potential competition, which is in fact welfare decreasing. Where have the profits gone? The answer is quite simple – they have been used up by the incumbent firm creating excessive capacity. Consider the case of a natural monopoly in which all costs are sunk. Suppose the capacity has a life of $T$ years. Sunk costs deter entry and so the firm can charge the monopoly price, maximizing profits. But the firm fears what will happen in year $T$ when capacity is depreciated and needs to be replaced. This fear will influence the monopolist's behaviour. A rival could enter the market at some date close to but prior to $T$ because it pays it to do so. During the period of time in which there are two firms in the market, Bertrand competition will drive profits to zero. Once the machine is, however, fully depreciated in year $T$, the initial firm in the market will not wish to replace the machine. The new incumbent could then charge a monopoly price and make monopoly profits.

E

Recognising the above possibilities, the initial firm in the industry could adopt the following survival strategy. At some date prior to the date $T$ at which time the existing capacity is scrapped the incumbent firm will purchase a new machine. It is no longer profitable for a rival to enter under these circumstances. Potential competition has resulted in over-capacity; price remains at the monopoly level and profits are driven towards zero. This result becomes stronger the shorter the life of the machine becomes.

These examples can be summarised as follows. The more intense competition is after entry (*ex post* competition) then the less effective is the power of potential competition (*ex ante*). When large sunk costs arising from R & D spending and learning-by-doing are considered, then monopoly power can be even greater. Is some degree of monopoly power beneficial for progress as Schumpeter suggested? Despite the insightful analysis of Dasgupta and Stiglitz (1980a,b), Salop (1979), Gilbert and Stiglitz (1979) and Sah and Stiglitz (1987), we do not know what degree of monopoly power is best, let alone whether or not this comes close to the real world.

## Distributive justice

Economists have traditionally used the device of the social welfare function to deal with the problem of distributive justice. This, however, leaves another problem unresolved – which social welfare function embodying alternative ethical postulates is to be chosen? What principles would guide us in dividing up society's wealth? This is the problem of distributive justice and a society will be judged not only in terms of the efficiency of its allocation of resources but also by how well it deals with distributive justice.

Any discussion of distributive justice will be wide ranging, covering an extensive literature drawn not only from economics but also from politics and philosophy. This review is highly selective. Many economists argue against the notion of weighting the utility of the poor more than that of the rich, claiming that a 'dollar is a dollar' no matter who spends it and that social welfare is maximised by the unweighted addition of individual utilities. Harberger (1971), Parish (1976) and Ng (1984) agree with this approach: Ng's argument is that, wherever we start, there is always a Pareto-superior policy which makes everyone better off and that we should aim for this rather than giving one group in society preferential treatment compared with another group.

Four approaches to distributive justice will be considered: (a) utilitarian, (b) egalitarian, (c) libertarian, and (d) Marxist.

Utilitarianism is a social philosophy that is now generally out of favour. Stated in its simplest form, utilitarianism (also called Welfarism) argues that what makes something (a rule or an act) good or bad is its effect on individual welfare. The utilitarian philosophy wishes to maximise social welfare by producing the greatest good of the greatest number (Bentham). To maximise total social welfare requires the equalisation of marginal utilities of different individuals. Some (Acton, 1963) have advocated negative utilitarianism. This version gives priority to the relief of suffering over the promotion of pleasure.

The problem with utilitarianism is that, by simply concentrating upon the maximising of welfare (the sum of individual utilities), it ignores the distribution of utilities.

Egalitarians concentrate upon the way in which individuals are treated. In particular, each individual is to be treated equally, but what does this mean? It could mean either equal distribution of output or equal opportunity. Aristotle, in his *Nicomachian Ethics*,[10] argued that egalitarianism involved treating equals equally but treating unequals unequally. This, however, leaves a number of unanswered questions. Over what dimensions should inequality be defined; how easy is it to implement the appropriate policies (how much information is required), and what disincentive effects are created and how important are these? Aristotle recognised that complete egalitarianism would fail because of disincentive effects. Success required a change in human attitudes – individuals would wish to participate in an egalitarian society and would gain satisfaction from such participation, thereby compensating those who would lose wealth as a result of living in a more equal society. Marx (1891) also recognised that unless human nature changed then disincentive effects would constrain the move towards equality.

Egalitarianism comes in different forms. There are those who argue for equality of welfare across individuals as the objective of policy. This assumes that interpersonal comparisons of utility can be made – a problem which has already been considered. Second, there are those who advocate equality of opportunity; Dworkin (1981) calls this 'starting gate equality'. This approach justifies final outcomes that are unequal if it is assumed that individuals have equal opportunities and are free to trade voluntarily. Between these two versions there are intermediate cases of equalisation of basic capabilities or an equalisation which allows individuals to meet basic needs.

Recognising that unbridled egalitarianism is both destructive and infeasible, Rawls (1971), in his seminal contribution to the theory of justice, presents a modified egalitarian philosophy. For Rawls, a just society must guarantee a system of equal basic liberties; all social goods other than liberty must also be distributed equally except when unequal distribution benefits the least well off and even then only if the position of the least well off in society is open to all. This is called the 'difference principle' or the 'maximin principle'.[11] In summary, the maximin principle states that society should select the reward structure which favours the least well-off person.

Rawls considers society to be a cooperative enterprise for mutual gain. Through bargaining and contracting, individuals collectively achieve outcomes that would not be available if they acted in isolation. There therefore exists a set of cooperative reward structures; the problem is, which should be chosen? Rawls' view is a liberal one. Society is a voluntary association for mutual gain. When forming a society individuals will wish to protect one another from coercion. 'Each person is to have an equal right to the most extensive basic liberty compatible with a similar liberty for others' (Rawls, 1971, p. 60). The basic rights and duties of individual members of society would be assigned and defined in an 'economic constitution'. This would determine the distribution of benefits and costs from social co-operation. The problem is, what rules should guide the writing of such a constitution? Whatever scheme is chosen, society must be stable: individuals must accept the basic rules and act upon them willingly. But they will only do so if they see them to be just, and no one will join or cooperate if they are going to be made worse off.

These ideas can be illustrated by means of Figure 4.4. The

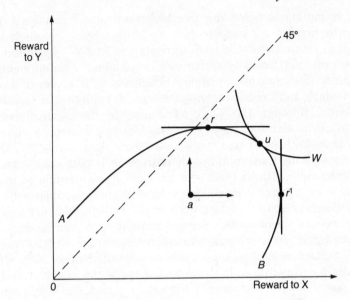

Fig. 4.4

point *a* gives a combination of rewards to X and Y if they do not cooperate. The locus *AB* shows combinations of rewards which result from X and Y cooperating. Any point in the north-east quadrant drawn from *a* is an improvement for either X or Y or both.

The 45° line indicates points of equal reward to X and Y. Each move from complete equality requires justification: 'social and economic inequalities are to be arranged so that they are both (a) reasonably expected to be to everyone's advantage and (b) attached to positions and offices open to all' (Rawls, 1971, p. 60). Inequality can widen, provided everyone is better off (compare with Little's critique of the compensation tests). How-ever, there will come a point at which someone is made worse off. At this point the least well-off person is as well off as poss-ible. This is the maximin outcome; i.e. the minimum of all re-wards is at a maximum. This is given by point *r*. The difference principle is one approach to distributive justice: it is unjust for a person or a group of people who are already at least as well off as another to demand a greater reward for cooperation if it is at the other's expense.

The just outcome is held to emerge from Rawls' idea of 'fairness', which is based upon the 'veil of ignorance' and an 'initial situation of equality'. Principles of fairness need to be chosen impartially and they must be universal, i.e. apply equally to all (Rawls, 1971, pp. 108–12). Principles of fairness are chosen in ignorance of our own vested interests. When people are together in the initial state of shared ignorance, then the just distributive principle is that which free and rational self-interested people will choose.

It is now possible to compare the utilitarian and egalitarian (Rawlsian) positions. In Figure 4.4 the rewards of both X and Y are increasing up to $r$. Inequality is widening after the 45° line is crossed, but this is justified because the rewards of the least well off (Y) are increasing. Between $r$ and $r^1$ the rewards of X increase but those of Y fall. Between $r$ and $u$ the rate at which the rewards to X increase is greater than the rate at which the rewards to Y decrease. Therefore, total social welfare is a maximum at point $u$. This is the utilitarian position. Utilitarians would be prepared to accept more inequality than egalitarians.

Utilitarians see that there are extra gains (efficiency) to be obtained from trade. They are prepared to sacrifice one person's loss of utility (reward) in order to obtain these gains. For a utilitarian the opportunity cost of staying at $r$ is too high and it is irrational to do so. The egalitarian reply is that individuals have a basic right to stay at $r$ and that justice demands that these rights should not be violated.

Libertarians such as Hayek (1960) and Nozick (1974) are critical of the redistributions implied by the utilitarian and egalitarian views. Hayek argues that the unfettered market mechanism guarantees individual liberty and that justice is nothing more than the rule of law. Government's role (a minimal one) is to set rules and regulations that will facilitate market transactions. Thus Hayek's focus is upon procedural justice. Nozick's is a rights-based theory of justice, but his set of rights is much narrower than Rawls'. Nozick argues that government intervention to redistribute wealth violates individual rights and liberties: its actions are coercive. Income or wealth transfers are just only if they are voluntary (altruism). A redistribution is just if the procedures of market exchange are just. Given a just initial distribution, the outcomes of market transactions will be just.

The libertarian approach is full of problems. How do we decide if the initial distribution is just? Libertarians have a narrow and simplistic view of liberty and freedom, which focuses upon negative freedom, i.e. 'freedom from', such as freedom from interference from government. Berlin (1958) demonstrates that there is another dimension to freedom, namely 'positive freedom', i.e. 'freedom to do'. Dasgupta (1986) builds upon this, arguing that individuals' freedoms are constrained in a positive sense if they face binding income constraints which are arbitrarily imposed by chance. A legitimate role of government is to extend positive freedoms by providing positive 'freedom goods' such as basic amounts of education, health, etc. This is an egalitarian's critique based on the idea of starting gate equality.

Nozick's entitlement theory of justice argues that transfers between individuals are just only if they are voluntary. The idea of voluntary giving is closely associated with the concept of altruism. Hochman and Rodgers (1969), in an interesting paper on Pareto-efficient transfers, attempted to explain why it was rational for individuals to make transfer payments. They argued that the utility of the rich depends upon the income of the poor (and vice versa). Thus if the existence of poverty enters into the utility functions of the rich in a negative way, then the utility of the rich can be increased by altruistic giving up to the point at which the marginal utility gain to the rich from a reduction in poverty is equal to the marginal utility loss from giving. Thus, altruism arises when an individual prefers state $X$ to state $Y$ because they know others are better off in state $X$ compared with state $Y$, even though they will be relatively worse off in state $X$.

Others have used the self-interest approach to explain altruism in terms of social exchange or reciprocal altruism. Help is provided in the expectation of someone helping you in the future (see Becker, 1976; Wintrobe, 1981). Children's welfare will, therefore, appear as arguments in the utility functions of parents as in the bequest motive in overlapping generation models.

This rational approach to altruism can be criticised for a number of reasons. The rich need to admit that their utility depends upon the income of the poor, otherwise there will be no transfers. Moreover, since transfer payments have a public good element it will be rational not to make transfers but, instead, to free-ride on others' giving. It is also argued that, because the redistribution depends upon the self-interest of the rich, then it is not a theory of altruism at all. A Kantian approach to altruistic giving would emphasise the notion of duty and an individual's sense of moral obligation rather than self-interest.[12]

Altruism can create incentive problems like those in the moral hazard problem. If the recipient knows that an altruist will always help out then they might squander their resources or shirk. Saving for old age might be reduced. Buchanan (1975) refers to this general problem as the 'Samaritan's dilemma'.

The classical economists such as Smith and Ricardo had, in their models of the market, assumed the atomistic dispersal of individual power. Marx criticised this as being unrealistic given that ownership of the means of production granted power to their owners. There are two theories of distributive justice found in Marx. First, there is the notion of a 'socialist society'. Each person receives rewards in accordance with the contribution of their labour to the social product (after a contribution has been made for investment). Complete equality is not achieved in this kind of society. This is contrasted with the second theory of distributive justice, which is to be found in a communist society. In this case rewards are distributed according to needs.

The problem with the Marxist view is that it often ignores disincentive effects. Marxists do, however, emphasise that in a capitalist system products are produced for profit, not for the satisfaction of basic human needs. This means that in a capitalist system the basic needs of many individuals will not be satisfied if it is not profitable to do so. Like Libertarians, Marxists don't believe that governments will always act to serve the public interest.

Each approach to distributive justice produces a different preferred position on society's grand utility possibility frontier, as shown in Figure 4.5. The libertarian minimalist state of Hayek and Nozick might be given by a point such as $N$. Here the only role of the state is to provide protective services that will safeguard entitlements. The solution produced by maximising a Bergson utilitarian social welfare function is given by $W$, whereas the Rawlsian maximin solution is at $R$. The egalitarian solution is $E$.

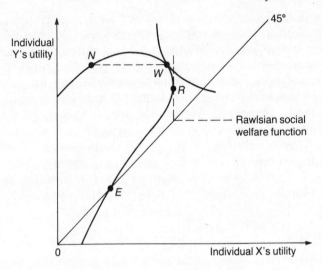

Fig. 4.5

The final concept that will be examined is that of 'fairness'. When dividing up society's wealth, two guiding principles are used. The first is Pareto optimality, which has been examined at length. When possible, the opportunity should be taken to make everyone better off. The second principle is that there should be no envy in the final state. That is, the final distribution of goods (income) should not give rise to envy in the sense that no individual should strictly prefer the bundle of goods of any other person to their own. An allocation which is both Pareto optimal and envy free is called 'fair' by Varian (1976) and 'superfair' by Baumol (1986). If there is no one who envies anyone else then there is no clear Rawlsian worse-off person who has been treated unfairly. Moreover, if individuals are not to envy each other, then individuals with identical preferences must get equally good bundles. This amounts to 'equal treatment of equals'.

## Conclusion

This survery has been wide ranging but by no means exhaustive. Welfare economics is again an active branch of economics.

Establishing the criteria that are to be used to judge the performance of an economy which is characterised by incomplete markets and asymmetric information is at the frontier of current theoretical research. The debate about competing theories of distributive justice is incomplete and enables economists to join with the research agenda of social and political philosophers.

The value of welfare economics is found in this application to informing policy debates. Areas such as the optimal design of tax systems (Mirrless, 1971, 1972), the design of incentive structures, social choice, and industrial organisation have all benefited from the revival of welfare economics since the early 1970s. Most of the exciting work remains to be done.

## Notes

1 See Mueller (1989) for a useful broad-based treatment of public and social choice. The breadth of welfare economics is readily seen from standard textbook treatments such as Boadway and Bruce (1984), Ng (1979) and Sugden (1981).
2 The development of welfare economics from Pigou's 1920 contribution is usefully provided in Hicks (1975).
3 Myrdal had a similar impact on the Scandinavian and German-speaking world. For the link between Myrdal and Robbins see Hicks (1954).
4 Carnap (1935), a philosopher of the 'Vienna circle' of logical positivists, argued that a value judgement is merely a disguised imperative which is devoid of empirical content, which cannot be proved or disproved and in the end is nothing more than an expression of a personal subjective wish. Ayer's influential *Language, Truth and Logic* (1934) argued that ethical statements either are a disguised form of the empirical propositions of sociology or psychology or, if they are value judgements, are 'simply expressions of emotion which can be neither true nor false' (p. 103).
5 A whole group of economists based at the LSE or having a connection with the LSE during the period 1935–55 made significant contributions to welfare economics. This was undoubtedly due to the influence of Robbins; see for example, in addition to Hicks, Kaldor (1939), Lerner (1944), Lange (1942), Baumol (1952), Mishan (1963). Other significant contributions included Bergson (1938), Samuelson (1947), Scitovsky (1941).
6 Arrow and Debreu (1954). See also Arrow (1951), Koopmans (1957), Arrow and Hahn (1971) and Malinvaud (1972).

7 Pigou, for example, thought that the competitive equilibrium is for the common good because it maximises national output.

8 The use of compensation tests is found in Dupuit (1844) and Marshall (1890), who considered the problem in partial equilibrium terms by comparing consumer supluses to distinguish efficient from inefficient states.

9 Samuelson (1947) also developed the Bergson social welfare function and made use of it in his 1954 paper on the analysis of public spending.

10 See Polanyi (1968).

11 This approach appeared earlier in Benn and Peters (1959): 'to act justly then is to treat all men alike except where there are relevant differences between them' (p. 111). But what constitutes relevance?

12 See also Titmuss (1971) and Singer (1972).

# References

Acton, H. B. (1963), 'Negative utilitarianism', *Proceedings of the Aristotelian Society*, Supplementary volume 37, pp. 83–94.

Akerlof, G. (1970), 'The market for lemons: qualitative uncertainty and the market mechanism', *Quarterly Journal of Economics*, 84, pp. 488–500.

Arrow, K. J. (1951), 'An extension of the basic theorems of classical welfare economics', in J. Neyman (ed.), *Proceedings of the Second Berkeley Symposium on Mathematical Statistics and Probability*, Berkeley, California.

Arrow, K. J. (1963a), 'Uncertainty and the welfare economics of medical care', *American Economic Review*, 53, pp. 941–73.

Arrow, K. J. (1963b), *Social Choice and Individual Values*, New York: John Wiley.

Arrow, K. J. (1971), *Essays in the Theory of Risk Bearing*, Chicago: Markham.

Arrow, K. J. and Debreu, G. (1954), 'Existence of an equilibrium for a competitive economy', *Econometrica*, 20, pp. 265–90.

Arrow, K. J. and Hahn, F. H. (1971), *General Competitive Analysis*, Edinburgh: Oliver & Boyd.

Atkinson, A. B. (1973), 'How progressive should the income tax be?' In M. Parkin (ed.), *Essays on Modern Economics*, London: Longman.

Ayer, A. J. (1934), *Language Truth and Logic*, Harmondsworth: Penguin Books.

Bator, F. M. (1957), 'The simple analytics of welfare maximisation', *American Economic Review*, 47, pp. 22–59.

Baumol, W. J. (1952), *Welfare Economics and the Theory of the State*, London: LSE; Bell and Sons.

Baumol, W. J. Panzer, J. C. and Willig, R. D. (1982), *Contestable Markets and the Theory of Industrial Structure*, New York: Harcourt, Brace, Jovanovich.

Baumol, W. (1986), *Superfairness*, Cambridge, Mass.: MIT Press.

Becker, G. (1976), 'Altruism, egoism, and genetic fitness: economics and sociobiology', *Journal of Economic Literature*, 14, pp. 817–26.

Belloc, B. (1986), 'Some normative aspects of Akerlof's problem: an example', *Economics Letters*, 20, pp. 107–10.

Benn, S. I. and Peters, R. S. (1959), *Social Principles and the Democratic State*, London: Allen & Unwin.

Bergson, A. ' (193?), 'A reformulation of certain aspects of welfare economic., *Quarterly Journal of Economics*, 52, February, pp. 310–34.

Berlin, I. (1958), *Two Concepts of Liberty*, Oxford: Clarendon Press.

Boadway, R. W. and Bruce, N. (1984), *Welfare Economics*, Oxford: Blackwell.

Boulding, K. R. (1969), 'Economics as a moral science', *American Economic Review*, 59, March, pp. 1–12.

Bowen, H. (1972), 'Towards humanist economics', *Nebraska Journal of Economics and Business*, 11, Autumn, pp. 9–24.

Buchanan, J. (1975), 'The Samaritan's dilemma', in E. Phelps, (ed.), *Altruism, Morality and Economic Theory*, New York: Russel Sage Foundation.

Carnap, R. (1935), *Philosophy and Logical Syntax*, London: Kegan Paul, Trench, Trubner.

Christianson, V. and Jansen, E. S. (1978), 'Implicit social preferences in the Norwegian system of indirect taxation', *Journal of Public Economics*, 10, October.

Dasgupta, P. (1986), 'Positive freedom markets and the welfare state', *Oxford Review of Economic Policy*, 2(2), pp. 25–36.

Dasgupta, P. and Stiglitz, J. E. (1980a), 'Uncertainty, industrial structure, and the speed of R & D', *Bell Journal of Economics*, 2, Spring, pp. 1–28.

Dasgupta, P. and Stiglitz, J. E. (1980b), 'Market structure and the state of innovative activity', *Economic Journal*, 90, pp. 266–93.

Demsetz, H. (1968), 'Why regulate utilities?' *Journal of Law and Economics*, 2, pp. 55–66.

Dixit, A. K. and Stiglitz, J. E. (1979), 'Monopolistic competition and optimal productivity diversity: reply', *American Economic Review*, 69 (5), December, pp. 961–3.

Dupuit, F. (1844), 'De la mesure de l'utilité des travaux publics',

*Annales de Pouts et Chassées*; English translation in K. J. Arrow, and T. Scitovsky, *AEA Readings in Welfare Economics*, Homewood, Ill: Irwin, 1969.

Dworkin, R. (1981), 'What is equality? Part 1: Equality of welfare' and 'What is equality? Part 2: Equality of resources', *Philosophy and Public Affairs*, 10, pp. 185–246, 283–345.

Feldstein (1973), 'On the optimal progressivity of the income tax', *Journal of Public Economics*, 2.

Geanakoplos, J. and Polemarchakis, H. (1986), 'Existence, regularity and constrained suboptimality of competitive allocation when the asset market is incomplete', in W. P. Heller, R. M. Starr and D. Starrett (eds), *Uncertainty, Information and Communication, Essays in Honour of K. Arrow*, Cambridge: Cambridge University Press.

Gilbert, R. and Stiglitz, J. E. (1979), 'Entry, equilibrium and welfare', NBER Working Paper, mimeo.

Graff, J. de V. (1957), *Theoretical Welfare Economics*, Cambridge: Cambridge University Press.

Greenwald, B. and Stiglitz, J. E. (1986), 'Externalities in economics with imperfect information and incomplete markets', *Quarterly Journal of Economics*, 101, pp. 229–64.

Grossman, S. J. (1981), 'Nash equilibrium and the industrial organisation of markets with large fixed costs', *Econometrica*, 49, pp. 1149–72.

Harberger, A. C. (1971), 'Three basic postulates for applied welfare economics', *Journal of Economic Literature*, 1.

Harrod, R. F. (1938), 'Scope and method of economics', *Economic Journal*, 48, September, pp. 383–412.

Hart, O. (1975), 'On the optimality of equilibrium when the market structure is incomplete', *Journal of Economic Theory*, 11, pp. 418–43.

Hayek, F. (1960), *The Constitution of Liberty*, London: Routledge & Kegan Paul.

Hicks, J. R. (1939), 'Foundations of welfare economics', *Economic Journal*, 49, pp. 696–712.

Hicks, J. R. (1954), Review of Myrdal's *The Political Element in the Development of Economic Thought*, *Economic Journal*, 64, December.

Hicks, J. R. (1969), 'Preface and a Manifesto', in K. J. Arrow and T. Scitovsky (eds), *AEA Readings in Welfare Economics*, Homewood, Ill: Irwin, pp. 95–9.

Hicks, J. R. (1975), 'The scope and status of welfare economics', *Oxford Economic Papers*, 27, November, pp. 307–26.

Hildreth, C. (1953), 'Alternative conditions for social orderings', *Econometrica*, 21(1).

Hochman, H. M. and Rodgers, J. D. (1969), 'Pareto optimal redistribution', *American Economic Review*, 59, September, pp. 242–57.

Inman, R. P. (1987), 'Markets, government and the new political economy', in A. J. Auerbach and M. S. Feldstein (eds), *Handbook of Public Economics*, vol. II, Amsterlam: North Holland.

Kaldor, N. (1939), 'welfare propositions of economics and interpersonal comparisons of utility', *Economic Journal*, 49, pp. 549–52.

Kemp, M. C. and Ng, K.-Y. (1977), 'More on social welfare functions; the incompatibility of individualism and ordinalism', *Economica*, 44, February.

Knight, F. (1921), *Risk, Uncertainty and Profit*, Boston: Houghton Mifflin.

Koopmans, T. J. (1957), *Three Essays on the State of Economic Science*, New York: McGraw Hill.

Laffont, J. J. (1975), 'Optimism and expert against adverse selection in a competitive economy', *Journal of Economic Theory*, 10, pp. 284–308.

Lange, O. (1942), 'The foundations of welfare economics', *Econometrica*, 10, pp. 215–28.

Lerner, A. P. (1944), *The Economics of Control*, London: Macmillan.

Little, I. M. D. (1950), *A Critique of Welfare Economics*, Oxford: Oxford University Press.

Malinvaud, E. (1972), *Microeconomic Theory*, Amsterdam: North Holland.

Malinvaud, E. (1973), 'The allocation of individual risks in large markets', *Journal of Economic Theory*, 5, pp. 312–28.

Marshall, A. (1890), *Principles of Economics*, London: Macmillan.

Marx, K. (1891), 'A critique of the Gotha Plan', *Neue Zeit* (Stuttgart); English translation R. C. Tucker (ed.), *The Marx, Engels Reader*, New York: W. W. Norton, 1972.

Mirrlees, J. A. (1971), 'An exploration in the theory of optimum income taxation', *Review of Economic Studies*, 38, pp. 175–208.

Mirrlees, J. A. (1972), 'Producer taxation', *Review of Economic Studies*, 39, pp. 105–11.

Mishan, E. J. (1963), 'Welfare criteria: are compensation tests necessary?' *Economic Journal*, 73, pp. 342–50.

Mishan, E. J. (1969), *Welfare Economics: An Assessment*, Amsterdam: North Holland.

Mishan, E. J. (1984), 'The implications of alternative foundations for welfare economics', *De Economist*, 32(1), pp. 75–85.

Mueller, D. C. (1989), *Public Choice II*, Cambridge: Cambridge University Press.

Ng, Y.-K. (1979), *Welfare Economics*, London: Macmillan.

Ng, Y.-K. (1984), 'Quasi-Pareto social improvements', *American Economic Review*, 74, pp. 1033–50.

Nozick, R. (1974), *Anarchy State and Utopia*, New York: Basic Books.

Pareto, V. (1896, 1897), *Cours d'économie politique*, 2 vols, Lausanne: F. Rouge.

Pareto, V. (1906) *Manuale de Economia Politica*, Milan: Società Editrice Libraria (referred to as the Manuel). Revised and translated as *Manuel d'économie politique*, Paris: Giard et Briere, 1909; English translation, *Manual of Political Economy*, London: Macmillan, 1927.

Parish, R. M. (1976), 'The scope of cost–benefit analysis', *Economic Record*, 52, pp. 302–14.

Pigou, A. C. (1920), *The Economics of Welfare*. London: Macmillan.

Polanyi K. (1968), 'Aristotle discovers the economy', in *Primitive, Archaic and Modern Economics: Essays of Karl Polanyi*, New York: Doubleday; from K. Polanyi, C. Arensberg and K. Pearson (eds), *Trade and Market in the Early Empires*, New York: Free Press, 1957.

Radner, R. (1979), 'Rational expectations equilibrium: generic existence and the information revealed by prices', *Econometrica*, 47, pp. 655–78.

Rawls, J. A. (1971), *A Theory of Justice*, Oxford: Clarendon Press.

Robbins, L. (1932), *Essay on the Nature and Significance of Economic Science*, 2nd edn, London: Macmillan.

Robbins, L. (1938), 'Interpersonal comparisons of utility: a comment', *Economic Journal*, 48, December, pp. 635–41.

Sah, R. and Stiglitz, J. E. (1987), 'The invariance of r and D to the number of firms in the industry: equilibrium and efficiency under Bertrand competition', *Rand Journal of Economics*, 18.

Salop, S. C. (1979), 'Strategic entry deterrence', *American Economic Review*, 69, May, pp. 335–8.

Samuelson, P. A. (1947), *Foundations of Economic Analysis*, Cambridge, Mass.: Harvard University Press.

Scitovsky, T. (1941), 'A note on welfare propositions in economics', *Review of Economic Studies*, 9, November, pp. 77–88.

Sen, A. K. (1970), *Collective Choice and Social Welfare*, Edinburgh: Oliver & Boyd.

Singer, P. (1972), 'Altruism and commerce', *Philosophy and Public Affairs*, 2, pp. 312–19.

Smith, A. (1759), *The Theory of Moral Sentiments*. Edited by D. D. Raphael and A. L. Macfie, Oxford: Clarendon Press, 1976.

Smith, A. (1766) *Lectures on Jurisprudence*. Edited by R. L. Meek, P. G. Stein and D. D. Raphael, Oxford: Clarendon Press, 1978.

Smith, A. (1776), *An Inquiry into the Nature and Causes of the Wealth of Nations*. Edited by R. H. Campbell, A. S. Skinner and W. B.

Todd, Oxford: Clarendon Press, 1976.

Stiglitz, J. E. (1981), 'Potential competition may reduce welfare', *American Economic Review*, 71, pp. 184–9.

Stiglitz, J. E. (1982), 'The inefficiency of the stock market equilibrium', *Review of Economic Studies*, 64, pp. 241–62.

Stiglitz, J. E. (1988), 'Sunk costs, competition and technical progress', *Brookings Papers on Economic Activity*.

Sugden, R. (1981), *The Political Economy of Public Choice*, Oxford: Martin Robertson.

Telser, L. (1980), 'A theory of self-enforcing agreement', *Journal of Business*, 53, pp. 27–44.

Titmuss, R. M. (1971), *The Gift Relationship: From Human Blood to Social Policy*, London: Allen & Unwin.

Varian, H. (1976), 'Two problems in the theory of fairness', *Journal of Public Economics*, 5(3), pp. 249–60.

Weisbrod, B. A. (1968), 'Income distribution effects and cost benefit analysis', in S. B. Chase Jr (ed.), *Problems in Public Expenditure Analysis*, Washington DC: Brookings Institution.

Wintrobe, R. (1981), 'It pays to do good, but not to do more good than it pays', *Journal of Economic Behaviour and Organisation*, 2, pp. 201–13.

# 5

*Michael Artis*

# Macroeconomic theory

## Introduction

Developments in macroeconomics, as in other fields of scholarly enquiry, reflect the influence of several forces. Some of these relate to the pure momentum of ideas as successive scholars pursue the logic of a particular paradigm, some have to do with the influence of new technologies on the methodology of the subject, and some reflect nothing higher than the need for academic scholars to differentiate their products in the interests of self-promotion.

There is, however, in the case of macroeconomics, a particular reason for expecting that its development should, over the not so long run, reflect the promptings of real-world problems. This is because the stuff of macroeconomics is precisely the behaviour of the large aggregates of economic activity and the price level, which are important to human welfare and are believed to be potentially capable of being influenced by the actions taken by governments. This immediately political context is no doubt one reason why the discussions between rival schools of thought in macroeconomics so often take on the appearance of sanguinary conflict, at some variance with the 'scientific' image that economists like to promote for their subject. Whilst real-world developments and the concerns of policy-makers and electorates thus provide an essential part of the background to the development of modern macroeconomics, this must not be read naively: for example, one of the 'messages' of recent work is precisely that the expectations of policy-makers and their electorates are often unrealistic and ask too much of macroeconomics and macroeconomic policy; indeed, it is not too much to say that a good part of the momentum of the subject today derives from experiences in the 1970s and 1980s in which indeed it did appear that macroeconomics had claimed too much for its real-world applicability.

It is not only developments in the real world that drive macroeconomics. Other factors are in play as well. We have already referred to the influence of new technologies: what stands out here is the mathematisation of the subject and the advent of the electronic computer. The latter has made possible the building and solution of models tuned to correspond to features of the real economies they represent and allows their operators to study the effects of certain types of intervention with speed and precision. The former has made possible the solution of economic models which could not have been solved even a few decades ago. If at one remove, this combination puts within the reach of many what was previously the arcane art of policy-making. Then there is the logic of pure scholarly enquiry, which ensures that ideas will continue to be pursued to their bitter end even if the 'relevance' of these ideas to real-world concerns is not immediately obvious: a snapshot of the subject taken at any one point of time reveals not one, but several, schools of thought and many different strands of work pursuing different basic insights. The professionalisation of the subject is also a remarkable phenomenon, hardly without its repercussions on the content of the subject, though these may not always seem desirable. The large numbers of economists specialising in macroeconomics or well acquainted as a part of their broader training with the subject stand in stark contrast to the position prevailing when modern macroeconomics was born, when in the UK at least there were only a handful of economists engaged on the subject concentrated in Cambridge, Oxford and the LSE. An obvious consequence of the larger numbers and the organisation of the profession is the competition to publish and a desire for professional differentiation. Whilst this can make for a frenetic intellectual atmosphere in which game-playing and position-taking compete with the generation of new ideas in academic life, it also makes for a more rapid turnover of ideas and ensures their wide dissemination and speedy testing.

In what follows, I begin by backcasting briefly over the development of macroeconomics and the macroeconomic environment, then look in more detail at the principal schools of thought. If the contention is right that macroeconomics feeds off real-world problems, this is a good way to proceed, as it makes sense of the evolving agenda of the subject. That agenda is currently dominated by the attempt to reconcile some of the method-ological instincts of the new classical school with some awkward facts, notably the persistence of unemployment and the stickiness of wages and prices. For most – but not all – economists this means that equilibrium approaches have been found wanting and 'new Keynesian' approaches which embody – but attempt to underpin – assumptions of market failure are the dominant focus of interest. But there are many minorities in macroeconomics today, some comment on which is attempted in the penultimate section. In the concluding section I pick up the theme of the introduction to reflect briefly on the impact on macroeconomics of some apparent current trends going beyond the problem of unemployment persistence.

## Modern macroeconomics

The birth of modern macroeconomics can be dated to the 1930s with the ferment of ideas that led to the publication of Keynes' *General Theory* (1936). The problem to which that book was addressed was explicitly that of unemployment. We shall discuss below how the particular framework laid out in the book was later developed; for the moment we are interested simply in identifying, in the broad, the real-world developments which have prompted – in combination with other influences – sub-sequent changes and developments in macroeconomics. In par-ticular, we have in view the down-grading of the Keynesian paradigm, the rise of monetarism and the so-called 'new classical' school and then the resurgence of 'new Keynesianism'.

After the successful establishment of a multilateral trading and monetary regime to govern international economic relations and the widespread adoption by governments of a 'Keynesian' policy stance, the world economy experienced unparalleled sustained high employment and growth in trade and output through the 1950s and early 1960s. The first obvious check to this 'golden age' progression was provided by the world's experience of inflation, starting in the late 1960s. This was amplified by the first oil price shock in 1973–4. Then followed a period of 'stagflation', with low growth, high unemployment and inflation becoming the norm. A second oil shock followed in 1979, which was succeeded by a prolonged period of falling inflation and persistent high unemployment. If this was all, it would be natural to expect that the macroeconomics of the 1930s would be applicable to the 1980s, and indeed there was (as will be indicated below) a revival in Keynesian ideas in this decade in a new form; but other developments were going on which have helped shape new ways of doing macroeconomics. These are long-term changes in the environment, not transitory shocks. I refer to three such trends. The first is the development of capital and credit markets, assisted by the growth of wealth and by deliberate acts of liberalisation and deregulation. Over the 1980s this was to accomplish, in the most advanced countries of the world at least, a substantial shift away from regimes of rationed finance to quite liberalised systems. As argued below, this has important consequences for the functioning of the macro-economy and for the leverage of macroeconomic policy. There has also been a drastic cut in the costs of communication and information-processing; this, too, has important consequences both for the kinds of assumption it is appropriate to make in macroeconomic modelling and for the kinds of policy that can be effective. A third trend has been that of globalisation, with the increasing openness of economies and diminution of sovereignty implied; this, too, has had important impacts on the direction of macroeconomic policy-making and on macroeconomic analysis.

### The Keynesian paradigm

The activity following the publication of Keynes' *General Theory* endowed macroeconomics with a framework for thought which has proved remarkably resilient and durable. Indeed, it is not too much to say that the framework as such – the Hicksian *IS/LM* version of Keynes – can be adapted to yield modifications which result in policy messages far from those normally described as 'Keynesian'.

The post-war Keynesian consensus was largely built around the basic income–expenditure model, embodying the separate treatment of the principal elements of demand. Supply was passive, being demand determined. Fluctuations in investment were seen as being the principal cause of fluctuations in output, through the mechanism of the multiplier, with consumption as endogenous to income and tax policy, whilst government expenditure could be seen as an element of demand which the government could in principle readily vary to offset unwanted changes in private sector investment. Prices and wages in this first version of the model were thought of as being determined by 'off-model' forces: Keynesian economists were not so foolish as to suppose that prices and wages were unaffected by the level of activity but to begin with they held (e.g. Worswick, 1944) that:

(a) this influence was not a finely graded one which could easily be quantified; and

(b) the level of full employment output might very well be high enough to invite undesirable inflation; in this event the answer was an incomes policy.

One of the great attractions of the Keynesian model was that it was systematic and quantifiable. It was also quite flexible: in principle all kinds of accounts might be given of additional influences on consumption and investment (for example, in the latter case, the 'accelerator' was readily admitted). In this version, the one popular with treasuries and ministries of finance throughout most of the world, not only was supply passive; so also was money. This assumption could readily be defended, however, by noting that, whilst money might be neglected, monetary policy was not – or at least not in principle – for the rate of interest was typically thought of as the instrument variable, and quite logically this implies an assumption of endogenous money (this very same practice is widespread today in models of the economy of the type used by policy-makers). The model was implicitly addressed to a world in which the shocks to worry about were those that might arise on the demand side and to a world in which inflation was not a problem, either because it was taken care of by an incomes policy or because it just happened not to be. On these suppositions the model lay behind the widespread commitment by post-war governments to the ideal of full employment; because of its characteristic neglect of money it is sometimes represented as the 'fiscalist' model and the model indeed gives a ready rationale to counter-cyclical fiscal policy.

In later versions of the model the wage–price sector was

modelled along lines suggested by Phillips (1958): the integration of a Phillips curve in the model allowed incomes policy to slip out of the picture and permitted inflation and employment objectives to be lumped together as that of 'internal balance'. Modelling the external side was substantially completed in the mid-1960s following the fundamental contributions of Fleming (1962) and Mundell (1963) and the *IS/LM* framework was augmented by the *BB* curve depicting positions of 'external balance'. Modifications of this model kept pace with the changing nature of the international monetary system as international payments were freed from restrictions and the world's capital market bacame progressively more integrated.

### Inflation and the challenge of monetarism

The rising tide of inflation towards the end of the 1960s was a problem for this model. It posed a critical policy problem because there appeared to be no way in which the goal of full employment could be reconciled with an acceptably low inflation rate. Instead of being accompanied by lower unemployment, the higher inflation was accompanied by a rise in unemployment; the concept of a stable Phillips curve providing alternative combinations of inflation and unemployment for policy-makers to choose from (Rees, 1970) no longer appeared viable.

The analytical solution offered for this apparent instability in the Phillips curve – the expectations-augmented Phillips curve (APC) – brought with it the concept of the 'natural rate' of unemployment (Friedman, 1968). This proved capable of being absorbed into the conventional model on the understanding that expectations processes were backward-looking (the so-called adaptive expectations assumption), while the causation continued to be read Phillips' way round: that is, from unemployment (as proxy for excess demand) to prices (now conditional on slowly moving expectations).[1] On these terms the expectations-augmented Phillips curve with a natural rate of unemployment could still give demand management policy considerable potential scope, as had always been assumed in the conventional Keynesian framework. As in the earlier model, disinflation would be costly in terms of unemployment, even if the description of the process was a little different. Now one would say that a period of unemployment above the natural rate would be necessary to start

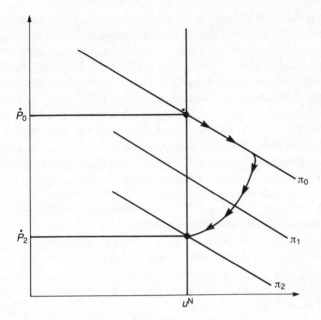

Fig 5.1   Disinflation in the APC world

a decline in the inflation rate, which would, in turn, bring down
inflation expectations: the economy could follow a path like that
depicted in Figure 5.1, running out along a short-term APC
indexed on the high expected inflation rate ruling at the start
of the process ($\pi_0 = \dot{p}_0$), then down successive short-term
Phillips curves as actual and expected inflation decline, eventually
stabilising at the natural rate again at an acceptable steady rate of
inflation ($\pi_2$ in the figure).

Curiously, the notions of the augmented Phillips curve and
the natural rate of (un)employment were late exhibits in the
monetarist case. Neither had anything to do with money as such,
whereas it was this that monetarists had always stressed. Nor was
the Keynesian model at large at very serious risk from the charge
that it neglected money. First, as already noted, practitioners
treated the interest rate as the monetary policy instrument and
were only being consistent in endogenising money. Second,
the Keynesian model to be found in universities was the more

141

expanded *IS/LM* model, which not only gave money an explicit role but also illustrated precisely that a modelling choice could be made to exogenise the interest rate and to endogenise the money supply. Third, the *IS/LM* framework could itself be used to illustrate all those issues which allegedly divided Keynesians from monetarists except those arising from the treatment of the supply side; in other words, a Keynesian framework could be used to describe differences between Keynesians and monetarists as differences about expected parameter values and the margins of error to be attributed to them.[2] At this level the basic monetarist model could be seen as a differentiation of a basically Keynesian model, with the differentiation driven by empirical observations of a kind which could easily prove ephemeral, rather than by profound analytical distinction. In fact, the augmented Phillips curve and the natural rate were to prove the more decisive contributions, for, when these were taken up and redefined, they formed the basis for the new classical macroeconomics which can be seen analytically as a stronger challenge to Keynesianism than monetarism had ever been.

Events in the outside world rubbed in the message that Keynesian economics was deficient in its handling of the supply side. The huge supply shock delivered by the OPEC countries in 1973–4 found policy-makers and their advisers floundering, attempting to adapt their apparatus for dealing with demand shocks to the novel situation confronting them. The weaknesses of incomes policies served to emphasise the need for alternative solutions. In desperation, countries abandoned their full employment goals and adopted monetary targets. Whilst this might be thought a vindication of monetarism, the circumstances of its introduction lent support to a new school of economics, ultimately to differentiate itself as strongly from monetarism as from Keynesianism – the so-called 'new classical macroeconomics'.

## New classical macroeconomics

The new classical macroeconomics (NCM), which began to come to the fore in the mid-1970s, offered a more powerful critique of Keynesian economics than anything that had appeared in monetarism. The key assumptions of this school, that markets clear and that expectations are formed rationally, were used to mount root-and-branch attacks on the Keynesian orthodoxy.[3] Superior technology, especially the device of rational expectations, gave this critique an analytical cutting edge which monetarism as such had never achieved. The assumptions of the NCM could be used, first, to show that demand management policy would be ineffective: in effect, well-informed agents would 'see through' government policies and act in such a way as to offset them. Second, even rather milder assumptions in similar spirit could be used to show that the conventional method of policy analysis by model simulation was conceptually faulty since the coefficients estimated in the model would themselves depend on the regime in force – this was the 'Lucas critique'. Third, Barro (1974a) showed that in this kind of setting it was immaterial to the outcome whether a given rate of government spending was financed by bond issue or covered by taxation, contrary to the Keynesian analysis of deficit financing. Fourth, Kydland and Prescott (1977) illustrated the problem of time-inconsistency, which suggested that, even when solved for optimal policy solutions, Keynesian models would succumb to a fatal inconsistency; on this foundation Barro and Gordon (1983) went on to demonstrate the superiority of reputational policies to those of the discretionary ('Keynesian') policy-maker. Finally, the new classical macroeconomics made a strong plea that theorising should begin with a clear description of the individual agents' optimising behaviour 'rather than with curves'.

All these propositions are sufficiently important, either in their own right or on account of their provocation, as to deserve some further spelling out. The key insight of the NCM arguably comes from Lucas' famous 'islands paradigm'. This provides a micro-'story' for the augmented Phillips curve. By analogising the position of agents as being akin to that of dwellers on an island, well informed about their immediate environment but ill informed about conditions on the rest of the archipelago, Lucas emphasised imperfections in information as the source of decisions to change the supply of effort. A rise in the local price would be read as a promise of an improvement in the terms of trade with other islands. Agents would agree to expend more effort (some forward commitment is implied, as otherwise on the receipt of the correct information the influence of disinformation obviously ceases), perhaps finding afterwards that the terms of trade improvement was illusory. This signal extraction problem – the problem of discriminating the change in the terms of trade (i.e. relative wages and prices) from changes in the general price level – is a central problem for agents in the NCM world. Generalising, the argument is that the augmented Phillips curve portrays the effect on aggregate supply (unemployment translated to employment and hence output) of relative price mistakes. So, if in (5.1) below $y$ is output, $y^n$ is equilibrium or 'natural' rate output, and $p^e$ and $p$ are expected and actual prices:

$$y - y^n = \alpha(p - p^e). \tag{5.1}$$

If the demand side is depicted as a simple quantity theory relationship (all the variables in logs), we have:

$$m = y + p \tag{5.2}$$

whence

$$p^e = m^e - y^e. \tag{5.3}$$

With rational expectations:

$$y^e = y^n. \tag{5.4}$$

Substituting yields:

$$y = y^n + \frac{\alpha}{1 + \alpha}(m - m^e). \tag{5.5}$$

According to (5.5), changes in $y$ around $y^n$ involve 'surprises' in monetary policy. Yet the rational expectations hypothesis says that agents would be able to guess any policy which systematically affects $m$: $(m - m^e)$ is essentially zero. Hence, policy is essentially ineffective – this is the (in) famous 'policy ineffectiveness proposition' due to Sargent and Wallace (1975). Figure 5.2 is a graphical illustration. In it, the aggregate demand schedules corresponding to equation (5.2) above are shown, dependent on the stock of money $(m_0, m_1)$, intersecting with aggregate supply schedules corresponding to equation (5.1). Starting from a position like $A$, an increase in the stock of money, if unexpected, would permit output to rise to $A^1$. At this point, however, price expectations are for $p = p_0$, whereas prices will be higher than this. Under the adaptive story, receipt of this information will cause successive upward shifts in the short-run $AS$ schedule

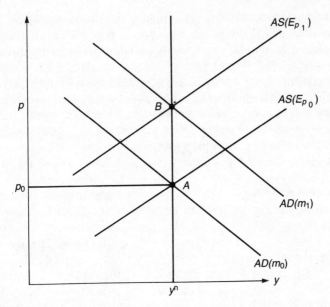

Fig 5.2   The 'surprise' supply function

until the new equilibrium at $B$ is reached. In the NCM account, however, if the money stock increase is perfectly anticipated the economy will move directly to the new equilibrium at $B$.

Clearly the rational expectations assumed reduces effective monetary policy to random shocks – not what we mean by a policy at all! A policy is systematic, yet systematic policy is known to agents and automatically accommodated in their price-level expectations.

If in practice econometricians were to estimate a version of (5.5), with $m^e$ as an unobservable, they would probably end up with an equation containing several lags of $m$, as a proxy. Lucas, in his famous 'critique' (Lucas, 1976), very reasonably objected that this not only would be a poor representation of (5.5) but would be sensitive to the actual processes driving $m^e$. Thus, if there were a change in policy and those processes changed, the previous estimate would no longer hold. In particular the old estimate could not be used to unravel the effects of the change in policy. Of course, in a framework as simple as (5.1)–(5.5), the

145

point of having any policy other than a fixed stock of money, let alone of changing it, is hard to see – but the point can be regarded as a parable, and has been taken to heart by macro-econometricians.[4]

In fact, the policy ineffectiveness proposition is not too hard to overturn; even 'minor' changes in assumptions can reintroduce a role for policy in principle (see e.g. Minford, 1990). New classical macroeconomics, however, also questioned whether policy, if effective, would be well used. This critique arose from the analysis of time-inconsistency by Kydland and Prescott (1977). Their point was the general one that, in a system in which expectations of the future affect current behaviour, an optimal trajectory for policy instruments devised and announced this year will no longer be optimal next year, since the starting conditions for a new optimisation will have been changed by agents' experience of the first year of the previously optimal plan and their belief that it will be maintained in the future. A pertinent example arises when the inception of a plan for monetary dis-inflation results in an immediate appreciation of the exchange rate and consequent reduction in the inflation rate. Once this has happened it is no longer so worthwhile pressing on with the rest of the disinflation plan and in fact optimising calculations will dictate a new policy trajectory. This criticism was especially effective in that it undermined the basis for optimal control of macroeconomic models: if optimally controlled policy trajectories are bound to be revised, who will believe in them?

Barro and Gordon (1983) were more specific in their critique, in which they confronted two policies – one of 'discretion' and one of 'precommitment'. The objective function is a quadratic cost-minimising function of unemployment around its desired value ($\bar{u}$), somewhere below the natural rate, and of inflation around its desired value (say, zero). Because the model is a natural rate model, the equilibrium outcome must be at $u^N$, so the only question at issue is how to guarantee the optimal (zero) inflation rate. If the policy-makers are able to 'credibly pre-commit' to zero inflation, then the best outcome is achieved. A good deal of discussion has since ensued about how this might be done – making the central bank independent, targeting the exchange rate against such a central bank, providing the government with strong incentives to maintain its reputation.

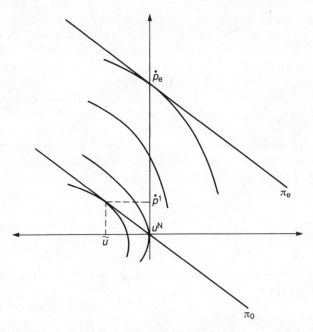

Fig 5.3   Discretionary equilibrium in the Barro–Gordon model

The reason why this is seen as important is provided by the 'discretionary' solution. Here, the government is open to the temptation to spring 'surprise inflation' on the economy to reduce unemployment. For example, in Figure 5.3, if the government is initially believed to be committed to zero inflation, the relevant APC is the one labelled $\pi_0$. But the government can achieve $\tilde{u}$ by springing 'surprise inflation' of $\dot{p}^1$. Naturally, this is not the end of the story. The public will distrust the government's promises because the temptation for the government to renege is so obvious. There is an equilibrium at $p_e$, however. At this 'bad' equilibrium the inflation rate is already so high that the government would gain no utility from springing a surprise increase in it. This model has provided the impetus, as already indicated, for more careful thought about the design of policy-makers' incentives, and constitutions; once again, although the initiating model now seems rather crude it has served to change the rules of the game in policy evaluation exercises.

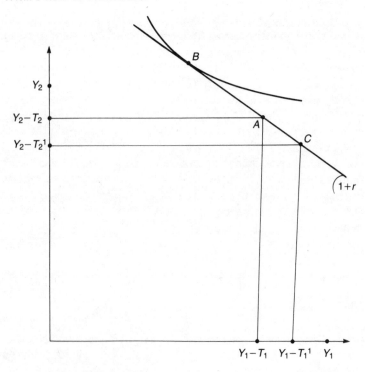

Fig 5.4   Ricardian equivalence

Whilst the Sargent–Wallace and Barro–Gordon critiques were aimed explicitly at monetary policy, the NCM challenge extended to fiscal policy also. Barro (1974a) launched the proposition that, for a given level of government expenditure, the composition of the corresponding tax and bond finance was immaterial. The basis for the assertion is very simple, as Figure 5.4 shows. Here we assume that the agent has lump sum income of $Y_1$ in period 1 and $Y_2$ in period 2. Initially he faces lump sum taxes of $T_1$ and $T_2$ in the two periods. The budget line drawn through $A$ (corresponding to $Y_1 - T_1$, $Y_2 - T_2$) gives the agent's opportunity line. It has a slope of $-(1 + r)$, where $r$ is the rate of interest at which he can borrow or lend. The preferred point is shown as $B$, which implies saving in the current period and dissaving in period 2. Now suppose that, with the level of government disbursements given, the decision is taken to substitute bond finances for tax finances. This permits a cut in period 1 taxes from $T_1$ to $T_1^1$ and a rise in disposable income from $Y_1 - T_1$ to $Y_1 - T_1^1$. The bonds are to be redeemed with interest in the second period. So, in the second period, the representative agent's taxes will be increased from $T_2$ to $T_2^1$. Allowing for the interest to be paid, $(T_2^1 - T_2) = (1 + r) (T_1 - T_1^1)$. Thus $C$, the point corresponding to the new disposable income, is on the same budget line as before, and $B$ remains the chosen point. The tax–bond finance change has altered nothing. This model clearly requires agents to be forward looking. Given this assumption, further assumptions needed are that the capital market is perfect and that the agent expects to survive until the next period (or that his welfare is linked in some other way to the next period, perhaps via a bequest to his heirs). Subsequent discussion of the Barro proposition (see e.g. Tobin, 1980) has examined all the qualifications carefully; although there are many of these, the impact of this simple Barro proposition (known as 'Ricardian equivalence') has none the less been significant for policy evaluation.

Whilst attacks on the Keynesian orthodoxy fell on receptive ears given the very obvious policy difficulties of the 1970s, it was to prove ironic that the attacks should come from a school that emphasised the efficiency of the market and equilibrium outcomes. Unemployment, in this framework, is due to informational errors, and appears to be essentially transitory.[5] Yet the problem of the next decade, that of the 1980s, was to be that of persistent unemployment.

## New Keynesianism

Most mainstream macroeconomics in recent years can be seen as a response to the methodological issues raised by the new classical macroeconomics and to the brute facts of global economic behaviour in the 1980s, in particular to the revealed problem of persistent unemployment. Rational expectations has ceased to be controversial in model-building and is no longer a monopoly of new classical macroeconomics. Recognising that expectations are important, the model-builder finds himself almost obliged to assume rational expectations; to do otherwise is to grant himself a wisdom not allowed to the agents in his model, which seems indefensibly arrogant as well as arbitrary.[6] Granted this, where new Keynesians have parted company with new classicals is over the market-clearing assumption, or more specifically over the twin assumptions, first that the market would, if prices and wages were flexible, solve the problem of coordination; second, that wages and prices can in fact be read as flexible or at least as being capable of being rendered so by feasible institutional reforms. It is interesting to note that this double-barrelled approach parallels the original treatment of the issue by Keynes himself in the *General Theory*. For most of the book Keynes assumes fixed money wages; then he spends some time discussing why, in fact, they might be expected to be sticky; finally he discusses what it would be like if, hypothetically, wages and prices were flexible. Notably, he does not conclude that in this event the coordination problem would be solved and in fact draws the moral that a degree of rigidity in money wages is a social good.

Most of the new Keynesian recovery of the late-1970s and the 1980s has focused on wage–price stickiness. Whilst it is relatively trivial to show that even under rational expectations such stickiness will prevent full equilibrium and may yield a case for government intervention,[7] meeting the NCM challenge has required economists to spell out why wages (and/or prices) might in fact be sticky. The reasons offered will, *inter alia*, affect the robustness of the conclusion that government intervention is justified and will certainly have implications for the form of that intervention.

### Approaches to wage–price stickiness

In his *General Theory*, Keynes stressed the stickiness of nominal wages, explaining that in a system of asynchronous wage bargaining interpersonal comparison would lead to a resistance to nominal wage cuts since these would be seen (correctly) as a reduction in the relative wage of the bargaining group affected. This foundation is thus not a casual appeal to, or assumption of, anything so crude as money illusion, though many discussions overlook this. Be that as it may, it is worth noting that, whilst Keynes was explicitly referring to nominal stickiness, in many Keynesian extensions prices themselves and thus real wages are taken as sticky.

Rationales for price stickiness have been predominantly empirical, scores of econometric relationships for example depicting consumer prices as a mark-up on costs, predominantly made up of wage costs with the costs of imports and indirect taxes also taken into account. The argument has been that the mark-up itself is not particularly responsive to demand pressures (under the 'normal cost' hypothesis, not at all). It was always evident at this level that a distinction should be drawn between the prices of manufactured products and those of certain kinds of commodities traded on world markets which seemed to be more like asset prices in that they exhibited complete flexibility. One of the principal analytical activities of the 1970s and 1980s was the attempt to provide some foundations for this difference in behaviour.

The explanations involve some departure from the assumption of perfect competition; Barro (1974b), for example, introduced a simple model of monopolistic competition with price-change cost (which can be thought of as, literally, the cost of printing new price lists or as an adverse impact on demand). With lump sum costs of price change and a downward-sloping demand schedule, a degree of price stickiness in the face of demand shocks is imparted: in an intuitively obvious way the degree of stickiness depends on the expected magnitude and duration of the shocks. The idea that part of the cost of price change is the forfeit of 'goodwill' was taken up by Stiglitz (1979), Okun (1981) and others. Okun's account employs the insights of 'search theory' to pioneer a distinction between 'auction' markets and 'custom' markets. In the latter, shopping costs are important, perhaps because the goods are not quite standardised, and as a result the firm obtains a degree of monopoly power and can indulge in strategic thinking. Thus, in contemplating the consequences of a price cut, the firm will have to take into account the fact that shoppers' knowledge is localised; they will know about the prices offered by the firm with whom they customarily shop but not about other firms' prices – so a price cut will attract the business only of those customers who are still searching the market and otherwise will simply reduce revenues per unit. Similarly, with a price rise: the firm may reckon that the effect of this will simply be to send its customers off on a search of rival firms' offerings. These considerations suggest that the effective demand curve

151

F

facing the firm is kinked at the current price – much as in the classic oligopoly case, but for different reasons. In any event, the consequence is sticky prices. The analysis of 'conjectural equilibria' (e.g. Hahn, 1978) is in similar vein. Given some degree of market power for the firm for whatever reason, strategic considerations must immediately come into play and the firm's actions will reflect its awareness of interdependencies. The search for underpinnings to a sticky-price 'Keynesian' macroeconomics in this respect leads away from perfect competition to alternative and, many would say, more 'realistic' models.

Although it was nominal wage stickiness which Keynes stressed and which has been regarded as the key to Keynesian macro-economic phenomena in the analytical literature, real wage stickiness has good claim to be regarded as Keynesian too. As Hicks pointed out (Hicks, 1974), the appeal to 'fairness' in Keynes' argument for nominal wage stickiness can be extended to supply a reason for expecting resistance to real wage cuts. Certainly, in the 1970s, it was a matter of empirical observation that many bargaining groups arrived at contracts which were explicitly indexed to the cost of living, and empirical exploration of wage formation has stressed both real and nominal wage rigidity (a classic example of the use of this distinction arising in comparisons between wage behaviour in the US, where long nominal contracts ensure real flexibility and nominal rigidity, and in Europe where it seems that shorter contract lengths produce the opposite combination).

Okun (1981) based his explanation of nominal rigidity on the firm's need to minimise turnover costs: this requires it to have a wage system which is regarded as 'fair', which includes a commitment to compensate its employees at a particular wage, agreed in advance. Since the existence of fixed nominal wages is the proximate 'cause' of unemployment of the classic Keynesian type, this approach appears to run into a paradox: it seems that the firm's attempt to be fair by committing to a fixed money wage results in lay-offs. It might be asked, 'Where is the fairness in that?' Okun turns the paradox to his own advantage: he argues that the lay-offs are seen as a convincing demonstration that times are bad, whereas wage cuts would be seen as an instance of the firm 'taking advantage of a weak labour market to enlarge its share of the bilateral surplus'.

There have been other attempts to construct a basis for wage rigidity. One of these is the idea that long-term wage contracts (whether explicit or not) are a Pareto-improving bargain in which risk-averse workers trade with risk-neutral firms (well reviewed in Taylor, 1987). This asymmetry in attitudes towards risk allows a bargain to be struck in which workers receive a fixed (real) wage, the certainty-equivalent value of which is less than that of their expected, stochastically variable, marginal product. In effect, real wages fall below the marginal product of labour in good states of the world by the amount of a premium paid by the workers to the firm, and exceed the marginal product in poor states of the world by the amount of an insurance payout from the firm to the workers. (A side argument is necessary to show that the firm is in a better position than an insurance company to provide these services – perhaps because it has better access to relevant information.) This approach is not as popular as it was, partly because it was initially looked to to provide underpinnings for the staggered nominal wage contract models of Fischer (1977) and others, and underpins neither staggering nor nominal fixity (real fixity being the point of the model).

Another approach is that of insider–outsider theory (see e.g. Lindbeck and Snower, 1986). This approach is built to try to account for why it is that the unemployed do not succeed in undercutting the wages of those already employed. The approach exploits a distinction between an 'inner' group (the insiders) and the rest (the outsiders). For Okun-type reasons the firm itself may encourage its labour force to rely on fixed wages and upon other perks related to seniority and length of stay. The insiders may fortify themselves by various devices which deter the outsiders – hassling new hires, for example; when a recession arrives the firm will fire first those whom it has most recently taken on, and its subcontracted labour. These unemployed have no influence on the bargaining strength of those who remain in employment because they are marginalised outsiders. The approach is less clear about what happens when the recession eventually hits the insiders. If these become outsiders as soon as they are fired, the approach would sustain complete immunity of the wage bargain to the unemployed, but it is not so clear why former insiders should suddenly become outsiders – though it could well be that over a period of time they would do so as their skills atrophy and their work attachment lessens. If the approach is a little vague about the criteria that separate insiders from outsiders, it nevertheless has a ring of plausibility to it.

An alternative approach to wage stickiness is provided by the 'efficiency wage' concept. The key to the efficiency wage approach is provided by the observation that direct control of its employees' work effort is prohibitively costly to the firm in many situations. If work effort is positively related to the wage paid, then the wage payment itself is an instrument that may be used to encourage productivity. But this subverts the role of the wage payment as a stabiliser. For example, a reduction in the wage may, if the positive connection exists, so reduce work effort as actually to raise wage costs per unit of output – in one version the negative impact of the wage cut is mediated through a damaging effect on morale (in its original Third World application, the mechanism envisaged went through a decline in nutritional levels); a similar result can be obtained by appeal to the impact on turnover costs, as in Okun, or through 'adverse selection' effects (in which the lower wage attracts a lower-quality labour force). These and other ideas are spelt out by Akerlof and Yellen (1986) in the introduction to their book, which brings together a number of important papers in the area.

There is an important 'loose end' in much of the discussion of sticky wages, and this is the casual labour market. Whilst the ideas put forward by Okun have their obvious application at the level of the large, established firm with a personnel department and well-established practices in relation to wage payment, promotion and the rest, and it might be argued that the same is true of some of the other notions discussed above, especially that of the insider–outsider approach, the fact remains that there is a casual labour market. This is a market of which it may make good sense to say that it clears, and can be regarded as a residual of the labour market as a whole: unless social policy puts a generous floor underneath wages in this market the functioning of the casual labour market may in fact be absorbing much of what the rest of the market is unable to absorb. To this extent, the wage-stickiness theorising may simply be accounting for the *relative* performance of the organised and the casual labour markets rather than for the overall behaviour of the macro-economy.

*Is wage–price flexibility enough?*

Whilst most of the Keynesian recovery seems to have looked to wage–price stickiness as the key to coordination failure, an alternative strand of work has pursued the question whether even full flexibility in wages and prices would necessarily solve the coordination problem. This strand of work responds directly to the 'bootstrap' nature of Keynesian equilibria as they are often described: the economy is where it is because demand is where it is. No individual firm has an incentive to schedule higher production, yet firm A would expand demand if firms B, C, D, E, . . . etc. were to do the same. A government shock to demand can move such an economy to a higher-level position, which will also be an equilibrium in the same sense; it may even be able to withdraw its demand stimulus without prejudice to that equilibrium once it is reached, as in the old 'pump-priming' analogy. These equilibria are positions in which 'there are no dollar bills lying on the sidewalk' (to paraphrase Lucas' famous admonition): there is no contradiction of individual profit-maximising behaviour.

How can such equilibria be underpinned? General equilibrium theorising proceeds on the assumption that there are locally decreasing returns, but the opposite assumption of increasing returns would provide the opportunity for an externality of the kind described to arise, and writers like Weitzman (1982) and Howitt (1990) have taken up this idea. In Howitt's version, economies in selling costs provide the source of increasing returns; the argument is that the cost of making sales falls with an increase in the probability of making a successful market contact, which itself rises with aggregate demand. On suitable assumptions about the form of this function, multiple equilibria may be described, and economies stuck in a low-level equilibrium will need a demand shock to push them to a superior position.

## Open economy extensions

It would be wrong to suggest that the whole of macroeconomics in recent years has been dominated by the new Keynesian response to the new classical macroeconomics, even though that may be the most striking aspect of it. In fact, it should be said that there has been a considerable increase in the amount of macroeconomics directed at questions arising in an open economy framework and for some reason there does not seem to have been a very large distinctive new classical contribution in this area (though Frenkel and Razin, 1987, are an exception) and most of the work has a distinctly Keynesian flavour to it.

Two important areas should be mentioned. The first of these is the development of open economy macroeconomics to take on board the stylised distinction between sticky-price goods and labour markets and flex-price foreign exchange markets; the second is the incorporation of issues pertaining to the co-ordination of policies between economies. Once again this can be seen as a response to events, in that the 1970s and 1980s witnessed a return to floating exchange rates after a lapse of several decades and with it a decline in the practice of inter-national policy coordination, a trend which was to be reversed in the mid-1980s on the initiative of the United States.

The floating rate experience very quickly produced the famous 'Dornbusch overshooting' model (Dornbusch, 1976), in which Dornbusch showed, in a model which effectively incorporated rational expectations, that a rise (fall) in the money supply would cause an appreciation (depreciation) in the exchange rate which would be in excess of that warranted by the new long-run equi-librium, i.e. where the exchange rate would 'overshoot'. The model is illustrated in Figures 5.5a and 5.5b. The top half of the diagram illustrates the case of a stationary, fixed-output, money-neutral open economy which undergoes a once-for-all increase in its money supply. The simplicity of the model tells us that, if the initial equilibrium is at $A$, the new one will be at $C$, where prices and the exchange rate increase in the same proportion (equal to the increase in the money supply), the real exchange rate remaining constant. The initial equilibrium is determined at the intersection of the two schedules labelled $\dot{e} = 0$ and $\dot{p} = 0$, which correspond to the solutions for dynamic equations of motion for these two variables. The new equilibrium $C$ is, cor-respondingly, on the intersection of the $\dot{e}^1 = 0$ and $\dot{p}^1 = 0$ schedules. The schedules $QQ$ and $Q^1Q^1$ are stable trajectories for $e$ and $p$ given any displacement from the corresponding equi-librium. (Begg, 1982, gives a lucid account of the phase diagram apparatus.) Dornbusch assumes that whereas $e$, the exchange

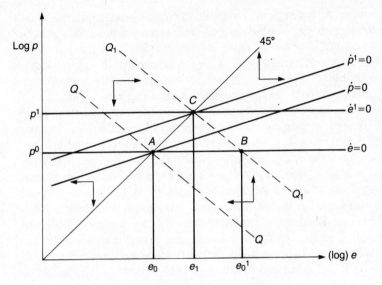

Fig 5.5a   Dornbusch overshooting: a money supply increase

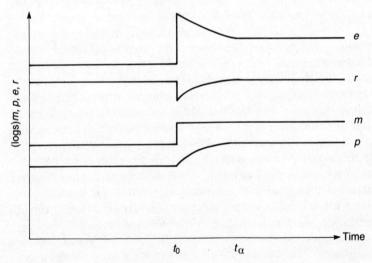

Fig 5.5b   The 'time track'

rate, is an asset price determined in flex-price markets, $p$ is a slowly moving variable (formed in 'custom' rather than 'auction' markets). If, starting from $A$, the money supply is increased, the new equilibrium is $C$, and the relevant stable trajectory is given by $Q^1Q^1$. The disturbance to the money supply is absorbed initially by asset prices: in the top part of the figure, the exchange rate depreciates to $B$ immediately and then appreciates towards $C$, prices moving slowly upward at the same time. The exchange rate $e_0^1$ clearly has overshot its new equilibrium value $e_1$.

The 'time track' version of the model shown in the lower part of the figure gives another perspective on the model's responses. At $t_0$ the shock to the money supply is introduced. In the new equilibrium, at $t_a$, the real money shock (given by the distance between the lines representing the (log of) $m$ and $p$) will be the same as at $t_0$, as will the nominal rate of interest ($r$) and the real exchange rate (the distance between the $e$ and $p$ schedules). On impact, the money stock increase is absorbed by a decline in the rate of interest and an over-depreciation of the exchange rate. The excess fall in the exchange rate permits a rationally anticipated appreciation to combine with the fall in the interest rate to satisfy the uncovered interest parity condition, given the unchanged foreign interest rate.

Dornbusch's framework proved capable of a number of extensions, not least to the macroeconomics of natural resource discoveries or shock increases in the prices of existing natural resources. Buiter and Miller (1981) applied the model to analyse the early years of the Thatcher government in Britain, when the pound sterling appreciated in an unparalleled fashion. A lesson from that episode, that restrictive monetary policy could achieve quick counter-inflationary gains through an over-appreciation of the exchange rate, was one of the incentives for looking at the question of international policy coordination; after all, one country's appreciation is another's depreciation, as the European countries were to complain bitterly of the appreciation of the US dollar through the early years of the Reagan administration.

The approach of macroeconomists to the issue of international coordination has been predominantly in the Keynesian vein, even whilst using models solved under rational expectations and with natural rate supply sides; for the approach has predominantly viewed the issue of coordination as a matter of efficiency at the macroeconomic level. The fact that one country's policies spill over onto other countries is an externality; the usual response to an externality is to invoke the government to provide a tax–subsidy framework to handle it. The market fails and the government is invoked to provide a solution which is preferable on efficiency grounds. In the international context there is no government, and indeed no market in policies, but the analogy is nevertheless an apt one: in lieu of invoking a world government, policies must be consciously coordinated and this solution is recommended on grounds of efficiency. The basic technique employed is that of game theory, with equilibria named after their industrial economics' progenitors: the Nash equilibrium corresponding to a situation where the individual countries optimise their own positions myopically, taking other countries' policies as given; the Stackelberg, where one of the countries acts as leader and sets its own policies in the light of the reactions of the follower(s) whilst the follower(s) in turn simply take the leader's position for granted. The locus of cooperative policies can be derived on the assumption that all externalities are internalised; this provides a superior set of possibilities, though the theory does not generally attempt to say which one of these will actually be chosen. Oudiz and Sachs (1984) provide one of the first and one of the most exciting examples of this kind of work.

## Other schools of thought

Whilst I have described the dominant strand of contemporary macroeconomics as new Keynesian and the dominant feature of recent developments in the subject as being the new Keynesian response to the challenge of the new classical macroeconomics, this is by no means an exhaustive (or even uncontentious) description. Certainly there are other minority schools with influence in particular areas, and, whilst space limitations forbid a full treatment, some brief comments will be made here, distinguishing just three minority 'schools'.

First, there is the post-Keynesian school. Among the distinctive claims of this school is one that the assumption of rational expectations is not applicable to serious macroeconomic analysis. The post-Keynesians' point here harks back to a passage of the *General Theory* in which Keynes emphasised the essentially arbitrary nature of entrepreneurs' expectations of the future and the consequent tendency for investment to be affected by waves of optimism or pessimism. The logical distinction between risk and uncertainty (the former bearing the statistical inter-pretation applicable to the outcome of a repeated experiment, the latter to the outcome of a unique event) which is involved is unassailable and the school's survival from the onslaught on conventional Keynesian positions launched by the new classicals is partly attributable to this fact. Another typical position is the proposition that 'money is endogenous', which proved a durable position in the earlier monetarist onslaught. Equally typical would be the claim that markets must be thought of as imperfect for the Keynesian position to be articulated properly and that taking short-cuts in this respect is likely to lead to trouble (as it can be argued that it did). With so many good points why is this school not more influential? Many reasons might be cited, of which one is that the 'research programme' of the school is somewhat static: the propositions cited above are not particularly new. The challenge is for the school to progress further and in ways that occupy some leading ground, a challenge acknowl-edged in a recently published statement by a leading post-Keynesian, Basil Moore (1989).

Another school of thought is represented by the 'Austrians', similar in some respects to the post-Keynesian school; that is, the central proposition(s) of this school, whilst undeniable 'truths', seem yet to be insufficient to guarantee a progressive research programme that can command the attention of many adherents. Most typical of this school is its claim that what passes for optimisation in conventional economics – and optimisation is claimed to be at the heart of economics – is in fact 'mere' calculation, that economics short-changes the processes of choice in favour of writing them down as processes of calculus. In this way, it is argued, conventional economics overlooks some important features – of the learning process, of agents' per-ception of events, of the development of tastes, and so on. Worse still, perhaps, an Austrian criticism of much conventional macroeconomics would be that it does not even try to put optimisation at the centre of the picture, but talks in (from the Austrian point of view) meaningless aggregates which cannot be said to have any purposive life. But, if this sounds like a state-ment which makes Austrian and new classical economics first cousins, the Austrian would certainly criticise the new classical habit of 'aggregating' across 'representative agents' as misleading both because the 'representative agent's' optimisation problem is falsely represented as excluding choice in the real sense of the word and because the aggregation is a fraudulent means of assuming that everyone is the same.

A third school to be mentioned here is that of the 'supply-siders', an ill-defined grouping of which it might be said that the essential feature is an empirical disagreement with Keynesians about the nature of the shocks which have to be dealt with most frequently by policy and thus the best direction for policy thinking and formulation. Thus, in contemplating tax reform, supply-siders emphasise the effects on incentives to work, or to accumulate capital, as opposed to the effects on demand, and scrutinise proposals for deficit finance or for expanding government expenditure from a similar perspective. Perhaps the most distinguished and successful example of this school of thought would therefore be represented by the dominant official line of economic policy advice in the Federal Republic of Germany, where Keynesian economic policy advice seems highly distrusted (see Helmstadter, 1988, for an account). Adherents to this approach might (as Helmstadter does) claim Schumpeter as their inspiration; but it is well known that Schumpeter left no direct disciples and indeed it is hard to recognise a significant body of literature supporting this school despite what seems to be its success, if indeed the German success is due to its advice. (It may be significant that the OECD, which has sought a new role in recent years as international adviser on the supply side, has found much to fault in German arrangements – despite which the German economy has recently resumed a high growth rate.)

The 'minority schools' mentioned in this section are small compared with the mainstream, and do not appear to have a dynamic research programme; indeed, critics accuse them of nihilism. Nevertheless, each has substantial points to make which are salutary for the mainstream.

## Conclusions: the relevance of macroeconomics

In this last section I return briefly to the themes introduced in the opening sections of this chapter – to the questions of those broad

161

developments in the real world that might be read as underlying developments in modern macroeconomics. Clearly, if macro-economics is to be 'relevant', some such connection is necessary. Indeed, there are a number of ways in which it is evident.

An obvious, powerful and important trend in the real world is the development of the financial sector, partly in response to the impact of new technologies (the reduction in information – processing costs, the steep decline in communication costs), amplified by legislative and regulatory change. This liberalisation process applies across the world. An obvious consequence is that it makes access to the capital market easier for the individual agent (firm, household or government). Developments like this underpin the acceptability of the dominant 'consumption-smoothing' paradigm of consumer behaviour, which, with the incorporation of forward-looking expectations, has translated Friedman's backward-looking 'permanent income' model of consumption into the 'surprise' model of consumption. The basic logic is straightforward. Consumption depends on expected income; the first difference of consumption depends then on the change in expected income between two periods. Rationally formed expectations change only with the access of genuinely new information, not previously available, i.e. with surprises. Similar logic has added 'surprise' or 'news' models of the exchange rate, investment and money demand to the surprise model of consumption.

These developments have important consequences for the leverage of policy – for example, the forward-looking model of consumption indicates that temporary tax increases will have little or no effect; in the limit, the neo-Ricardian model (see above) suggests a zero effect. At the international level, financial liberalisation has the effect of rendering the current account of the balance of payments a residual of no normative significance, as stressed by modern intertemporal balance of payments theory (Sachs, 1981; Frenkel and Razin, 1987). The response of macro-economics to these developments is two-stage. In stage one, new paradigms are devised and policy conclusions revised. In stage two, there is empirical testing. The results of the testing often enough are to suggest that the world does not yet conform to the new paradigm. A new round of revisions to policy thinking ensues.

Close partner to the financial revolution is the process of globalisation of economic activity. A rising proportion of the world's traded output is due to the activities of genuinely multi-national firms and traded output is rising in proportion to total output. This also affects the nature of useful assumptions: it becomes more appropriate to treat international macroeconomics as interregional economics. The policy independence of the nominally sovereign units assumed in conventional analysis is less obvious, the traditional concepts of the import propensity and export and import elasticities less relevant. In the limit, the balance of imports and exports becomes a simple residual of aggregate demand and supply (Mckinnon, 1976), the level of activity determined by the real wage and productivity conditions of the economy. The scope for traditional demand management diminishes, almost to zero.

Once again, there is a tension between the process of constructing the new paradigm with its revolutionary policy proposals and testing the relevance of the underlying assumptions, a process which usually produces some reversion towards the older models.

There is every reason to believe that the progress of modern macroeconomics reflects, among other things, trends in the real economy. The relationship between the two is a complex one, however. Macroeconomic theorists like to abstract severely, so as to highlight the implications of the particular set of 'unrealistic' assumptions with which they are concerned. The relevance of the sometimes radical policy conclusions which follow, however, obviously depends on 'how well' the theorists' choice of assumptions reflects the real world. Empirical testing is vital at this stage and there is a close relationship between theoretical and empirical macroeconomics, though that relationship is a surprisingly complex one which would deserve another chapter to itself to explain in full. Suffice to affirm, for present purposes, that developments in modern macroeconomics and underlying trends in the real world are far from unconnected.

## Notes

1 Though widely read this way, by monetarists just as much as by Keynesians, Friedman's own words in fact indicate the opposite line of

causation: from the inflation expectations 'mistake' to the deviation of unemployment from its natural level. This, of course, was to be the essential message of the new classical macroeconomics.

2 Exhibits include Laidler (1971), who looked at parameter slopes, Poole (1970), who stressed margins of error, and Friedman himself (Friedman, 1970), who appealed to wealth effects to supply a missing stabiliser from the Keynesian model. Subsequent pursuit of the role of wealth effects in the Keynesian model was to produce some bizarre results (e.g. the Blinder–Solow, 1973, 'super multiplier' for bond-financed fiscal policy), but in essence simply confirmed new mechanisms reinforcing standard *IS/LM* conclusions on the ability of monetary policy to formulate fiscal policy. No fundamental revision of the Keynesian model was involved.

3 The NCM has been very well served by texts which combine rigour with candour – see e.g. Begg (1982), Minford and Peel (1983), Pesaran (1987) and Hoover (1988).

4 The practice is to attempt to identify the expectations variables separately, together with the process which drives them, which may be 'rational'. This feature is to be found in most British macro-models today.

5 The account given in the islands parable focuses on labour supply variations induced by information errors. Changes in the supply of labour representing equilibrium (full information) responses to changes in relevant determining factors are obviously not thereby excluded and in fact such responses (building on the early Lucas–Rapping, 1969, intertemporal model of labour supply) have taken centre stage in the more recent development of the 'real business cycle'. This development, however, has not yet occupied the core of the macroeconomic debate in the way that the earlier surprise supply function did.

6 In deterministic models this amounts to the assumption of perfect foresight. Obviously, this is a quite inappropriate assumption to make when discussing actual historical episodes or indeed when discussing the feasibility and stability of general equilibrium. Its assumption in modelling simply guarantees that the results obtained are not due to expectational 'inefficiencies'.

7 For example, in Fischer's (1977) overlapping wage contract model, agents have rational expectations and strike their contracts accordingly. If however, a shock should occur, government intervention is optimal if it can take place more frequently than the contracts can be revised.

# References

Akerlof, C. A. and Yellen, J. C. (1986) (eds), *Efficiency Wage Models of the Labour Market*, Cambridge: Cambridge University Press.

Barro, R. J. (1974a), 'Are government bonds net wealth?' *Journal of Political Economy*, 59(2), pp. 93–116.

Barro, R. J. (1974b), 'A theory of monopolistic price adjustment', *Review of Economic Studies*, 41.

Barro, R. J. and Gordon, D. B. (1983), 'Rules, discretion and reputation in a model of monetary policy', *Journal of Monetary Economics*, 12(2), pp. 101–21.

Begg, D. K. H. (1982), *The Rational Expectations Revolution in Macroeconomics*, Oxford: Philip Allan.

Blinder, A. J. and Solow, R. M. (1973), 'Does fiscal policy matter?' *Journal of Public Finance*, 2, November.

Buiter, W. H. and Miller, M. H. (1981), 'Monetary policy and international competitiveness', *Oxford Economic Papers*, July (Supplement).

Dornbusch, R. (1976), 'Expectations and exchange rate dynamics', *Journal of Political Economy*, 84.

Fischer, S. (1977), 'Long term contracts, rational expectations and the optimal money supply', *Journal of Political Economy*, 85, pp. 191–205.

Fleming, J. M. (1962), 'Domestic financial policies under fixed and under floating exchange rates', *IMF Staff Papers*, IX, November, pp. 209–22.

Frenkel, J. A. and Razin, A. (1987), *Fiscal Policies and the World Economy*, Cambridge, Mass.: MIT Press.

Friedman, M. (1968), 'The role of monetary policy', *American Economic Review*, 58, March, pp. 1–17.

Friedman, M. (1970), 'A theoretical framework for monetary analysis', *Journal of Political Economy*, 78, March/April, pp. 193–238.

Hahn, F. H. (1978), 'On new Walrasian equilibria', *Review of Economic Studies*, February.

Helmstadter, E. (1988), 'The irrelevance of Keynes to German economic policy and to international economic cooperation in the 1980s', in W. Eltis and P. Sinclair (eds), *Keynes and Economic Policy*, London: Macmillan.

Hicks, J. R. (1974), *The Crisis in Keynesian Economics*, Oxford: Basil Blackwell.

Hoover, K. D. (1988), *The New Classical Macroeconomics*, Oxford: Basil Blackwell.

Howitt, P. (1990),*The Keynesian Recovery*, Oxford: Philip Allan.

Keynes, J. M. (1936), *The General Theory of Employment, Interest and Money*, London: Macmillan.

Kydland, F. E. and Prescott, E. C. (1977), 'Rules rather than discretion: the inconsistency of optimal plans', *Journal of Political Economy*, 85(3), pp. 20–100.

Laidler, D. E. W. (1971), 'The influence of money on economic activity: a survey of some current problems', in G. Clayton, J. Gilbert and R. Sedgwick (eds), *Monetary Theory and Monetary Policy in the 1970s*, Oxford: Oxford University Press.

Lindbeck, A. and Snower, D. J. (1986), 'Wage rigidity, union activity and unemployment', in W. Beckerman (ed.), *Wage Rigidity and Unemployment*, Baltimore, Md: Johns Hopkins University Press.

Lucas, R. E. (1972), 'Expectations and the neutrality of money', *Journal of Economic Theory*, 4, April, pp. 103–24.

Lucas, R. E. (1976), 'Econometric policy evaluation: a critique', in K. Brunner and A. Meltzer (eds), *The Phillips Curve and Labour Markets*, Carnegie-Rochester Conference Series on Public Policy, 1, pp. 19–46.

Lucas, R. E. and Rapping, L. A. (1969), 'Real wages, employment and inflation', *Journal of Political Economy*, 77, pp. 721–54.

McKinnon, R. I. (1976), 'The limited role of fiscal policy in an open economy', *Quarterly Review of the Banca Nazionale del Lavoro*, September.

Minford, A. P. L. (1990), 'Rational expectations and monetary policy', in T. Bandyopadhyay and S. Ghatak (eds), *Current Issues in Monetary Economics*, Brighton: Harvester/Wheatsheaf.

Minford, A. P. L. and Peel, D. (1983), *Rational Expectations and the new Macroeconomics*, Oxford: Martin Robertson.

Moore, B. J. (1989), *Horizontalists and Verticalists: the macroeconomics of credit money*, Cambridge: Cambridge University Press.

Mundell, R. A. (1963), 'Capital mobility and stabilization policy under fixed and flexible exchange rates', *Canadian Journal of Economics and Political Science*, 29, November, pp. 475–88.

Okun, A. M. (1981), *Prices and Quantities*, Oxford: Basil Blackwell.

Oudiz, G. and Sachs, J. D. (1984), 'Macroeconomic coordination among the industrial countries', *Brookings Papers in Economic Activity*, 1, pp. 1–75.

Pesaran, H. (1987), *The Limits of Rational Expectations*, Oxford: Basil Blackwell.

Phillips, A. W. (1958), 'The relation between unemployment and the rate of change of money wage rates in the United Kingdom, 1861–1957', *Economica*, November, pp. 283–99.

Poole, W. (1970), 'Optimal choice of monetary policy instruments in a simple stochastic macro model', *Quarterly Journal of Economics*, 84, June, pp. 197–216.

Rees, A. (1970), 'The Phillips Curve as a menu for policy choice', *Economica*, 38(147), pp. 227–380.

Sachs, J. D. (1981), 'The current account and macroeconomic adjustment in the 1970s', *Brookings Papers in Economic Activity*, 1, pp. 201–68.

Sargent, T. J. and Wallace, N. (1975), '"Rational expectations", the optimal monetary instrument and the optimal money supply rule', *Journal of Political Economy*, 82, pp. 241–54.

Stiglitz, J. (1979), 'Equilibrium in product markets with imperfect information', *American Economic Review*, 69, May, pp. 339–45.

Taylor, M. P. (1987), 'The simple analytics of implicit labour contracts', in J. D. Hey and P. J. Lambert (eds), *Surveys in the Economics of Uncertainty*, Oxford: Basil Blackwell.

Tobin, J. (1980), *Asset Accumulation and Economic Activity*, Oxford: Basil Blackwell.

Weitzman, M. L. (1982), 'Increasing returns and the foundations of unemployment theory', *Economic Journal*, 92, December, pp. 787–804.

Worswick, G. D. N. (1944), 'The stability and flexibility of full employment', in Oxford University Institute of Statistics, *The Economies of Full Employment*, Oxford: Basil Blackwell.

# Monetary economics

### Introduction

Hicks (1967) stated the creed of monetary economics by stressing that it had to be policy relevant in a way that no other branch of economics had to be.

> Monetary theory is less abstract than most economic theory; it cannot avoid a relation to reality, which in other economic theory is sometimes missing. It belongs to monetary history, in a way that economic theory does not always belong to economic history. Indeed, it does so in two ways which need to be distinguished.
>
> It is noticeable, on the one hand, that a large part of the best work on money is topical. It has been prompted by particular episodes, by particular experiences of the writer's own time. All theorising is simplifying, cutting out the unimportant and leaving what is thought to be important in the hope that by simplifying we may increase understanding. Sometimes what is sought is a general understanding; but with monetary theory it is more often a particular understanding, an understanding directed towards a particular problem, normally a problem of the time at which the work in question is written. So monetary theories arise out of monetary disturbances . . . Topicality is one way in which monetary theory is conditioned but there is another also . . . money itself has been evolving. (Hicks in Clower, 1969, p. 255).

This approach has been adopted here. What is new 'is' what is topical, in Hicks' two senses. The unifying theme of modern monetary economics is that it should not be regarded or analysed as a separate, arcane branch of economics using specialist techniques to tackle peculiar (in both senses) problems. Instead it should as far as possible be integrated into the central core of economic theory using standard microeconomic technical analysis. Keynes (1930, 1936) began this by arguing that money was an asset and should be analysed in just the same way as all other assets. Hicks (1935) had a similar message: not only could the result be more rigorous, it would also be simpler. Friedman (1956) was consciously Keynes' heir in this respect and deliberately reformulated the quantity theory of money as a theory of stock adjustment. Individuals, like companies and financial institutions, hold a portfolio of assets. In many cases the most important assets are houses and consumer durables. They will usually be in equilibrium. Monetary shocks, such as changes in monetary policy, will disturb this equilibrium. Economic agents will then readjust their portfolios and in consequence income will change.

This process is easy to observe in the UK. On three occasions (1971–3, 1977–8, 1984–6) there have been rapid monetary expansions. On each occasion the consequent excess monetary demand has led to increased demand for housing and consumer durables. House prices have therefore exploded, thereby causing a much smaller but significant rise in house-building. The extra demand for consumer durables has been satisfied from overseas sources, causing in turn large balance of payments deficits, expecially in 1973–4 and 1988–9. In addition, the extra corporate liquidity seems to cause companies to increase wages. Hence this approach to monetary theory seems of practical as well as theoretical relevance. Therefore this approach has become central to monetary theory in the 1980s; it is topical in the Hicks' sense. Keynesians, notably Tobin (1969), have adopted and developed Friedman's portfolio approach to monetary theory. The approach so permeates modern macroeconomic and international economics as well as monetary economics that precise territorial demarcation is no longer possible; hence much of 'what's new' in monetary economics can be found in other chapters. In particular, the asset approach to exchange rates (Dornbusch, 1988) is the latest and most general application of model-building which rests on these Keynes–Hicks–Friedman foundations.

The new frontier of monetary economics narrowly defined in the 1970s and 1980s has been the application of a similar approach to banks and banking. The seminal text of this approach is Tobin (1963), which inaugurated the slogan of theorists in this area: banks are firms just like any other and should be analysed

in the same way. There have been a large number of consequences of the application of marginal cost, marginal revenue
and risk-preference to banking. One is the almost total triumph
of the 'new view' of banking; that is, the credit multiplier models
are neither theoretically useful nor practically relevant. Indeed,
most monetary specialists are both irritated and annoyed that
these troglodytes appear so regularly in macroeconomic texts.
Modern banking theory is presented as the application of sales
and profit maximisation to a constrained portfolio-selection
problem whereby banks choose the total of deposits and loans so
as to maximise a utility function. This approach fits in quite well
with the banker's approach of asset and liability management.

The regulatory consequences of this modern approach can
be startling. The imposition of a compulsory reserve ratio on
banks can have a perverse effect by inducing banks to lend more
(Jaffee, 1975; Courakis, 1986; see the survey by Di Cagno, 1990).
Similarly such ratios can also lead a bank to take more risks,
since the higher return on a riskier portfolio is more attractive
after the imposition of reserve ratio which acts as a tax. Nowhere
is the Hicksian *dictum* cited above more relevant than in regulatory theory. The 'gathering crisis in deposit insurance' was
not only predicted by economists, especially Kane (1985), but it
stimulated them to further analysis of this device. What had
seemed a benign and arcane method of protecting depositors
turned out to be very dangerous and expensive. In 1989 the US
government had to face a bill of at least $362 billion as a con-
sequence of the Savings and Loans Association fiasco.

Another initial application of this general approach has been
to credit rationing. Elementary microeconomics suggests that an
agent can buy as much as they like of a good at the prevailing
price if they are 'small', that is, a price taker. If they are large
then they can obtain as much as they want so long as they are
prepared to pay a sufficiently high price. In credit markets this is
not so. Agents sometimes discover that no one will make a loan
to them at all, irrespective of the interest rate they are prepared
to pay (Type 1 rationing). More frequently, a would-be borrower
discovers that financial institutions will assess their credit-
worthiness and offer a loan of a maximum of £$x$, at an interest
rate of $y$ per cent. It is unusual that they can bargain for an
increase in $x$, even if they are willing to pay more than $y$ (Type 2

rationing). Price does not clear the market. This has led to a massive literature[1] analysing credit rationing as a normal micro-theoretic response to imperfect information and to the revival of the Keynesian 'creditiste' position abandoned in the 1950s. Ben Friedman (for example, 1983) and Blinder (for example, 1989) have revived a full-blown new Keynesian approach to economic policy based on natural or optimal imperfections in the credit market. These are considered in the final section. Again the topical element is clear. In the 1980s there was a debt explosion in the USA as the public, household and corporate sectors all increased their borrowing massively and, to many commentators, with disastrous consequences (B. Friedman, 1989; Kaufman, 1986).

## Banking models

It is conventional in textbooks to illustrate the nature of banking models and their objectives by reference to stylised descriptions of early banks. From one point of view this is absurd since there is very little in common between the Midland Bank and a seventeenth-century goldsmith. On the other hand, it does demonstrate the generality of the models and can be used to emphasise the chief characteristics of the two rival schools of analysis: the multiplier and the 'new view'.

Modern banking emerged from the Italian financiers of the late twelfth century, of whom the Bardi are the best known. They came from the Lombard and Tuscan cities of northern Italy, especially Sienna and Florence. These entrepreneurs operated an extensive money-transmission mechanism, designed to serve the Pope (who received taxes in all countries, but wished to spend them in Rome), various kings (fighting wars abroad) and the merchants who traded at the great fairs of Champagne, where merchants from northern and southern Europe met to trade goods. The Italian firms operated by receiving cash (usually gold and silver) in one centre and giving a receipt that could be encashed at another one of their branches; formal branches seem to have been established about 1290. Hence, a London merchant could hand over gold in London to the Bardi, who would give him a receipt. He might then travel to Champagne and buy silk from an Italian merchant. He would pay with the receipt which the Italian could cash in, say, Siena. Thus, neither merchant had to transport cash. Moreover, the Bardi also dealt with the very complex foreign exchange problems that emerged. Some of these transactions would offset each other, but the Bardi would have to ship enough gold to meet any net claims. If, for example, English merchants had bought more than they sold in Champagne, it would be necessary to ship bullion from London to Italy. The Bardi made a profit by charging a commission for their services.

The Italian financiers also started to lend funds, originally by extending credit to customers who bought goods from them; the Bardi and others were traders as well as bankers. At some point they found it convenient to make loans by issuing certificates that entitled the holder to receive bullion from one of their branches. For example, if the King of England wished to send an ambassador to the Pope in Rome, he could finance the trip by a loan from the Bardi. He would do this by obtaining a certificate entitling his emissary to draw gold in Italy. The Italian financiers quickly realised that they could issue more certificates than they had bullion; indeed it is unlikely that their Paris agent had much idea how much cash was held in Siena, or vice versa. Hence, modern banking emerged. By issuing certificates to a borrower, the Italian bankers were creating money. They chose to lend and in doing so created liabilities on themselves which were money.

In the eighteenth century, English banks performed the same operation by printing notes so that they could lend them. Modern banks do the same, but the creation is concealed behind entries in ledgers and on computer tape. A bank can make a loan in two ways. It can increase the balance of the borrower as in the USA and in the UK with a personal loan, as exemplified by the ubiquitous TSB advert. Alernatively, it can increase the balance of a third party at the request of the borrower, as happens with the overdraft system. In either case a deposit is created; every loan creates a deposit.

Banking economists have sought to answer two questions about this process. The first is why it emerged (and continued). The second is what determines the amount of credit a bank extends (that is, the quantity of money it creates). The first can be answered easily. The Bardi and their confrères made loans because it was profitable (or in many cases because powerful monarchs coerced them). This is still true for banks, although residual finance is a smoother method of borrowing than some of, say, Philip the Fair's methods. The second is a much more complex and crucial question. Indeed, the question can be posed as the converse of the first problem – why is money not created? It might seen that, if banks can create money, the natural result would be creation on a infinite scale. If a bank literally has a licence to print money, restraint is not the most likely result. Models of banking seek to analyse the constraints on money creation and so explain the quantity created. Basically, there are two answers: the multiplier and the 'new view'. Both of these can, however, be viewed as special cases of the portfolio model of banking.

The Italian banks, according to the multiplier approach, were constrained by the need to redeem the certificates they had issued. The banks had to exchange certificate for gold (more or less) on demand. Thus, a reserve had to be held to meet these claims. Prudence and experience revealed what was the best ratio; that is, what proportion of deposits it was sufficient to hold as reserves to meet likely claims. This might be, for example, 40 per cent. Critically, for multiplier analysis, the ratio was constant. In this case the main determinant of loans extended was gold inflows and outflows. When the reserves were depleted by the encashment of certificates, the bank would cease to make loans until more cash was deposited. If extra deposits were received, the bank would choose to extend more loans, i.e. issue more certificates (in fact equal to over twice the inflow) without the ratio falling below the critial level.

This 'old view' or multiplier approach has been subject to devastating analysis by monetary economists (for example, Goodhart, 1984). The approach is often found in general textbooks but is largely discredited in more specialist analysis. It is usually presented as some sort of stochastic cash model. Banks receive deposits and encash them as their customers receive income and make payments. These flows can be modelled as statistical series with means, standard deviations, etc. Banks calculate optimal reserves so as to trade off the possibility of running out of reserves against their cost. While these models are rigorous and would describe, say, a bank in the Wild West in the 1830s quite well, they assume that obtaining reserves is exogenous to a bank. A bank in practice can obtain reserves in

173

the modern world. Thus the old view assumes a perfectly inelastic supply of reserves to a bank. Hence reserves determine loans: a bank makes a loan whenever but only when it has the necessary reserves. The 'new view' would regard this as an over-mechanistic and simplistic model. Banks would have to hold reserves but not as a fixed proportion of deposits. The quantity of loans would depend upon the number of customers wanting to borrow, what security they offered, and so on. Banks, in short, were profit-maximising firms. They should therefore be analysed using the normal marginal tools of microeconomic analysis.

This second approach to the modelling of banking starts with the concept that the important constraint upon a bank is that it has to persuade enough depositors to hold claims on it so that its liabilities are equal to its desired assets. In other words, the emphasis is on all deposits, not just the marginal deposit as in the old view. In a simple form this is currently practised by UK banks (liability management). These are usually run by those who give priority to lending and then consider where to find the necessary deposits. In the short run this will almost inevitably be the case as the maturity of deposits is so much less than that of loans. Hence, day-to-day management of a bank is very much a question of finding deposits to match assets. Marginal deposits are often obtained on the overnight inter-bank market.

More generally, however, a very simple model of banking can be constructed from this basic idea so long as an objective function for the bank is added. The simplest and most obvious is profit maximisation. A bank therefore has to calculate its marginal cost and marginal revenue schedules for different levels of output, that is, for different levels of loans. If a bank makes a loan it incurs two sorts of costs. The first are administrative costs, shown as *MAC* in Figure 6.1. These include the costs of processing a loan, of attracting customers, perhaps by advertising, and so on. In addition, a bank must induce or obtain a total of deposits equal to its loans (less any own capital). It therefore has to calculate the cost of attracting deposits – interest payments, advertising, free gifts, free or subsidised services such as cheque clearing. All of these are shown in Figure 6.1 as *MIC* and the sum of *MAC* and *MIC* as *MC*. The bank can in principle calculate the demand for its loans. It has, however, to allow for default risk; customers may not pay back. If it is maximising expected

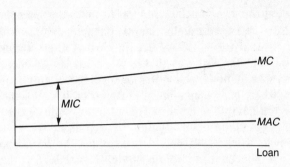

Fig 6.1

profit, it calculates revenue by deducting the risk of default from interest payments to calculate the marginal revenue from a loan. This is a reasonable approach for lending to the personal sector since with a large number of loans an actuarial approach is possible. If not, a risk preference has to be assumed (see below). The resulting curves are just like those of any other firm and so profit maximisation occurs where they intersect (Figure 6.2) – so long,

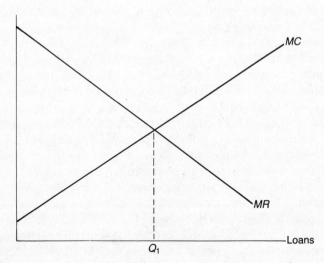

Fig 6.2

of course, as the firm switches from profit to loss at this point. The returns from loans are usually interest payments and so are some of the costs of deposits. However, the rate of interest receivable on loans is not the same as that paid on loans. An increase of the same size in both may not influence the quantity of loans supplied, whereas a change in the differential between them will influence the quantity supplied. This is an example of the supply of money depending upon relative, as well as absolute, interest rates (Gowland, e.g. 1991b). If desired, it is easy to incorporate a reserve-asset mechanism into this model (Figure 6.3). If there is a reserve ratio of 20 per cent, then, to lend £100, £125 of deposits must be raised so that £25 can be held as reserves and £100 lent out. In this case the cost of £100 of loans includes the interest paid on £125 of deposits rather than on £100, as would be the case if no reserve ratio existed. In consequence, the *MC* curve shifts upwards to reflect the higher inducement costs. A reserve ratio works like a tax and its impact, if any, is through increasing

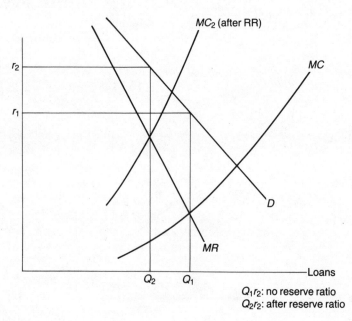

Fig 6.3

interest rates (Bank of England and HM Treasury, 1980). In the new view, loans create reserves and are in elastic supply to the banks.

If banks are competitive, then it is possible to derive the supply curve for loans (credit), and this will normally be upward sloping. In this case one has arrived at the same analytical model as in the multiplier model but without the need either to treat banks as special or to use such a distinctive and dubious apparatus. As Tobin puts it (1963, p. 122), 'thus the new view is a very simple and very flexible approach to the analysis of banks'. Marginalist tools, always so powerful in economics, render monetary analysis very simple. For example, it is easy to incorporate different utility functions for the banks, such as sales maximisation or risk aversion. Indeed the whole of modern banking theory is based upon this approach. It seems reasonable to assume banks are risk averse, especially with large loans – although their behaviour in practice often suggests that this plausible assumption is ill founded. The Third World debt crisis has made this topical and made economists focus upon it (especially Hefferan; see the survey by Ciarrapico, 1991). In general, portfolio models of banking incorporate many assets with different risk–return frontiers. A bank then maximises its utility subject to any constraints, such as minimum legal reserve ratios.

Moreover, the 'new view' has other advantages: the importance of private sector behaviour is emphasised by the need to examine the private sector's demand for loans, which determines the banks' marginal revenue schedule, and the private sector's demand for deposits, which determines the banks' marginal cost curves. It is worth emphasis that Friedman, Brunner and other soi-disant monetarists would regard the 'new view' as being appropriate in analysing an individual bank or even banking as an industry. However, for macroeconomic purposes they believe that the multiplier model is more appropriate to explain money creation by the banking system as a whole. Individual banks can always obtain reserve assets at a price. However, if the total of reserves is fixed, this price will be such as to make the quantity of loans equal to the prediction of the ratios model. In other words, at a micro level loans determine reserves, but at a macro level causality is reversed.

Practising bankers tend to analyse banking by reference to

asset and liability management. In the case of asset management, a bank takes its deposits (liabilities) as predetermined and adjusts its assets to maximise its objective function. It is easy to see that asset management is a necessary condition for a reserve base system. In this model, banks adjust the size of their assets, loans and reserves according to exogenous shifts in deposits (and reserve inflows). With liability management a bank determines its assets and then obtains the necessary deposits. This necessarily implies the 'new view', although this is not true in reverse because the 'new view' is consistent with either asset or liability management.

The consensus of opinion is that liability management is practised in the UK. The overdraft system, which accounts for a large if declining proportion of loans, means that the customer not the bank determines the level of loans. Banks usually delegate the determination of many loans to branch or regional level – for example, with personal customers by using the score card system.[2] Thus loans are exogenous to the banks' central decision-makers in the short term. A bank therefore has to practise liability management but then adjusts the terms on which loans are given to achieve equilibrium.

If a bank were to seek to manage both assets and liabilities, it would be practising portfolio management, which is the most general approach to banking. In fact, both multiplier and profit maximisation can be regarded as special cases of the portfolio approach. The bank has a portfolio of assets. These include cash, any other reserve assets and loans, as analysed earlier. However, in most portfolios the menu of assets is much richer, as loans are categorised by type of borrower (for example, public sector, industrial companies, personal sector), degree of risk, liquidity, and so on. The banks' liabilities are constrained to be equal to assets, but again there is usually a richer menu of choice for the bank as different types of deposit may be taken. The bank maximises its utility function by appropriate choice of the size and composition of its assets and liabilities. Profit is likely to appear in the utility function, but so may risk aversion, liquidity, the size of assets and, indeed, many other variables. The reserve base model is a special case of this model, where the desire to maintain a minimum quantity of reserves is the only relevant consideration, because reserves are the only relevant consideration, because reserves are exogenous (that is, in inelastic supply and so a binding constraint upon banks). If a bank's objectives are restricted, then the 'new view' emerges. For example, if profit maximisation is the sole objective of banks, this simplifies the asset choice facing a bank such that the basic 'new view' model is appropriate. An adherent of the new view argues that some portfolio model is bound to be correct because it is so general, but to be useful it has to be simplified. The simplification is usually a profit-maximising model of some sort, hence proponents of the 'new view' would argue that their approach is correct and the portfolio approach is merely a slight elaboration of their basic model.

## Regulation of banks

The most startling application of the new view is to the analysis of the impact of regulation upon banks, especially the impact of reserve ratios. A plausible special case of the portfolio model generates a multiplier model with a *negative* coefficient; that is, extra reserve assets (or an increase in bank lending to the public sector) lead to a fall in bank lending to the private sector. Jaffee (1975) argues that such a model is highly plausible in the USA. His elegant presentation rests upon an assumption of credit rationing (see next section). The results can also be generated by plausible assumptions about bank objectives, for example:

(1) Banks (in managerial-coalition theory, of the firm style) have a target level of assets. Accordingly, extra public sector assets (or reserves) imply fewer private sector ones.
(2) Banks' utility functions include size (positive) and risk (negative); that is, their controllers desire to be as large as possible but to take as few risks as possible. Public sector assets are less risky than private sector ones. Extra government spending causing an increase in bank holdings of public sector debt means that they can both take fewer risks and be larger (but reducing private sector lending as a proportion of assets). Including leisure or profits or both in the utility function complicates this analysis but does not change the result.

179

In particular, the textbook reserve ratio/reserve base system cannot work without exchange control and an ability to prevent market forces eroding the impact of the control. The problem is even greater with credit ceilings (as in the UK in 1952–71 or France 1946–89) or deposit ceilings (UK, 1974–80). All of these are direct controls which create an incentive to evade them. This is an application of the black market theory of elementary microeconomics: any restriction on economic activity creates an incentive to evade it. In financial markets, conditions are such that evasion is usually possible – low transaction costs, homogeneous products, many economic agents, good information and the rest of the criteria listed by textbooks. Certainly innovation designed to evade regulation has been very common in the last thirty years. The Eurocurrency market, now $15,000 billion, originally developed in the 1960s as a device to evade Regulation Q (Gowland, 1979, Chapter 3; Johnson, 1983). This was a restriction on the maximum interest paid on bank deposits. Hence American banks could not pay the market interest rate to their customers if they took a deposit in, say, Dallas. If, instead, the deposit was made with a London branch of the same bank, they could pay whatever interest they liked. Moreover, other regulations prevented traditional customers from borrowing from banks in the USA. These included foreign borrowers such as the Kingdom of Denmark and US firms wishing to finance overseas expansion. As a result, American banks switched a large chunk of their business to London, where neither deposit-taking nor lending were subject to Federal Reserve and Treasury regulations.

Many institutions grew up in London in the 1960s to evade ceilings on bank lending – secondary banks for example. They aimed to perform banking business in substance but not according to the strict letter of the law, in a legal form chosen so as not to be subject to the ceiling (rather as clubs, especially in Wales, often fulfil the functions of pubs while evading the legal restrictions on pubs).

Evasion of the UK ceiling on bank deposits (IBELs ceiling or 'corset') in the 1970s also occurred but mainly in two other ways. One was *offshore banking*, as with the Eurocurrency market; the deposit was 'booked' to a foreign banking centre and any loan made from this branch (I can deposit money in a York bank and the amount credited to an account with a branch in London or

Paris; it is then said to be 'booked' to London or Paris). This was especially prevalent in the last few months of the ceiling, after the abolition of exchange control in November 1979.

Earlier in the 1970s, evasion of the 'corset' occurred via the 'bill leak' or letter of acceptance leak (named after a particular form of bill). Normally, without any controls, A deposits money with a bank and receives a security (a bank deposit) in exchange. This is matched on the bank's balance sheet by a loan to B, who thereby obtains funds. Instead, A may go into a bank and receive in exchange for his deposit not a claim on the bank but a bank-guaranteed claim on B (that is, a bill of exchange). In reality all is the same; A has a security, B has his loan, the transaction has occurred because A trusts the bank, etc. However, legally A no longer has a deposit, so the control has been evaded. This was often called disintermediation in the UK, but is now usually termed *off-balance-sheet lending*.

More generally, off-balance-sheet and offshore banking can be used to evade a wide range of controls on banks – reserve requirements, constraints on the quantity or type of lending, and, of current significance, capital adequacy ratios. There have been introduced or increased in most countries in recent years and are part of the G10 pact, and of the European Commission's scheme to regulate banks. In the USA and UK, to achieve the structural objectives of monetary policy the regulatory agencies rely largely on a combination of capital adequacy ratios and deposit insurance (see below).

A bank has three sources of funds: equity capital, deposits and non-deposit loan capital of various sorts such as bonds. These are then invested in both fixed assets and various types of loan and investment. Hence a bank's balance sheet might appear as follows:

| Assets: | loans | 100 |
|---|---|---|
| | fixed assets and other non-loan assets | 25 |
| represented by | | 125 |
| Liabilities: | deposits | 90 |
| | bonds | 15 |
| | equity | 20 |

A capital adequacy ratio imposes the requirement that equity (and sometimes bonds) be at least a specified percentage of total assets. The purpose is to increase the security of depositors' funds. In the above example assets could decline in value to 90 and depositors' funds would still be safe as they have a claim on the assets which takes precedence over bond holders' and equity interests. The greater are bonds and equity, the more the bank's assets can decline in value and still be sufficient to repay depositors. However, a number of problems arise with such a regulation, all of which have been tackled by both G10 and the EC:

(a) Definition of assets. In the above example, if the bank were allowed to write its fixed assets up to 40 from 25 then the value of its equity would also rise by 15 and so capital adequacy would rise from 29 per cent (35/125) to 35 per cent (50/140). This means that a common set of valuation rules must be laid down, otherwise competition in laxity (Gowland, 1990) amongst regulators would allow banks to meet a ratio by writing up the value of their assets, as, for example, NatWest did in the UK in 1988. Particular problems arise with property, profits on share holdings (especially in the case of Japanese banks) and valuation of dubious loans, for example to the Third World. If a bank fails to write off bad debts this also artificially boosts its assets.

(b) Some loan capital is a permanent investment in the business, like equity, but some has to be repaid in the near future and cannot really be regarded as a protection to depositors. In the above example, if the bonds had to be repaid the capital adequacy ratio would fall to 18 per cent (20/110). To deal with this, various capital adequacy ratios have to be observed, each to satisfy a different definition of capital'.

(c) Different banks' portfolios of loan embody different risks, so a uniform ratio is both unfair and inefficient.

(d) A capital adequacy ratio may encourage banks to hold more risky loans (see the survey in Di Cagno, 1990). The basic idea is simple: a capital adequacy ratio reduces a bank's profits so it may seek to counteract this by holding riskier assets. In economic jargon, a capital adequacy ratio has both an income and a substitution effect. The latter induces a less risky portfolio but the former a riskier one. This is an important application of the Jaffee–Courakis result presented above. Banks respond to reserve ratios not only by lending more but by lending in a riskier fashion.

The solution to both (c) and (d) adopted by the European regulators (like G10 and the anglo-American banking pact) is the *risk-weighted capital adequacy ratio*. An immediate and obvious improvement on the simple capital adequacy ratio is that the optimal capital adequacy ratio should depend on the riskiness of the assets. If 5 per cent (however measured) is adequate for bank A with assets of riskiness 80 (however that is measured), it is not adequate for bank B with assets of riskiness 200. This proposition is undeniable and the Bank of England pioneered the development of such risk-weighted (or adjusted) ratios. They were incorporate into the Anglo-American banking pact of 1986 and the G10 pact of December 1987 and in subsequent EC regulations. Unfortunately, what seemed to the Bank to be the only practicable method of doing this is controversial.

The Bank's method is to divide a bank's assets into categories. Each category is viewed as having a different risk and so a different capital adequacy ratio is assigned; for example, asset A might be riskless and have a zero requirement, B might be riskier and have a 10 per cent requirement, and so on. Hence a bank's overall capital adequacy requirement is a weighted average of the requirements of the various types of assets it holds. This approach is illustrated hypothetically in Table 6.1. A conventional capital adequacy ratio would be calculated as a proportion of total assets (500) and a risk-weighted one as a proportion of the

Table 6.1

| Asset | Amount | Risk weight | Adjusted amount | After switch | Adjusted amount |
|---|---|---|---|---|---|
| Cash | 50 | 0 | 0 | 50 | 0 |
| Government securities | 100 | 0.5 | 50 | 100 | 50 |
| Loans to large companies | 200 | 1 | 200 | 300 | 300 |
| Loans to small companies | 150 | 2.00 | 300 | 50 | 100 |
| Total | 500 | | 550 | | 450 |

risk-adjusted column (550). Hence, if the requirement were 10 per cent, the requirement would be 55. If the bank were to switch 100 from loans to small companies to loans to large companies, a conventional capital adequacy ratio would be unaffected. The hypothetical risk-weighted one would be reduced by 10–that is, to 10 per cent of the new final column, which would then sum to 450 (see the final column).

The Bank's and *a fortiori* the EC's method of measuring the riskiness of assets seems unexceptionable. For example, for quoted securities, it bases the risk partly on the volatility of the price of this type of security, and partly on the 'thickness' of the market (if there are few dealings on the stock exchange – that is, it is a 'thin' one – then there may be problems in disposing of large holdings of shares, even if past quoted prices show little variation). Methods of measuring the risk of unquoted assets (that is, loans) are equally pragmatic, but equally reasonable.

Where the Bank's method is controversial is in the assumption that the overall riskiness of a portfolio of assets can be measured in this way. For the statistician, the critique is simple: the Bank has committed the classic howler of assuming that the variance of the sum is equal to the sum of the variances (that is, it has ignored covariance). No one, of course, suggests that the Bank's experts are ignorant of elementary statistics – but they have chosen to behave as if they are.

For non-statisticians, the critique can best be understood using an example drawn from betting. Imagine betting on the toss of a coin. A bet on heads is risky, so is a bet on tails. However, a bet on each taken together is riskless. This can be extended to that riskiest of all activities, roulette. A European roulette wheel has 37 slots (1–36, plus zero) and, when spun, a ball drops into one of the slots, the pay-outs to the gamblers being determined by which slot (number) this is. This example considers three bets:

A: $18,000 on high (19–35)
B: $18,000 on low (1–18)
C: $ 1,000 dollars on zero

The first bet will be lost if either zero or any number between 1 and 18 appears. However, if any number between 19 and 36 appears, the gambler will receive his stake of $18,000, plus winnings of $18,000 (that is, $36,000). The second bet will produce similar results, with a return of $36,000 if a number between 1 and 18 appears, but it will lose if either zero or 19–36 turns up. Finally, the $1,000 bet on zero will be lost, unless zero turns up; however, if zero does turn up, the gambler receives the stake ($1,000), plus winnings of $35,000 (35–1 is paid on a bet on a single number).

Each of the above three bets is highly risky, the third exceptionally so. However, the combination is riskless! Whichever number turns up, the gambler will receive $36,000 (from B if 1–18 turns up, A if 19–36 appears and from C if zero occurs). Of course, the gambler has staked $37,000 to ensure a return of $36,000 whatever happens, so it is an unlikely combination; however, it is conceivable – for example, if one were laundering funds or had been given complimentary chips and had to gamble them to convert them into cashable ones, or if gambling to impress others. More important, the example illustrates the two criticisms made of the Bank's methods:

(1) The overall riskiness of a portfolio (in this case three bets) may be less than the riskiness of any individual component.
(2) The addition of a very risky investment (the zero bet) may reduce the riskiness of the overall portfolio. More generally, a risk-weighted ratio may deter a bank from taking out a desirable risk-reducing strategy. The counterpart argument in the real world often involves the use of forward dealing, futures, options, etc. as means of reducing overall risk (Gowland, 1990, pp. 65–7).

Deposit insurance is widely practised in the Western world in a variety of forms. The common feature is that, in the event of a bank failure, depositors receive reimbursement for some or all of their losses from a government-backed insurance fund. Like all insurance, deposit insurance raises the problem of moral hazard. This occurs when insurance leads the insured agent to be more careless or otherwise take greater risks than they otherwise would. For example, a person insured against fire may be more careless with cigarettes. Economists in recent years have focused upon this problem with deposit insurance (especially Kane, 1985; see also papers by Kane and Horwitz reproduced in Gardener, 1986, and the review by Goodhart, 1987). This particular issue is topical in all Hicks' senses in the USA where insurance covers many bank deposits (over \$2,400 billion) and over \$2,000 billion of other assets in addition to thrifts (a thrift was the US equivalent of a building society prior to 1980; that is, a savings bank most of whose loans were in the form of mortgages). Thrifts are also known as Savings and Loans Associations (or S & Ls). It is in this area that problems have emerged – first with state insurance (Cargill and Garcia, 1985) and more recently with federally insured ones. A combination of bungled deregulation in 1980–2 and deposit insurance has produced the S & L fiasco in the USA. The cost to the US Treasury is officially estimated at \$362 billion and other estimates are higher – for example, the General Accounting Office estimate is \$500 billion, in addition to \$70 billion already paid out to depositors. Hence it is worth examining the cause of this problem in detail.

In the case of deposit insurance the basic problem is that economic agents place deposits heedlessly without thought to the safety of the institution – after all, they have no incentive to check since they will be reimbursed if it fails. The deposit-taker therefore can obtain funds without paying the market rate for the risk it takes. Hence it has an incentive to take risks since its owners gain all the reward but bear few of the costs. With a thrift, a depositor receives a fixed return so any increase in the return obtained by the institution accrues entirely to its owners. For example, if the depositor is paid 8 per cent and the thrift earns 9 per cent on its assets it has a gross profit equal to 1 per cent of deposits. If, instead, it can earn 10 per cent on its assets, its gross profits double, to 2 per cent of deposits. Hence there is an incentive to take excess risks. Imagine a thrift with a choice between a safe investment portfolio earning 9 per cent and one with a 50 per cent chance of paying 20 per cent and a 50 per cent chance of default. The latter has an expected rate of return of minus 40 per cent (the average of 20 and minus 100). However, the thrift may well prefer it to the safe 9 per cent! In the latter case, the thrift earns 1 per cent (9 less the 8 paid to depositors). If instead it invests in the risky portfolio, it receives either 12 (20 less 8) if the portfolio pays off or 0 (when the thrift defaults). This is an expected, if risky, return of 6 per cent, which may well be preferred to a safe 1 per cent. This is a classic example of a principal – agent problem and, although grossly over-simplified, illustrates the distortion of incentives produced by deposit insurance.

In a free market a bank is constrained from such actions because it either cannot obtain funds to pursue such a risky strategy or at least would have to pay such a high risk premium that the gambling strategy would no longer be attractive. Deposit insurance removes both constraints. A bank can obtain deposits from investors who neither check on its prospects nor demand a risk premium. Hence deposit insurance may be counter-productive and actually increase the risk of default. In the case of S & L's, this was reinforced by fraud – the criminally minded obtained funds from heedless depositors and siphoned them off by either embezzlement or loans to firms their associates controlled. By September 1989 half of all US thrifts were insolvent-in half of these cases because of legal but risky invest-ments, in half because of crime.

There are a number of devices designed to reduce moral hazard:

(a) restricting the size of deposit covered (as in fact was the case with thrifts, where only the first $100,000 was insured);
(b) coinsurance (where only a specified percentage of the deposit is insured);
(c) limiting the amount paid out in any one year (so that if claims exceed the limits they are scaled down *pro rata*); both (b) and (c) apply in the UK;
(d) risk-related premia whereby the amount paid by a bank to the insurance fund increases in accordance with the riskiness of its assets.

None are perfect answers to the problem. Partial insurance means that the risk of a run on a bank remains. This is the basic rationale of intervention to ensure bank safety (see the discussion in Gowland, 1991a). Ceilings on deposit coverage can be justified on equity and efficiency grounds. It seems reasonable to assume that the cost of monitoring a bank is independent of the size of one's deposit. It would therefore pay those with large deposits to investigate the riskiness of banks, but not those with small deposits. Hence it seems reasonable to require large depositors to check on the safety of their deposits. Small ones would find it uneconomic-hence the case for intervention, even if there were not the equity case for protecting 'widows and orphans'. However, these ceilings can be evaded by breaking deposits up into small parcels (brokered deposits). Moreover, the authorities may find it cheaper to assume responsibility for all the deposits than to liquidate the institution and pay out some depositors; usually this has been the case in the USA and even the UK in the case of JMB (Johnson Mathey Bankers), where eventually, somewhat to its surprise, the Bank of England avoided an accounting loss. Finally, political pressure may mean that limits cannot be adhered to in a democratic society: exemplified by the Barlow Clowes affair in the UK.[3] All in all, some scheme of deposit insurance or guarantee is probably essential to achieve the structural objectives of monetary policy, but the problems of practical implementation are serious.

## Creditisme and credit rationing

Keynesian economists have always placed considerable emphasis on the role of credit as opposed to money, even though there is only one *en passant* reference to credit in the *General Theory* (1936, p. 158). Credit is what an individual owes, the extent of his or her indebtedness, whereas money is what an individual owns, his or her stock of perfectly liquid assets. Milton Friedman and monetarists generally argue that the behaviour of economic agents is largely influenced by their stock of assets and by the liquidity of this stock. In the simplest form of monetarism, 'money burns a hole in your pocket'. Keynesians have always denied that money was very important in its own right, although it might be indirectly important through its effect on interest rates, exchange rates or credit. Keynesians stressed in the 1950s particularly the role of availability, known in Federal Reserve circles as the *availability* doctrine. The argument was originally ad hoc. Casual empiricism suggested that, especially in the days before effective financial liberalisation (1950s in the USA, 1980s in the UK), individual and small-company spending plans were frequently frustrated by an inability to borrow. Keynesians at this period therefore often argued that credit restraint could halt economic expansion but not promote it (Hansen, 1953; Radcliffe Committee 1959). This assumed that credit availability was the only possible money transmission mechanism and that its role was restricted to 'the bank manager says No'. Johnson, in a whole series of articles, trenchantly attacked this (for example, 1972).

In response, the Keynesian position was reformulated by Radcliffe (1959). In addition to the classical definition of liquidity in terms of the cost, speed and certainty of converting assets to purchasing power, a fourth dimension was added: *collateral value*. Assets were liquid if one could borrow against their security. Keynesian analysis developed further with Clower (1965) and Leijonhufvud (1968). They justified the Keynesian consumption function as a liquidity constraint. In a new classical world, economic agents use borrowing and saving to ensure a smooth path of consumption in the face of uneven income – as in the famous Ando–Modigliani (1963) life cycle or Friedman (1956) permanent income model. This follows from the principle of diminishing marginal utility. To consume $x + 1$ in period 1 and $x - 1$ in period 2, or vice versa, is less attractive than to consume $x$ in each, since the extra utility gained from the $x$'th unit is greater than that from the $x + 1$'th forgone to obtain it. Hence, individuals will not respond to shocks and the consequent variations in income by adjusting income. Instead they will borrow or dissave if their income falls. The marginal propensity to consume will thus be approximately equal to zero. Hence there will be magnification of shocks to the economy: the multiplier process will not exist. Clower and Leijonhufvud argued that the multiplier was an illiquidity phenomenon – individuals could not borrow as much as they wanted and therefore consumption plans were constrained by income. Hence effective demand (as predicted by a Keynesian consumption function) would differ from notional demand (as predicted by neoclassical analysis).

Soi-disant monetarists like Brunner and Meltzer (1972) followed suit by giving debt a role in their analysis. However, credit remained a theoretical curiosity to which little attention was paid until the 1980s when it became Hicks-topical. Then Benjamin Friedman argued that, statistically, credit aggregates were better predictions of income than monetary ones (1983). He and Blinder (1989) developed models in which there was a role for credit (bank assets or loans to the private sector). These models were part of a general realisation that many of the arguments for monetary targets were really arguments for *any* target expressed in terms of a financial aggregate – DCE, governments bonds, credit, etc. In a world of perfect certainty all would be equivalent, in that any one would imply values for the rest. In a world of uncertainty the form of the uncertainty would determine which is preferable.[4] Of course, such arguments are bound to be inconclusive and, as Laidler (1982) points out, miss the point of monetarism. If there were enough information to make it possible to determine whether a credit or money target were better, then there would be enough to select a still better policy, either discretionary or 'open loop', that is, some combination of the two.

However, what really gave impetus to the revival of creditisme was the discovery that credit rationing was not only prevalent but in many ways an optimal response to the market failure generated by imperfect and asymmetric information. Neither borrowers nor lenders have perfect information, but it is likely that the borrower will have more information than the lender about what he or she intends to do with a loan and the prospects of any investment project. This is reinforced by the possibility of bankruptcy. If borrowers default, they go bankrnpt. It is then immaterial to them whether their assets are sufficient to repay 50 or 60 per cent of their debts. On the other hand, the bank is concerned for obvious reason. At the other end of the distribution, the reverse is true for the reasons discussed in the analysis of thrifts above. Normally, either the bank receives a fixed return – agreed interest plus principal – or the borrower defaults and the bank has to *sauve qui pent*. However well the project prospers, it will receive none of the excess. Hence the borrower has an incentive to take more risks than the bank would like and so to pretend that the project is less risky than it really is.

To illustrate, assume that the interest rate on bank loans is 10 per cent. Consider a variety of projects all with an expected return of 10 per cent, and so all equally socially desirable. The borrower is taken to be a limited liability company investing only in this project an entirely financed by the bank loan. The first project offers 10 per cent with perfect certainty. The borrower will find this unattractive – its net return is zero. On the other hand, it would be very attractive to the bank – it would always receive its agreed interest. The next project offers a 50 per cent chance of a return of 5 per cent and a 50 per cent chance of a return of 15 per cent. If it pays 15 per cent, the borrower receives an amount equal to a net 5 per cent (15 − 10) of the amount invested on an investment of zero. The bank receives the agreed 10 per cent. If it pays 5 per cent, the borrower defaults (earns 0 per cent) and the bank recovers its investment plus 5 per cent − all the available funds. The borrower therefore has an expected net return of 2.5. The bank's expected return is 7.5 per cent. The bank would therefore prefer the less risky alternative, the borrower the riskier. Hence a borrower has an incentive to pretend that projects of the second type are projects of the first type or more generally to conceal the risk element.

This example illustrates the key proposition of the credit rationing school: the higher the interest rate, the riskier will be the loans demanded. Assume there are a large number of entrepreneurs, of whom some can invest in the safe project above and some in the risky. For simplicity, assume that the bank cannot distinguish them. If the interest rate is 9 per cent, both types will demand loans. The safe project offers a return to the borrower equal to 1 per cent (10 − 9) of the project's cost. The risky project offers the borrower either 6 per cent (15 − 9) or default. The bank receives a 9 per cent return from the first group and either 9 or 5 per cent (in the case of default) from the second, that is, 7 per cent. If there were equal numbers of each project it would receive an overall return of 8 per cent. If the bank raised the interest rate to 11 per cent, borrowers would not wish to borrow to finance the safe project: 9 per cent is less than 11 per cent. However, the second type of project is still attractive − offering either 4 per cent (15 − 11) or default. Thus the bank would find all its loans were to risky customers and it would receive a return of 8 per cent − 11 when the project paid 15, 5 when it did not and the borrower defaulted.

In general, therefore, a high interest rate has an adverse selection effect which may outweigh any risk premium effect even to a risk-neutral bank. In other words, charging a higher interest rate to a riskier borrower may have a lower expected return than a low rate to a safer one. It is interesting to muse on the effects of combining the deposit insurance analysis above with the analysis here. Banks are searching for risky loans when faced with borrowers who are pretending their loans are less risky than they are. Hence the thrifts may have sought a risky portfolio but obtained a still more risky one.

Banks can protect themselves from the problem in part by demanding collateral or by insisting that the borrower provide equity funds as a cushion for the bank and to ensure the borrower pays in the event of bankruptcy. Information about projects may be obtainable at a price (Williamson, 1986); for example, accountants can be asked to verify the data provided by a would-be borrower. Finally, the bank may demand that its return be related to the overall return on the project: an equity kicker. All of these are real-world phenomena and are termed equilibrium rationing by Jaffee. The crucial point is that all involve a limit on the amount a borrower is allowed to borrow, determined by his collateral or by available equity funds. This limit will not be relaxed by a willingness to pay more. In other words, there is a foundation for the availability doctrine.

The analysis can be extended to derive the familiar result that a bank would rather lend to a large company than to a small one to finance the same project – since its other activities provide collateral. Moral hazard may also apply. Once a loan has been obtained, borrowers have an incentive to change their behaviour so as to take more risks.

In general, credit rationing provides a micro-foundation for the availability doctrine and the Keynesian consumption function. To conclude, modern monetary theory analyses banks as if they were ordinary firms. The result is a rich portfolio of Hicks-topical analysis of current policy problems with many counter-intuitive results.

## Notes

1 The seminal works are Stiglitz and Weiss (1981, 1983); see also Stiglitz (1988). Surveys include Allen (1987), Cosci (1991), and Clemenz (1986).
2 With the score card system the borrower fills in a form and obtains points for having a permament job, owning a house, etc. The total determines his or her credit limit.
3 Barlow Clowes is discussed in Gowland (1990), especially pp. 35–6.
4 Poole (1970); for subsequent analysis, see Gowland (1985), pp. 241 ff.

# References

Allen, L. (1987), *The Credit Rationing Phenomenon: A Survey Literature*, New York: Salomon Brothers Center, New York University.

Ando, A. and Modigliani, F. (1963), 'The "life cycle" hypothesis of saving', *American Economic Review*, 55, June.

Bank of England and HM Treasury (1980), *Monetary Control*, Cmnd 7858, London: HMSO.

Blinder, A. S. (1989), *Macroeconomics under Debate*, Bringhton: Wheatsheaf.

Brunner, K. and Meltzer, A. H. (1972), 'Money, debt and economic activity', *Journal of Political Economy*, 80, pp. 951–75.

Cargill, T. F. and Garcia, G. G. (1985), *Financial Reform in the 1980s*, Stanford, lalif.: Hoover Institution Press.

Ciarrapico, A. M. (1991), *Sovereign Debt*, Aldershot: Dartmouth.

Clemenz, G. (1986), *Credit Markets with Asymmetric Information*, Heidelberg and London: Springer-Verlag.

Clower, R. W. (1965), 'The Keynesian counter-revolution: a theoretical reappraisal', in F. H. Hahn and F. P. Brechling, *The Theory of Interest Rates*, London: Macmillan; reprinted in R. W. Clower (ed.), *Monetary Theory*, Harmondsworth: Penguin, 1969.

Cosci, S. (1991), *Credit Rationing and Asymmetric Information*, Aldershot: Dartmouth.

Courakis, A. S. (1986), 'In what sense do compulsory ratios reduce the volume of deposits?' in C. Goodhart, D. Currie, D. T. Llewellyn (eds), *The Operation and Regulation of Financial Markets*, London: Macmillan.

Di Cagno, D. (1990), *Regulation and Bank Behaviour Towards Risk*, Aldershot: Dartmouth.

Dornbusch, R. (1988), *Exchange Rates and Inflation*, Cambridge, Mass.: MIT Press.

Friedman, B. M. (1983), 'The Role of Money and Credit in Macro-economic Analysis' in J. Tobin (ed.) *Macroeconomics, Prices and Quantities*, Oxford: Blackwell.

Friedman, B. M. (1989), *Day of Reckoning* (English edition), London: Pan Books.

Friedman, M. (1956), 'The quantity theory of money – a restatement', in M. Friedman (ed.), *Studies in the Quantity Theory of Money*, Chicago: University of Chicago Press.

Gardener, E. P. M. (ed.) (1986), *UK Banking Supervision*, London: Allen & Unwin.

Goodhart, C. A. E. (1984), *Monetary Theory and Practice: The UK Experience*, London: Macmillan.

Goodhart, C. A. E. (1987), 'Financial regulation and supervision: a review of three books', *National Westminster Bank Review*, August, pp. 55–64.

Gowland, D. H. (ed.) (1979), *Modern Economic Analysis*, London: Butterworths.

Gowland, D. H. (1985), *Money, Inflation and Unemployment*, Brighton: Wheatsheaf, Brighton.

Gowland, D. H. (1990), *The Regulation of Financial Markets in the 1990s*, Aldershot: Edward Elgar.

Gowland, D. H. (1991a), *The Microeconomics of Monetary Policy*, Aldershot: Edward Elgar.

Gowland, D. H. (1991b), *Monetary Control in Theory and Practice*, London: Routledge.

Hansen, A. H. (1953), *A Guide to Keynes*, New York: McGraw Hill.

Hicks, J. R. (1935), 'A suggestion for simplifying the theory of money', *Economica*, 2, February, pp. 1–19; reprinted in F. A. Lutz and L. W. Mints (1951), *Readings in Monetary Theory*, Homewood, Ill.: Irwin.

Hicks, J. R. (1967), *Monetary Theory and Policy: A Historical Perspective*, the Seventh Edward Shawn Memorial Lecture in Economics, Perth: University of Western Australia Press; partially reprinted in R. W. Clower (ed.), *Monetary Theory*, Harmondsworth: Penguin, 1969.

Jaffee, D. W. (1975), *Credit Rationing and the Commercial Loan Market*, New York: Wiley.

Johnson, H. G. (1972), *Further Essays in Monetary Economics*, London: Allen & Unwin.

Johnson, R. B. (1983), *The Economics of The Euro Market*, London: Macmillan.

Kane, E. J. (1985), *The Gathering Crisis in Federal Deposit Insurance*, Cambridge, Mass.: MIT Press.

Kaufman, H. (1986), 'Debt: the threat to economic and financial stability', *Economic Review* (Federal Reserve Bank of Kansas City), 71(10), pp. 3–11.

Keynes, J. M. (1930), *A Treatise on Money*, 2 vols, Macmillan; reprinted in *The Collected Writings of John Maynard Keynes*, London: Macmillan for the Royal Economic Society, 1971, vols V and VI.

Keynes, J. M. (1936), *The General Theory of Employment, Interest and Money*, London: Macmillan; reprinted in *The Collected Writings of John Maynard Keynes*, London: Macmillan for the Royal Economic Society, 1971, vol. VII.

Laidler, D. E. W. (1982), *Monetarist Perspectives*, Cambridge, Mass.: Harvard University Press.

Leijonhufvud, A. (1968), *On Keynesian Economics and the Economics of Keynes*, New York: Oxford University Press.

Poole, W. (1970), 'Optimal choice of monetary instruments', *Quarterly Journal of Economics*, 84, pp. 197–216.

Radcliffe Committee (1959), *Committee on the Workings of the Monetary System*: Report Cmnd 827, London: HMSO.

Stiglitz, J. (1988), 'Money, credit, and business fluctuations', *Economic Record*, 64, pp. 307–22.

Stiglitz, J. and Weiss, A. (1981), 'Credit rationing in markets with imperfect information', *American Economic Review*, 71, pp. 393–410.

Stiglitz, J. and Weiss, A. (1983), 'Incentive effects of terminations: applications to the credit and labor markets', *American Economic Review*, 73, pp. 912–27.

Tobin, J. (1963), 'Commercial Banks as Creators or Money', in D Carson (ed.), *Banking and Monetary Studies*, Homewood, Ill.: Irwin; reprinted in J. Tobin, *Essays in Economics*, vol. 1: *Macroeconomics*, Amsterdam: North Holland, 1972.

Tobin, J. (1969), 'A general equilibrium approach to monetary theory', *Journal of Money, Credit and Banking*, 1(1), March.

Williamson, S. (1986), 'Costly monitoring, financial intermediation, and equilibrium credit Rationing', *Journal of Monetary Economics*, 18, pp. 159–79.

# International trade

## Introduction

International trade theory in recent years has developed principally but not exclusively along the lines established by a series of important articles in the late 1970s and early 1980s which began the organised incorporation into it of imperfect competition and game theory.

To explain this development, we must return briefly to the dissatisfaction felt in the 1960s with older trade theories in elucidating the nature of gains from international trade and in accounting for certain trade patterns, including the growth of intra-industry trade and the dominance of world trade by trade among developed countries with similar factor proportions and levels of per capita income. This dissatisfaction led to the construction of several well-known trade models such as Posner's technological gap, Vernon's product cycle, and Linder's theory of representative demand. These sought variously to overcome the neglect of technological change and the role of consumer tastes, and to relax the common, although not universal, assumptions of international immobility of factors of production and constant costs.

These new theories rejected perfect competition, proposing instead that firms may possess quasi-monopolistic advantages in international markets, exploitable in different ways. Research ensued into two related topics – the source of these advantages; and ways in which firms could extend and obtain maximum gain from them. International capital flows and the establishment of subsidiaries abroad entered the literature as alternatives to international trade. Pride of place went to the possession of scarce knowledge as a source of temporary comparative advantage and to ideas concerning the transmission of technology and the changes over time in products and production processes. Valuable contributions were made in explaining some aspects of modern international trade, but intra-industry trade was not satisfactorily accounted for until the late 1970s when increasing returns to scale and product differentiation were incorporated more fully into models.

### Normative aspects of trade theory

Attempts to explain international trade patterns went hand-in-hand with the development of normative trade theory. Neoclassical theory, with its emphasis on the welfare advantages of free trade and its inherent rejection of protection, had to be supported by attempts to understand the universal existence of protection. If all countries stood to gain from freer trade, why was there such resistance to it?

This was not a question of great import while GATT negotiations were succeeding in reducing average rates of nominal tariffs on industrial products. It was true that there was some scepticism over the significance of these reductions with the development of the theory of effective protection, which highlighted the impact of tariffs on levels of value-added in production rather than on final prices of goods. It was true also that the agricultural and textile industries remained problems, as did developing countries – but they could be treated as special cases with the construction of particular arguments for protection (such as the infant industry case), usually through the extension of the market distortions framework and the utilisation of second-best theory.

However, with the great increase in the use of non-tariff barriers in the 1970s, the question of why countries should so much wish to protect re-emerged as one of great importance. The immediate answer took the form of an investigation of the political economy of protection based upon the theory of pressure groups. After all, extensions of traditional trade theory had shown that, even when it was clear that a country could potentially gain from freer trade, in practice some groups in the economy would lose. The Stolper–Samuelson effect had long before shown that in a two-factor model a country's relatively scarce factor would lose from free trade and hence gain from protection. Further, models incorporating specific factors of production showed that those factors specific to the import-competing goods sectors of economies would certainly lose from freer trade. Indeed, in such models, mobile factors may either gain or lose; only factors specific to the exported goods sector clearly gain.

The specific-factors models produced the greater amount of real-world application. Granted that in the long run all factors become internally mobile, it remains true that trade unions and current owners of firms are concerned with the jobs and incomes of the present generation of workers, and the current profits of firms. Consequently, specific-factor models provided an explanation of why in many industries both workers and capitalists favoured protection. Allied to arguments from political theory concerning the regional concentration of many industries and the nature of the voting system, the prevalence of protectionist sentiment became explicable. None of this interfered with the ability of the economist as ethereal value-free spirit to argue for the desirability of free trade.

One problem remained – the need to explain the resurgence of protectionism in the 1970s. Informal arguments relating to levels of unemployment and growth rates abounded. However, Krugman provided a definite link between the positive and normative aspects of new trade theory.

Gains from trade in neoclassical theory arise only from changes in relative prices as countries change production patterns in line with comparative advantage. These changes produce gains for some groups within the economy and losses for others. However, the introduction of economies of scale and, crucially, consumer choice among product varieties allows further possible gains from trade. Krugman argued that, if increases in international trade were principally intra-industry in nature, the gains from additional trade would mainly take the form of greater consumer choice. All consumers could benefit in this way. Such gains might be sufficient to offset losses to some groups resulting from changes in relative prices of tradable goods. If all people in the economy were, then, becoming better off as a result of increased trade, we should not expect great pressure in favour of protection. If, however, increases in trade were principally intra-industry in form, consumer gains from product diversity would not offset losses from changing relative prices. It was then argued that trade expansion in the 1950s and 1960s had largely taken the form of increased intra-industry trade; whereas in the 1970s, growth in trade was mainly inter-industry in character, reflecting the strong performance of the newly industrialising countries. Consequently, in involved significant losses for some groups in developed economies – hence the resurgence of protectionist feeling. This also neatly explained the textiles and agriculture special cases as well as the tendency to adopt forms of protection which again permitted discrimination among countries.

But this was not the only impact on normative theory of the movement away from the assumption of perfect competition. For many years, trade theory had acknowledged only one beggar-my-neighbour argument for protection in which one country might gain by protection at the expense of others. This was the optimum tariff/export tax case in which countries might be able to use protection to change the terms of trade in their favour. This was applicable only to countries which consumed or supplied a high proportion of total world output of a product. All this was changed by Brander and Spencer who introduced the notion of strategic trade policy: the existence of imperfect competition made it possible for a government to adopt commercial policies which could shift profits from foreign to domestic firms.

In recent years the trade literature has been dominated by extensions of the work of Krugman, Lancaster, and Brander and Spencer. At the same time, other authors have sought to defend free trade by exploring the weaknesses of the strategic trade policy arguments for protection.

In the midst of this development of positive and normative trade models, work has continued on the generalisation and testing of traditional trade theories, examining the extent to which their predictions hold under a variety of assumptions. Also, we have seen the beginning or expansion of interest in topics of current policy relevance, notably trade in services, an issue of considerable importance in the Uruguay round of trade negotiations. Within Europe more attention has been paid to economic integration as the EC approaches 1992, the date set for completion of its internal market. In addition, much continues to be published on the question of foreign direct investment and the growth of multinational corporations. In this chapter we shall summarise many of the contributions within these areas.

## Generalisations of traditional trade theories

The extension of traditional comparative advantage theory has proceeded in many directions. Work has continued on the incorporation of uncertainty into Ricardian trade models. Helpman and Razin (1978) had introduced the possibility of international risk-sharing through trade in equities and had shown that comparative advantage could explain the pattern of trade in securities within a trade model. However, that conclusion had been based on the strong assumption of the perfect correlation across countries of industry-specific uncertainties. Grossman and Razin (1985) thus sought to consider variations in risk across countries. However, the assumptions were still limiting and the conclusions hardly exciting. Grinols (1985), pointing out that earlier work had assumed that securities markets were complete, extended the analysis to deal with incomplete markets. In doing so, he demonstrated that the welfare properties of the standard trade model as well as the factor price equalisation (FPE) and Heckscher-Ohlin (H–O) theorems do not generalise to incomplete markets.

Differences among countries have interested other writers. Gray (1985) considered the problem that, once imperfect competition was introduced, the possibility arose that industries may be domestically X-inefficient but relatively efficient internationally (in terms of comparative advantage). He suggested that such firms might be destroyed by changes in domestic conditions despite their international efficiency and put this forward as a possible justification for conditional protection – protection as long as the firms involved act to increase domestic efficiency.

Ethier and Svensson (1986) examined the relationship between goods trade and international factor mobility. This was part of the extension of the trade model beyond two goods and two factors. For the standard factor endowments theorems to hold in multi-commodity and multi-factor models, the number of goods needs to equal the number of factors. For example, Thompson (1986) investigated the effect of changing prices on factor payments in a three-factor, two-good trade model, showing that, when such an economy moves from autarky to free trade, payment to a relatively cheap factor may fall, polarising rather than equalising factor prices.

According to Ethier and Svensson, this dimensionality requirement derives from the unrealistic assumption that goods are internationally traded but factors are not. Allowing for trade in some factors, all of the strong versions of the basic trade theorems (FPE, the Rybczynski and Stolper–Samuelson theorems and H–O), with the exception of the price version of H–O, are shown to hold if the number of international markets for goods and factors is at least as large as the number of factors.

Deardorff (1986) considers another problem involved in the extension of the basic trade model beyond two goods. He uses a two-country, two-factor, four-good model in which free trade causes factor prices to be drawn further apart than they were in autarky, again contradicting FPE. The problem stems from the various patterns of complementarity and substitutability among goods once one moves beyond two goods.

Staiger (1987) attempts to generalize H–O to non-competitive product and factor markets, finding that factor intensities remain a good guide to the pattern of trade in the presence of factor market distortions but not in product market cases where the principal exercise of market power is in import-competing industries.

Markusen and Svensson (1985) develop a new general approach to trade stressing international differences in production technology. They show that, in the case of product-augmenting technological change, factor mobility leads to factor trade and commodity trade being complements, rather than substitutes as in traditional trade theory. Trade causes factor movements and these, in turn, reinforce comparative advantage, generating further trade.

In the model, countries on average export goods in which they have a technological lead. As a result, prices of factors used intensively in those export industries rise. Then, factors (notably labour and capital embodying technological knowhow) move in response to the newly created international factor price differences. This movement allows further technological developments, expanding and preserving the initial technological lead, consequently generating further trade. Although Markusen and Svensson's results are much less clear in the case of factor-augmenting technological change, they are important since they contrast with earlier technological-gap trade models in which trade based on technological leads is strictly temporary and is often followed by capital movements in the opposite direction (that is, *from* the country with the initial technological lead) as firms, through foreign direct investment, attempt to preserve the quasi-monopolistic position gained through technological advance.

Rauch (1989), in examining the relationship between increasing returns to scale and trade patterns, makes a novel link between trade theory and the costs of commuting. He proposes that the realisation of increasing returns, where this requires geographic concentration, will be limited by the optimal size of cities, given commuting costs. If this size is small relative to the country's population, the efficiency of city formation, rather than country size, will determine comparative advantage in increasing returns industries. Thus any country large enough to sustain an optimally sized city for a particular industry can compete in that industry on an equal footing with much large countries. This supports the view that country size may be irrelevant to trade patterns, conflicting with Helpman and Krugman (1985).

Several articles have added to the long line of empirical tests of the predictions of the basic trade theories which had been given such impetus by the Leontief paradox, which appeared to contradict directly the Heckscher–Ohlin factor proportions theorem. H–O has continued to fare badly. The most ambitious study has been that of Bowen, Leamer and Sveikauskas (1987), who tested the predictions of a development of H–O (the Heckscher–Ohlin–Vanek model) using data for 12 resources and 27 countries. Their study rejected the propositions that trade reveals gross and relative factor abundance. The authors argued that all previous tests of H–O had been inadequate because they had used inappropriate generalisations of the $2 \times 2 \times 2$ model to deal with multi-dimensional reality. Most had also used data on only two of the three elements with which H–O deals: trade; factor input requirements; and factor endowments.

Tamor (1987) found that studied using cross-country regression offered little support for the claim that H–O can explain the composition of trade in manufactures. Staiger, Deardorff and Stern (1987) found discrepancies between the theoretical predictions of H–O and the observed factor content of Japanese and American foreign trade. These discrepancies could not be explained by the existence of protection.

# Extensions and tests of newer trade theories

Trade models based upon differing types of imperfect competition have been the principal growth area within international trade theory. These have been particularly aimed at explaining the growth of intra-industry trade. Greenaway (1987) provides a good summary of this area, categorising models by type of market structure. He deals first with three types of oligopolistic models: with Cournot behaviour and trade in identical products; with natural oligopoly and vertically differentiated goods; and with horizontally differentiated goods. He then treats large number cases under the heading of intra-industry trade in structurally competitive markets, dividing these into three types: neo-H–O (with a vertically differentiated product in one sector and with consumers all preferring high-quality to low-quality goods); neo-Chamberlinian (with horizontally differentiated products with all consumers consuming some of each product), and neo-Hotelling (with horizontally differentiated products with consumers with different tastes each demanding only one differentiated product). A useful outline of important points from the new imperfect competition trade theories is also in Helpman (1987).

One of the more interesting extensions of intra-industry trade models has been the attempt to take account of imperfect information about product quality among consumers. Donnenfeld (1986) sets up a model in which consumers' information about the quality of products varies according to the suppliers' country of origin. He shows that the patterns of trade are determined by both production and informational comparative advantage.

The model has two countries with one industry. In each country a continuum of qualities is produced. The home country (H) is assumed to have a comparative advantage in the production of high qualities and will specialize in and export these high qualities, while the foreign country (F) has a comparative advantage in low qualities and will specialize in and export these. If transport costs and/or tariffs are introduced, there will be a range of intermediate goods which are not traded and are produced by both countries. Next, Donnenfeld assumes that the transport costs/tariffs are removed and these intermediate qualities become traded. But consumers in each country have no experience of

203

quality within this range of the other country's production. Thus potential exporters within this range cannot differentiate their product and face a uniform price regardless of the true quality they are producing. Because of our initial assumptions about comparative advantages, F will specialize in the lower part of this range and H in the upper, but there will be some overlap. Consequently, the model produces an explanation of two-way trade in identical products. It also contradicts the law of one price in that different-quality goods will be sold in the same market at the same price.

Flam (1987) stresses the importance for firms intending to buy expensive producer durables of the experience of others in relation to maintenance costs and performance. He constructs a model of a monopoly which sells products in two markets and two time periods – selling exclusively in the home market in the first period and exclusively in the foreign market in the second. He examines the profit-maximization conditions for both discriminating and non-discriminating monopolists. A discriminating monopolist who takes consumption externalities into account will lower domestic price in order to sell more in the domestic market and thus also in the foreign market at a higher price. This sets up a model of reverse dumping. The monopolist sacrifices some profits in the domestic market in order to increase foreign and total profits. Flam suggests that there may be scope for welfare-increasing policies, such as a subsidy to domestic sales, when an ignorant but price-discriminating monopolist does not take the dependence of foreign sales on domestic sales into account. Policy might also be used to allow price discrimination to occur, e.g. by preventing resale by domestic buyers to foreign buyers.

Models from the generation before imperfectly competitive models remain important. Linder's representative demand theory (in which consumer tastes differ with differences in their per capita incomes and countries export predominantly to countries with similar per capita incomes), and Vernon's product-life-cycle theory (in which comparative advantage originates with the development of new products and processes, reflecting differences in technology, R&D, and entrepreneurial skills, but shifts to other countries as the product matures) have continued to be tested and used in country studies of trade performance. However, the more interesting development has been the incorporation of ideas from these theories into models centred upon imperfect competition and increasing returns to scale.

Although the testing of Linder's model has been inconclusive, articles reporting studies of it provide good examples of some of the problems involved in carrying out regression analysis of the determinants of trade patterns. In an imaginative study, Greytak and Tuchinda (1990) seek to overcome problems arising from the influence on international trade data of such factors as currency conversion, exchange rate restrictions, most-favoured-nation trade treaties and the impact on trade patterns of colonial ties by using interstate commodity flows in the US as the basis for their test. With these data, they find more support for Linder than in many earlier studies.

Hughes (1986) looks at the roles of R&D expenditures and of skilled labour in the determination of the composition of UK exports and finds that the level of technology, the technological gap, and skilled manual labour all have positive effects on UK exports. No positive role was found for investment or the scale variable, while concentration had a negative effect. Hughes concludes that her results indicate at least three separate determinants of UK export composition: technology; skill; and industrial structure. The failure to find a positive role for the scale variable is at odds with much of the recent theorising on trade patterns. The work of Marvel and Ray (1987) contains an even stronger rejection of its role.

In a study of Israel's high-technology industries, Hirsch and Bijaoui (1985) also find support for both the neo-factor proportions model and the product cycle model of trade by demonstrating the importance both of the relative abundance in Israel of engineers, scientists and technicians and of high expenditure on R&D by innovative firms which attain market power through innovation.

Both Markusen (1986) and Flam and Helpman (1987) make use of Linder's ideas in North–South trade models. These have become popular since Krugman's development of the view that trade between industrial countries was likely to be intra-industry trade in differentiated manufactured goods, while that between rich and poor countries was likely to be inter-industry trade based upon factor endowments.

Markusen divides the world into a capital-abundant North and a labour-abundant South, subdividing the North into two identical regions, East and West. He then explains the volume and direction of trade by combining non-homothetic preferences with scale economies and differences in endowments. More specifically, Linder's view that people with similar per capita incomes consume similar bundles of goods is modelled as an assertion that income elasticities are different for different goods; the North produces a differentiated capital-intensive manufactured good with increasing returns to scale and a high income elasticity of demand; the South a labour-intensive homogeneous commodity with constant returns to scale and a low income elasticity of demand. The more differentiated the non-homogeneous good produced by the North, the greater is the volume of East–West trade and the smaller that of North–South trade.

Flam and Helpman's model has the North exporting high-quality and the South low-quality industrial products. The structure of international trade is determined by cross-country differences in technology, income and income distribution. Intra-industry trade derives from an overlap in income distribution, again introducing an element from Linder. Flam and Helpman use their model to consider what happens when the South experiences changes in income distribution, faster population growth, and faster technical progress. Faster population growth produces an increase in the share of intra-industry trade and a product cycle in middle-range quality products. Faster technical progress causes the per capita income gap between North and South to fall because it results in a lower wage rate in the North.

Another North–South model involving a product cycle is that of Dollar (1986), which modifies Krugman's (1979) formal model of the product cycle by allowing competition between factors in different regions in order to combine the product cycle with neoclassical tendencies toward FPE. Thus, Dollar adds the assumption that the rate of technological transfer is positively related to the differences in production costs between North and South; introduces capital as a second factor of production; and assumes that the movement of capital between regions takes place slowly over time. He then considers the effects of an increase in labour supply in the South. In the short run, the result is the same as in the Krugman model—the demand for North's goods increases, the supply of new goods is unaffected and

North's terms of trade improve as the wages of Northern workers rise. In the long run, however, North's improved terms of trade produce a more rapid rate of technological diffusion to the South. The flow of capital to the South also reduces the North's capital/ labour ratio. The net effect is that real wages in the North fall.

Jensen and Thursby (1986, 1987) introduce game theory into product cycle models. In their 1986 article they demonstrate how the optimal strategic behaviour of decision-makers can result in a constant technological gap between North and South. The 1987 article raises the possibility that the existence of technological transfer from North to South may lead to a less than optimal rate of innovation in the North.

As well as theorising about intra-industry trade (IIT), economists have continued to worry about the measurement of it. Globerman and Dean (1990) provide a useful summary of studies showing the growth of IIT. Amidst criticisms of it and attempts to improve it, most empirical studies continue to use the Grubel–Lloyd index, which measures IIT as the percentage of a country's total trade in a given industry in which trade is balanced (exports equal to imports). The average level of IIT for a country is then calculated as a weighted mean of IIT in the individual industries. Despite the dominance in practice of this index, articles dealing with measurement appear regularly. For example, Milner (1988) considers the problem of weighting and the way in which the Grubel–Lloyd index is used. He raises the possibility that a number of earlier econometric studies need to be reworked. One way in which writers have sought to modify the Grubel–Lloyd index has been to correct it for aggregate trade imbalances. Kol and Mennes (1989) review these attempts, criticising them as too mechanical.

Despite this concern about measurement, early doubts as to whether IIT is genuinely an important phenomenon, rather than just a by-product of inadequate data and measurement techniques, have largely disappeared and empirical work is more likely to deal with the determinants of it in particular countries or groups of countries. Balassa (1986) tested various hypotheses concerning the determinants of IIT in 38 countries exporting manufactured goods. The econometric estimates showed that IIT increases with: (a) the level of economic development (GNP per capita); (b) the size of domestic markets (GNP); and (c) the openness of national economies. Both (d) the existence of trading partners with common borders; and (e) geographic proximity also helped to explain IIT.

Balassa and Bauwens (1988) studied the determinants of intra-European trade in manufactured goods. The results suggested that inter-industry trade could be explained by factor endowments while intra-industry specialisation was shown to be related to a number of country and industry characteristics, positively to per capita income and country size; but negatively to inter-country differences in these variables. Unsurprisingly, distance and high trade barriers were found to hinder bilateral trade, while the existence of common borders, participation in integration schemes, and a common language and culture all promoted trade among European countries. Finally, product differentiation and offshore assembly were shown to contribute to IIT and product standardisation to reduce it. The results seem to provide incentives for overall trade liberalisation and for the completion of the internal market of the EC. Both of these studies provided support for the new models of intra-industry trade, including those based upon product differentiation.

The outcome of the Marvel and Ray (1987) study, mentioned earlier, was quite the reverse. Using more disaggregated data than many earlier studies, their results strongly contradicted the models of IIT which stress product differentiation and scale economies. Models which emphasise the role of trade liberalisation in creating larger markets with increased opportunities for specialisation do find support, but only if carefully interpreted. Clearly more studies with results such as these will begin to raise doubts. None the less, a good deal of confidence in the new models remains.

For example, Globerman and Dean (1990) express the growth of IIT as a function of (a) an *ex ante* measure of product scale economies which can be exploited over time; (b) a measure of taste for variety; and (c) a measure of similarity of revealed preferences among consumers in the relevant market. This fits in well with the theories we have been considering above.

Globerman and Dean suggest the possibility that the growth of IIT has been slowing down in recent years. They put forward three hypotheses to explain this: (1) that the recession of the early 1980s led to a fall in the demand for product variety; (2)

that geographically dispersed international trade has increasingly encompassed heterogeneous tastes and preferences, thus encouraging inter-industry trade relative to IIT; and (3) that there may now be negative returns to further specialisation within industries both because of the existing high levels of IIT and because changes in technology have been more favourable to economies of scope than to economies of scale. They test these hypotheses for 16 OECD countries for the periods 1970–80 and 1975–85. Their explanatory variables are: diminishing returns to scale as proxied by initial IIT levels and by country size; less rapid changes in taste for variety as proxied by real income growth; less trade expansion between consumers with similar preferences as proxied by an index of bilateral trade; growth in trade flows; and trade liberalisation (within the EC, between Canada and the US, and between Australia and New Zealand). All variables are significant except real income growth, country size, and trade liberalisation within the EC.

# Protection

### *The new arguments for protection*

Writers have applied many of the ideas we have come across above in addressing the question of the desirability of protection from the point of view of either national or world welfare and in considering the best form of commercial policy.

For example, Helpman and Razin (1978) had shown that, with appropriate risk-sharing arrangements among domestic consumers and producers, the traditional arguments for free trade remain intact in the presence of uncertainty. Grossman and Eaton (1985), however, suggest that domestic risk-sharing arrangements are likely to be incomplete, largely because of the existence of moral hazard and adverse selection. In this case, free trade may not be optimal and governments may be able to improve social welfare with commercial policies which act as a partial substitute for the missing insurance market, especially for small countries which are more likely to face uncertain terms of trade. An income tax to redistribute income is the first-best policy in this model, but if this is not possible interventionist commercial policy is the second-best solution.

As indicated earlier, the best known of the new arguments for protection is that of strategic profit-shifting based on the work of Brander and Spencer (1983, 1984, 1985). They rejected the assumptions of perfect competition, arguing that, in industries with only a few firms in effective competition, firms could earn supernormal profits and it would be possible for governments through protectionist policies to shift some of these excess profits from foreign to domestic firms. Assuming only two firms in the industry, one domestic and one foreign, a subsidy to the domestic firm would improve the domestic firm's competitive position and deter investment and production by its foreign competitor. Then, if both firms use Cournot conjectures (with each firm making its output decision on the basis of the existing output levels of other firms and believing its actions will not cause competitors to alter their production levels), the home firm will respond to the lower output of the foreign firm by increasing output, in the process taking advantage of economies of scale and lowering average costs. As a result, the profits of the domestic firm will increase by more than the amount of the subsidy. In effect, profits of the foreign firm would be captured by the domestic one, thus raising national income at the expense of another country. The same results occur with a tariff on imports from the foreign company.

In the simplest Brander–Spencer model, there are again only two firms (one domestic and one foreign) and everything depends on the order of entry into the market of the firms. Either firm could alone earn profits from the production of a particular good, but if both firms try to produce it, both will lose. Suppose the foreign firm has entered the market first and is currently making a profit. With no assistance from its own government forthcoming, the domestic firm will not enter. However, if the home government offers a sufficiently large subsidy to the domestic firm, it will become profitable for it to enter irrespective of the behaviour of the foreign firm. Then, again following Cournot, the foreign firm will respond to the entry of the domestic firm by reducing its output. In a very simple game, the final result is the complete replacement of the foreign firm by the domestic firm in the home market. Krugman (1984) goes a step further and, assuming that the cost functions of the two firms are interdependent, shows that the domestic firm may also out-compete the foreign firm in the foreign market.

Dixit and Kyle (1985) and Venables (1985) supported the Brander–Spencer approach. Dixit and Kyle considered the importance in high-technology industries of the order in which players move in a game-theoretic model and showed that under certain assumptions the inability of firms to appropriate all of the consumer surplus in the model can justify a policy to alter an oligopolistic market outcome even from the viewpoint of world efficiency.

Several authors have, however, demonstrated the special conditions needed for the Brander–Spencer result to hold. Crucially, the notion that the home government could help the domestic firm by imposing an import tariff or an export subsidy depends on the assumption of Cournot conjectures. Eaton and Grossman (1986) showed that, if firms used Bertrand conjectures (with each firm taking its competitor's price rather than its output as given), an export tax would be called for instead. Here, a tariff pushes up the price of the foreign competitor's product. The domestic firm raises its price in response, with the result being a reduction in the output of both firms. The domestic firm does not take advantage of available economies of scale. Similarly, with an export subsidy, the domestic firm does not lower its price and take advantage of its improved competitive position by expanding output. An export tax, on the other hand, forces the domestic firm to expand its output in order to remain competitive. The question of the sensitivity of optimal trade policies to the nature of competition is also dealt with by Cheng (1988).

However, it is not only the nature of conjectures made by firms which matters. Collie and de Meza (1986) show that an export tax is optimal if the elasticity of market demand is less than unity, even if Cournot conjectures are assumed. Horstmann and Markusen (1986) set up a model which differs from Brander and Spencer by allowing the possibility of free entry of new firms. They show that, even assuming Cournot behaviour, a tariff or export subsidy may lead to inefficient entry and be welfare reducing. Dixit and Kyle (1985) also point out that in the strategic policy game, with other governments simultaneously pursuing trade policies, a prisoner's dilemma can arise. The timing of policy actions and the degree of commitment to them become crucial.

This range of possibilities has led to the view that individual industries need to be examined to consider whether in imperfect competition strategic trade policy can lead to gains at a national or at a world level. Several studies have been carried out. Dixit (1987) in a study of the US car industry found a fairly weak case for intervention to produce gains at a national level and Laussel *et al.* (1988) applied his model to the EC with similar results. Other studies also tend to support the case for domestic production subsidies or tariffs in cases with no freedom of entry.

However, the industries concerned (Norwegian skis, computer chips, US footwear) were characterised by significant variations in the nature of strategic interactions among firms. This suggested to Norman (1989) that perhaps too much stress had been placed on these in the literature. After all, simulation experiments by Smith and Venables (1988) and by Daltung *et al.* (1987) in which optimum policies under Cournot and Bertrand assumptions were compared directly suggested that moving from one assumption to the other did not affect the direction of optimum policies and that, indeed, the difference between them was quantitatively small. Rather, such studies stressed the importance of the possibility and the nature of entry and exit.

Before moving on to other arguments for interventionist trade policy, we should note Baldwin and Flam's (1989) investigation of strategic trade policy in the market for 30–40-seater aircraft. They conclude that the evidence is consistent with two of the three governments involved having pursued such policies and with their having been reasonably successful in shifting profits away from foreign firms to the domestic firm. Although they note many caveats, they also suggest that world welfare has not necessarily been reduced as a result of this intervention.

A different argument for export subsidies has been based on the idea of their cross-market effects, with a subsidy-induced terms of trade loss in one market offset by a terms of trade gain in another market, leaving a possible national gain. Examples of this type include Feenstra (1986) and Itoh and Kiyono (1987). Feenstra suggested the possibility of a major role for trade policy within a competitive two-country three-good model, showing that (a) an export subsidy may benefit the exporting country; (b) a voluntary export restraint (VER) may benefit the importing country; and (c) a countervailing duty may benefit the importing country even if there were no effect on the foreign price of the good in question. As with Deardorff (1986) above, the difference between these results and those derived from two-good models stems from the patterns of substitutability and complementarity among goods.

Itoh and Kiyono also assume competitive conditions and more than two goods. Specifically, they distinguish between marginal and non-marginal export goods. Marginal goods are those exported in only small amounts or not at all under free trade but whose export can be promoted by export subsidies. Non-marginal exports, obviously, are those exported in significant amounts even with free trade. The authors argue that subsidising exports in a standard two-good model has the same effect as applying a uniform export subsidy within a model with many goods. Such a uniform subsidy worsens the country's terms of trade and thus lowers its trade welfare level. However, the use of a three-good model with two export goods allows us to consider what happens when a subsidy is applied to one export good but not to another. Itoh and Kiyono prove that, when subsidies are concentrated on marginal goods, the country's economic welfare increases. The proof depends on the country having a monopoly in non-marginal goods. Thus a subsidy on them expands their supply and worsens the terms of trade. However, a subsidy on marginal goods contracts the supply of non-marginal goods and may improve the terms of trade. In general, it is claimed that export subsidies improve economic welfare only when they expand the set of export goods, rather than simply increasing the volume of exports of goods which would in any case be exported.

In our discussion of causes of intra-industry trade above we came across the possible importance of informational asymmetries – with consumers' information about product quality varying with the country of origin of the good. This idea has been used to support government intervention in trade. Ignorance of product quality by consumers is regarded as a potential barrier to entry. Export subsidies may allow this to be broken and increase welfare. Bagwell and Staiger (1989) survey earlier work in this area as well as developing their own model in which asymmetric information about firm types stops producers of high-quality goods from selling their goods at prices which reflect their true quality, thus blocking their entry into the market. In this case, a subsidy on high-quality goods may be welfare enhancing. We have seen earlier also possible support for an export subsidy in Flam's (1987) article on experience goods.

A variation on the theme of imperfect quality information is found in Grossman and Shapiro (1988). They deal with an issue of considerable importance in recent multilateral trade talks – property rights and counterfeit goods. In their model, home firms own trademarks and have established reputations for high-quality products while foreign firms export both legitimate low-quality goods and counterfeits of home brand-name goods. Grossman and Shapiro reach a number of conclusions. Welfare in the home economy may fall because consumers unsuspectingly purchase copies and because the counterfeit production increases factor prices in the export sector of the foreign country, thus worsening the terms of trade of the home economy. However, the existence of counterfeits may change the nature of rivalry among home manufacturers, and this may have varying effects on the equilibrium price and quality of the home goods and hence on both home and global welfare. The authors show that with free entry the quality change lowers both home and global welfare, whereas with a fixed number of home firms, brand-name producers may increase product quality and home and global welfare may increase, since quality would have been initially undersupplied.

Falvey (1989) uses the same idea of unobservable product quality to explore the possible role of non-tariff barriers such as origin labelling requirements and minimum quality standards. Where countries differ in the average quality of their outputs but where market price depends on average quality across all countries, there is a problem of adverse selection – firms will have an incentive to lower the quality of their output. In such cases, origin labelling can have direct welfare implications by allowing consumers to identify outputs from different countries. Falvey's model contains the notion of a reputation premium being built into prices. The costs of establishing a reputation are assumed to be related to production costs. The model is used to put forward the idea that the imposition of minimum quality standards or mark of origin requirements may genuinely be justified on informational grounds and may not necessarily be done for protective reasons.

Possible effects of movements towards free trade

Instead of arguing positively for an interventionist trade policy, it is possible to look at what would happen from a movement towards trade liberalisation. Clearly, to cast doubts upon the benefits to be obtained from such a movement can be seen as an argument for the retention of at least the current levels of protection. Such doubts are cast by Buffie and Spiller (1986) who look at the short- and long-run effects of partly liberalising quota restrictions in a conjectural variations model of oligopoly.

Their model is of an industry of $N$ identical profit-maximising firms, using output as their strategic variable, in which economies of scale occur over an extended range of output. They investigate the response of domestic firms to an increase in the allowed import quota for the industry. In a standard competitive model, as quotas increase, domestic output will certainly fall. But Buffie and Spiller show that this need not hold in the short run under oligopoly. The quota increase acts to reduce residual demand facing domestic firms and the outcome depends on the relative magnitudes of the slope of the inverse demand function for the product, the domestic firms' share of total supply, the number of firms in the domestic industry, and the conjectural variations parameter (CVP), which is defined as the expected change in the strategic variable (in this case output) of competing firms following a small change in the variable by one firm. The CVP indicates the extent of oligopolistic coordination in the industry, and will be $-1$ in the case of perfect competition, zero with Cournot conjectures and 1 for a perfect cartel. Buffie and Spiller deal with both an exogenously set CVP and rational or consistent conjectures in which the conjectural responses are determined by the reaction functions within the model.

In essence, the argument is that, if each domestic firm assumes that other domestic firms will reduce output and that total output will fall, it is possible (depending on the sizes of the variables listed above) that perceived marginal revenue at each firm's existing output will increase and firms will then respond by increasing, rather than reducing, output. Naturally, prices and profits of domestic firms will fall in this process. However, in the long run, with free entry and exit, this will cause some firms to leave the industry. Then it is possible, depending now on

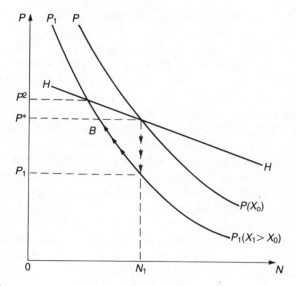

Fig 7.1

whether the degree of oligopolistic coordination of firms changes with the number of firms, for the perceived marginal revenue of firms remaining in the industry to fall. In this case, their equilibrium output will fall, and total output will fall beyond that needed to return price to its initial level. Thus, in the long run, prices may actually rise following an increase in import quota.

This process is illustrated in Figure 7.1 in which $PP$ shows the market clearing price and $HH$ the firm's average cost, both as functions of the number of firms in the industry. $HH$ may be positively or negatively sloped depending on whether entry lowers or increases output. Here it is assumed that domestic output is initially unaffected by the increase in quota and the $HH$ schedule does not change while the $PP$ schedule shifts horizontally to the left. In the short run, price falls to $P^1$, but in the long run firms leave the industry, driving the price up. If the only adjustment to output occurred through the exit of firms (with the equilibrium output of remaining firms being unchanged), price would return to its initial equilibrium level of $P^*$. However, if, as $N$ falls, firms do not believe that industry output will fall to that extent, their perceived marginal revenue will fall and equilibrium output of the remaining firms will fall. We move further up $P^1P^1$ to the higher price of $P^2$.

Buffie and Spiller point out that the possibility of such perverse output and price responses to a quota increase in both the short and the long run means that trade liberalisation through quota increases need not necessarily lead to increases in economic welfare.

Ross (1988) also finds that a movement towards free trade may lead to worse domestic market performance. In his model, domestic firms form a dominant oligopoly and foreign firms a competitive fringe. He shows that it is possible, especially where entry and exit are allowed, for a reduction in tariff to lead to a higher domestic price. His results lead Ross to propose that a strong competition policy may be complementary to freer trade.

Gasoriek, Smith and Venables (1989) investigate the pay-offs from trade policy in a model of trade under imperfect competition applied to world markets in motor vehicles and computers. They look particularly at the effects of countervailing duties and conclude that the relationship between the trade policies of different countries will vary from industry to industry and that it is impossible to construct a strong case on the basis of national welfare for the use of countervailing duties. However, they also argue that, while trade restrictions may be internationally undesirable, there are only some cases with scope for mutually beneficial tariff-cutting negotiations, at least if attention is confined to one good at a time.

Finally, Kowalczyk (1989) shows that, when both tariffs and subsidies are involved, approaching free trade may reduce world welfare. This proposition is derived from a two-country, two-good model which assumes a costless transfer of income among countries.

### Types of protection

Articles regularly compare the various types of commercial policies available to governments. This area of work was opened up by Bhagwati (1969) who demonstrated that tariffs were preferable to quotas under conditions of imperfect competition because quotas encouraged the establishment of domestic monopolies. Melvin (1986) provides a brief summary of other contributions to this question. These reinforced the idea of the non-equivalence of tariffs and quotas under various circumstances, e.g. in the presence of uncertainty; with changes in economies such as growth or price fluctuations; and with retaliation. In Melvin's own model, tariffs and quotas are not equivalent, even under conditions of perfect competition, if both countries in a two-country model pursue restrictive trade practices. In such a case, the retaliation equilibrium with quotas is unstable and the outcome depends on which country imposes the quota first. He shows that it is only in the special case where just one of the countries is assumed to have a tariff or quota that tariffs and quotas are equivalent.

With Rotemberg and Saloner (1989), we return to imperfect competition. They show that the usual finding that tariffs are Pareto-superior to quotas can be reversed in dynamic models of imperfect competition. To do this, they use a model of implicit collusion in which domestic and foreign firms achieve collusive outcomes by threatening to punish deviations. The actions of firms are assumed to depend on the history of their industry and they follow Bertrand competition. In this setting, quotas promote competition while tariffs do not. Thus, the imposition of a quota by one country can *reduce* the price in the country which imposes the quota. Results change if firms are assumed to play Cournot rather than Bertrand.

Levinsohn (1989) investigates the equivalence of tariffs and quotas, allowing the possibility of foreign direct investment. Then there may be a foreign supply response to domestic price changes even when a quota applies, since foreign firms now have the option of producing the good in the domestic economy. Many of the strategic interactions which differentiate a tariff from a quota disappear. Specifically, Levinsohn shows tariffs and quotas to be equivalent when the optimal tariff is greater than the difference between the marginal cost of foreign production in the domestic economy and of foreign production abroad. This result, however, requires the assumption of constant costs. The equivalence breaks down under increasing marginal costs.

Mai and Hwang (1989) show, in a conjectural variations model of duopoly, that the equivalence of tariffs and ratio quotas (quotas which limit imports to a fixed percentage of the domestic market) depends crucially on the particular value of the conjectural variations parameter and on the target ratio of imports to domestic production. The monopolistic behaviour of the domestic firm does not necessarily result in non-equivalence.

Rodrik (1986) considers the question of subsidies versus tariffs and shows that the usual view that subsidies are preferable to tariffs may be overturned if it is assumed that the form of the policy objectives themselves depends on the instrument chosen by the government to achieve them. This is because tariffs benefit all domestic producers in the same way and so individual firms will have no incentive to push for increased tariffs. Subsidies, on the other hand, may be more specific and benefit particular firms. Thus, pressure for protection may be greater when the chosen instrument is subsidies rather than tariffs.

By far the biggest interest in this area recently has been in the effects of voluntary export restraints (VERs). The majority opinion is that VERs are undesirable from the viewpoints of both the importing country and world welfare. However, some arguments have been presented in defence of them.

Harris (1985) mounts a strong attack on VERs. He analyses the effect on an oligopolistic equilibrium of the introduction of a VER set at the free-trade level of imports and shows that it will raise the profits of all firms in the industry. This occurs because the imposition of the VER facilitates collusion and lowers consumer welfare. Depending on the relevant elasticities, the imposition of the VER may even lead to the home firm reducing output. Thus, the VER acts mainly to sustain monopolistic forces rather than to bring about import substitution. Harris concludes that VERs are welfare reducing in comparison with both free trade and tariffs.

However, Mai and Hwang (1988) contradict one of Harris's conclusions by arguing that, in a conjectural variations model with VERs, the value of the conjectural variations parameter is the critical factor for determining the effect of the VER. They conclude that if the free-trade equilibrium is more collusive than Cournot (that is, with a CVP above zero) the imposition of VERs at the free-trade level of imports will lead to a fall in the profits of the foreign firm.

Krishna (1989) also modifies the Harris result in an article on the impact of quantitative restrictions in general on oligopolistic markets. The outcome is seen to depend on whether imports are substitutes for or complements with domestic products. If they are substitutes, if firms compete in prices, and move simultaneously, then the Harris result is confirmed: quantitative restrictions facilitate collusion by interfering with the ability of the foreign firm to compete in the domestic market. This causes prices and profits (of both home and foreign firms) to increase. Tariffs and quotas are definitely not equivalent in their effects. When goods are complements, however, a quota or VER set at the free-trade level has no effect and tariffs and quotas are equivalent.

Where profits of both home and foreign firms rise, there is no profit-shifting and the rise in profits is entirely at the expense of the domestic consumer. Trade policy leads to lower overall welfare in the home economy. Krishna recognises one possible exception – where the market for the domestic product is more distorted than that for the foreign product and, as a result of the quota or VER, domestic output increases. This might compensate for the reduction in imports and the increase in foreign profits.

Aw and Roberts (1986) take up another common criticism of VERs (although their article talks in terms of OMAs – Orderly Marketing Arrangements): that they cause the constrained exporter to move into higher-quality products in the importing country. They add that the country-specific nature of OMAs and VERs leads also to substitution among supplying countries. They calculate that product upgrading accounted for 12 per cent of the observed rise in the average price of footwear imports to the US in the period surrounding the US's 1977–81 footwear OMA with Korea and Taiwan.

Greenaway (1986), in a study of the non-leather footwear industry in the UK, concludes that the cost of VER protection is greater than that of tariff protection, while de Melo and Messerlin (1988) find that VERs negotiated by the UK, France and West Germany with Japanese car makers did not achieve the results expected by domestic car makers.

The issue of substitution among supplying countries is central to the argument of Dinopoulos and Kreinin (1989). Since VERs are inherently discriminatory, the usual two-country analysis comparing it to a quota is inadequate. They use a three-country model (the importer, the constrained exporter and an unconstrained exporter) to compare tariffs, quotas and VERs. In their comparison of quotas and VERs, they conclude that the welfare of the importing country is higher under a quota, while that of the non-restricted exporter is higher under a VER. The welfare position of the constrained exporter is uncertain.

Neary (1988) reverses the usual order of welfare effects of trade policy instruments in the presence of exogenous shocks. In a model with international capital mobility but which omits the complications of market imperfections, uncertainty and retaliation, the responses to exogenous shocks may be very different with different forms of trade policy in force. Much depends on the assumptions made about the disbursement of tariff revenues and rents from quotas and VERs. Neary assumes that tariff revenues and quota rents are returned in a lump sum fashion to domestic consumers, while rents from VERs accrue to foreign consumers and are thus lost to the home economy. Both types of quantitative restriction (quotas and VERs) are assumed to produce a fixed level of imports. The home country is assumed to be a net importer of capital, and rental payments to foreign owners of capital are assumed to be untaxed.

An exogenous increase in foreign capital inflow will then have different effects depending on the type of protection in force. The increase in total domestic capital stock (hom owned + foreign owned) leads to an increase in domestic output, displacing lower-cost imports. This involves a welfare loss to the economy and increases the welfare cost of tariff protection. With quantitative restrictions, however, this loss is removed since imports are fixed by assumption. The effect of the increase in output, then, is to lower the domestic price of importables and to reduce rents generated by the restrictions. In the quota case, since quota rents are assumed to be fully distributed domestically, this produces only an internal transfer between residents and national welfare is unaffected. However, with VERs, with rents accruing to foreigners, the lowering of them raises domestic welfare. Thus, increased international capital mobility lowers the cost of VER protection, leaves the cost of quota protection unchanged and raises the cost of tariff protection.

The effects are shown in Figure 7.2. Here we have two domestic supply curves, $S_{NCM}$ with capital assumed internationally immobile and $S_{ICM}$ with mobile capital. The supply response is greater with mobile capital because, as domestic prices rise with

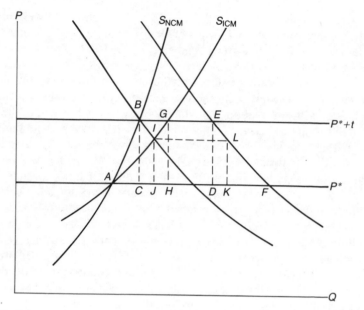

Fig 7.2

protection, foreign capital is attracted into the economy, producing an increase in domestic output. With immobile capital, the welfare loss from both tariffs and quotas is seen to be $ABC$ (production loss) + $EDF$ (consumption loss). With VERs there is the additional rent loss shown by $CBED$. With mobile capital, under tariffs, imports fall from $CD$ to $HD$ and the production loss increases to $AGH$. With quotas, imports are assumed to remain at $BE = IL$ but the price of the domestic good falls. The production loss becomes $AIJ$ and the consumption loss $KLF$, both clearly less than in the case of tariffs. With VERs, the production and consumption losses are the same as in the quota case but there is also a reduction in the rent loss to $JILK$. This does not, of course, provide an argument for the choice of VERs above tariffs as a form of protection since the lowered cost of VER protection outlined above arises because of the existence under VERs of an additional loss to the economy through the transfer of rents abroad. However, as Neary points out, it suggests that, if it is easier to remove controls on international capital movements than on trade, this should be done if trade restrictions are quantitative in nature, but not if they take the form of tariffs.

An entirely different basis for support for VERs is used by Donnenfeld and Mayer (1987). They show that VERs may increase the social welfare of the constrained exporting country in the presence of certain informational externalities. Here we return to buyers in the importing country having incomplete information about the product quality of foreign firms. In this version, they use the average industry quality of the exporting country as the indicator of the quality produced by each foreign firm. Since this determines the price consumers are willing to pay, competitive firms will produce socially suboptimal product qualities. As the enforcement of quality standards is costly, quantitative restrictions (including VERs) may act to raise product quality.

Another strand of argument relates to the comparison between doemstic policies and trade policy instruments. For example, de Meza (1989) shows that, in a standard Cournot model in a Brander–Spencer setting, price controls dominate export subsidies. We may also note the presence in the literature of articles on other types of non-tariff trade barrier including government purchasing practices (McAfee and McMillan, 1989; Finsinger, 1988) and local content schemes (Vousden, 1987; Hollander, 1987).

### The political economy of protection

Political economy approaches to protection have also been concerned with both the level and the form of protection. Two types of model can be distinguished. The first looks at levels of protection across countries and then uses regression analysis to try to discover the reasons for differences. For instance, Godek (1986) studied the trade policies of 15 countries. He found variations in trade restrictions across countries to be explained by such factors as per capita income, governement size (in terms of its share of national income) and country size. He had, however, arrived at the hypotheses he wished to test through the use of the second possible approach – the construction of a model of the political process. In Godek's model, government policy aims to maximise political success through a trade-off between competing groups with different lobbying efficiencies. In any particular market there will be a politically optimal level of taxes, subsidies and tariffs. Optimal trade policy is influenced by the range of policies available to government and the relative size of the groups seeking protection. Thus, if one assumes government has a vote-maximising redistributional goal, the larger is a group's share of national income, the more likely it is that income redistribution can be achieved by non-trade policies. Again, the smaller is the group being protected, the less is the cost of protection to the country as a whole. It follows that the bigger a country is and the more diverse it is in production, the smaller will be its import share and the lower will be the relative cost of protecting import-competing industries and the more easily can the country afford it. On this basis, one wuld expect government size to be negatively related and country size to be positively related to the level of protection.

Wellisz and Wilson (1986) also stress the advantage of smallness for an industry lobbying for protection. Their model has two organised groups spending real resources to influence tariff policy. A small group, it is argued, bears only a small share of the deadweight loss associated with the movement from free trade which the group is seeking. This strengthens its willingness to lobby strongly for protection. Cassing and Hillman (1986) contradict this view in explaining why industries suffering from a loss of comparative advantage often suddenly collapse rather than decline steadily. They suggest that such an industry initially contracts slowly but as it does so politicians see less advantage in pushing to protect it. Further, the cost of protection becomes more obvious to consumers. Thus, contraction leads to the withdrawal to existing protection and the industry collapses.

Some support for Wellisz and Wilson comes from a regression analysis of variations in the level of agricultural protection of ten industrial countries by Honma and Hayami (1986). They note that comparative advantage moves against agriculture during the process of economic growth, especially in land-poor countries. They then suggest that the greater the cost of intersectoral labour adjustments resulting from this shift in comparative advantage, the greater is the demand for agricultural protectionism. This is all the stronger because the contraction of the agricultural industry makes it easier for agricultural producers to organise political lobbying and also lowers the resistance of the non-agricultural population to agricultural protectionism. Whoever is correct over this issue, such studies provide good examples of how economic and political factors may be combined to explain the existence of protection.

Hillman and Ursprung (1988) use a political model to explain the popularity of VERs. They incorporate foreign interests in a country's trade policy into a model of political competition between candidates fighting for political office. Both foreign and domestic producers express their views through campaign contributions to candidates, who, in turn, attempt through statements on trade policy to maximise support from producers. Tariffs are divisive among producers but VERs may (as we have seen above) raise the profits of both domestic and foreign producers and thus attract all-round support.

Kaempfer, McClure and Willetts (1989) tackle a similar problem, seeking to explain the increasing use of quotas either instead of or in combination with tariffs. They argue that the relative efficiency of tariffs and quotas in achieving political objectives will vary with the nature of the market and the level of protection. As is common in political economy of protection models, considerations of income distribution drive the political processes which determine economic policies. At high levels of protection, quotas may become more politically effective than tariffs. Cassing and Hillman (1985), in a model based on the maximisation of a political support function by political officials and in which interest groups include both protection seekers and quota-rent or tariff-revenue seekers, had concluded that tariffs would dominate quotas in the absence of government revenue motives. Kaempfer, McClure and Willetts, however, point out that Hillman and Cassing were concerned with a straight choice between tariffs and quotas, whereas, in practice, industries are often protected by both.

Bhagwati (1989), in a spirited rejection of the new theories of protection, argues that the incorporation of imperfect competition into the theory of international trade is just an extension of the older theory of the effect on trade policy of the presence of domestic market distortions. This, he suggests, leaves the basic case for universal free trade intact since it concludes that tariffs are only a second-best policy and that the optimal policy in the case of domestic distortions is one aimed directly at the market failure. Tariffs become the appropriate policy only against monopoly power in foreign markets and even then could lead to retaliation which would make everybody worse off.

He then discusses the view of governments adopted in political economy models of protection – being seen at the two extremes as self-willed, with clear objectives of their own, or as clearing houses, acting only as an arena in which lobbies clash over policy. In both cases, governments become capable of perverse, national-welfare-reducing, actions. He also stresses the cost of unproductive pressure group activities. Both of these, he proposes, considerably add to the cost of protection and this strengthens the case for a movement to universal free trade. In other words, even if there is an economic case for protection, once protection is allowed as a possibility, the behaviour of governments and pressure groups will be such that protectionist policies will produce undersirable results.

## Other topics

### Trade in services

Markusen (1989) notes that, although most trade theory deals with trade in final goods, over half of all international trade is in intermediate goods. A rapidly growing category of these is in producer services (consulting, marketing, banking, insurance and other financial services). The best introduction to this area can be found in two articles by Nayyar. Nayyar (1988a) looks at the definition of and the extent of trade in services before going on to consider the views of the industrialised and developing countries towards service trade. Nayyar (1988b) presents a more detailed discussion of the nature of services and of the differences between goods trade and services trade. Hirsch (1989) combines goods and services within a single analytical framework while allowing for the major differences between them.

### Customs unions

Venables (1987) considers the formation and enlargement of customs unions within a model of an industry with market segmentation and price discrimination in which all firms produce an identical product and follow Cournot behaviour, ensuring the existence of intra-industry trade. This is a development of Brander and Krugman's (1983) model of intra-industry trade. The analysis supports the view that customs unions allow an increase in both firm scale and competition in member countries. Tariff reductions cause firms to expand production, while free entry leads to a reduction in the gap between price and marginal cost. However, the model does not produce unambiguous gains to either custom union membership or enlargement of a union. Countries which are net importers of the products of imperfectly competitive industries may suffer welfare losses from membership, while an expansion of the customs union may benefit those joining at the expense of existing members. Yannopoulos (1987) provides an interesting consideration of a customs union extension in practice in his study of Spanish accession to the EC.

Among several articles in a special edition of the *European Economic Review* devoted to issues to the completion of the internal market of the EC, Winters (1988) considers the potential dangers of members of the EC resorting to subsidy-based protection. He argues that there may be serious problems even where subsidies could be used to shift profits to the benefit of the EC as a whole, since subsidy wars could break out between member states as they competed for rent-generating industries. In the same volume, Smith and Venables (1988) study welfare effects of changes in the EC internal market in a partial equilibrium model of imperfect competition with economies of scale. They present two cases: (a) where there are small reductions in barriers to trade; and (b) where a fully integrated market is created. In (b) substantial welfare gains are generated.

At a more general level, Appleyard, Conway and Field (1989) examine the effects of customs unions on the pattern and terms of trade in a Ricardian model with very many goods by adapting the Dornbusch–Fischer–Samuelson (1977) continuum of goods model to three countries. They derive comparative static effects of changes in factor endowments and tariffs. Trade creation and trade diversion are shown to be influenced by the position of countries' traded goods on the continuum. In addition, the desirability of economic integration is found to be dependent on the level of country development. In particular, there are gains for mid-continuum countries such as the newly industrialising countries.

*Foreign direct investment*

The central issue among the many articles which relate to foreign direct investment (FDI) and multinational corporations (MNCs) is still the question of the reasons for the development of the multinational enterprise. The best-known explanation is that of internalisation theory (Rugman, 1986). This is defined by Parry (1985) as the notion that firms which operate across national boundaries act to replace various market functions with internal intra-firm transactions whenever the cost of internal transactions is less than the cost of market transactions. In particular, internalised transactions will arise in the presence of imperfections or failure in markets.

In a perfectly competitive world, all firms remain small and there is no possibility of FDI. Market imperfections (for example, possession by some firms of firm-specific knowhow, the lack of a fully developed market for the transfer of such information, the existence of differing tax regimes among countries, risks and uncertainties associated with the supply from abroad of raw materials or intermediate goods or with variable foreign exchange rates) all provide opportunities for firms to increase profits through the replacement of external contractual relations by internal, intra-firm transactions (leading to such things as vertical integration and transfer-pricing). The most common analysis of MNC decisions in economics is in terms of the choice made by an MNC in the exploitation of a quasi-monopolistic advantage between exporting and production abroad through FDI.

Smith (1987) deals with this especially in the presence of government protection policy. His model has only one multinational corporation (M) and one host-country firm (H) and does not consider licensing. In its home country, M has a plant where it has incurred a firm-specific and a plant-specific sunk cost. It produces output at a constant average variable cost. If it exports, it faces a constant transport cost per unit ($s$) and a per unit import tax ($t$). If it establishes abroad, it incurs the plant-specific fixed cost ($G$) but not the firm-specific cost ($F$). H may also produce but will incur both the firm-specific and the plant-specific fixed costs. The host country market for the good is described by a concave revenue function, $P(X)X$.

The model takes the form of a multi-stage game, assuming Cournot behaviour when both firms enter. Smith sets out the four possible solutions deriving from the available pairs of decisions: M may export or invest; H may enter or not enter. When H does not enter, M acts as a monopolist, choosing on the basis of figures for the above costs to invest rather than export if and only if:

$$P(X_H)X_H - cX_H - G > P(X_E)X_E - (c + s + t)X_E,$$

where $X_H$ is the profit-maximising output level when it invests and $X_E$ is the profit-maximising level of exports when it exports. Clearly, if M had chosen to invest in the absence of a tariff ($t = 0$), the imposition of the tariff has no effect. However, a tariff may persuade M to move from exporting to investing. If H chooses to enter and M chooses to invest with $t = 0$, again a tariff will have no effect. But with H in the market and M as an exporter, a tariff may either leave M as an exporter and change the balance of power within the duopoly in favour of H or lead to M switching from exports to investment abroad.

Yet again, consider the case where in the absence of a tariff it is not profitable for H to enter but the effect of the tariff is to make H profitable only if M exports and does not invest. M would prefer exporting over investing whether H is in the market or not, but it is more profitable for M to invest with H absent from the market than to export with H present in the market. Then, if M moves first, it may invest in order to deter entry by H. However, if H moves first it will enter and, as long as the tariff does not change the relative profitability of exporting and investing for M in H's presence, M will continue to export. The tariff will have changed the market equilibrium from a monopoly to a duopoly.

On the other hand, consider what would happen if, without a tariff, it was profitable for H to enter only if M did not invest, while with H present M will choose to export. Allow H to move first and it will enter while M exports. Suppose now that H's choice is unaltered by the tariff whereas for M it becomes more profitable to invest rather than to export with H in the market. Anticipating M's investment, H will not enter. In this case, the tariff will have induced FDI and acted to reduce competition.

These various examples show that tariffs may or may not induce foreign direct investment, may or may not change the market structure and may have a pro- or an anti-competitive effect.

Horstmann and Markusen (1987) develop a model to explain multinational production. They deal with a horizontal multinational enterprise which operates plants producing identical products in several countries. The technology of production is assumed to involve certain firm-specific activities like research, organisational activities and marketing which give rise to multi-plant scale economies and give the MNC a cost advantage over potential domestic producers. Branch plant production is encouraged by the existence of international transport costs which are, however, offset by plant scale economies. The model predicts that MNC production occurs if firm-specific scale economies and export costs are large relative to plant scale economies.

In a later paper, Horstmann and Markusen (1989) formalise the view that MNCs arise as a consequence of the existence of knowledge-based firm-specific assets. They demonstrate that the host country gains if either competition among MNCs or potential rivals drives price down to the MNCs' average cost (and the host country receives the services of the firm-specific assets free); or the host is too small to support a domestic firm. It loses if the MNC drives out a profitable domestic firm.

## Conclusion

The aim of this chapter has been to give a broad overview of developments in trade theory while referring briefly to many recently published papers in an attempt to give a feeling of both richness and confusion. Models have adopted ideas from many other areas of economics as well as trying to cope with difficulties raised by such things as uncertainty, asymmetric information, capital mobility, and the international transmission of knowledge. This explains the richness. The confusion comes from the fact that, depending on the assumptions chosen, models can be constructed to prove almost anything. As a result, many old certainties have disappeared and many old debates have been sharpened. Many valuable contributions to theory have been omitted here and some areas have been neglected entirely.

What should be clear, however, is the extent to which the use of strategic, oligopolistic models have become dominant within international trade theory.

# References

Appleyard, D. R., Conway, P. J. and Field, A. J. (1989), 'Effects on pattern and terms of trade in a Ricardian model with a continuum of goods', *Journal of International Economics*, August, pp. 147–64.

Aw, B. Y. and Roberts, M. J. (1986), 'Measuring quality change in quota-constrained import markets: the case of US footwear', *Journal of International Economics*, August, pp. 45–60.

Bagwell, K. and Staiger, R. W. (1989), 'The role of export subsidies when product quality is unknown', *Journal of International Economics*, August, pp. 69–89.

Balassa, B. (1986), 'Intra-industry specialisation: a cross-country analysis', *European Economic Review*, January, pp. 27–42.

Balassa, B. and Bauwens, L. (1988), 'The determinants of intra-European trade in manufactured goods', *European Economic Review*, September, pp. 1421–37.

Baldwin, R. and Flam, H. (1989), 'Strategic trade policies in the market for 30–40 seater aircraft', *Weltwirtschaftlichesarchiv*, August, pp. 484–500.

Bhagwati, J. (1969), 'On the equivalence of tariffs and quotas', in J. Bhagwati, *Trade, Tariffs and Growth*, London: Weidenfeld & Nicholson.

Bhagwati, J. (1989), 'Is free trade passé after all?' *Weltwirtschaftlichesarchiv*, February, pp. 17–44.

Bowen, H. P., Leamer, E. E. and Sveikauskas, L. (1987), 'Multicountry, multifactor tests of the factor abundance theory', *American Economic Review*, 77, December, pp. 791–809.

Brander, J. A. and Krugman, P. (1983), 'A reciprocal dumping model of international trade', *Journal of International Economics*, 13, pp. 313–21.

Brander, J. A. and Spencer, B. J. (1983), 'International R&D rivalry and industrial strategy', *Review of Economic Studies*, 50, pp. 707–22.

Brander, J. A. and Spencer, B. J. (1984), 'Tariff protection and imperfect competition', in H. Kierzkowski (ed.), *Monopolistic Competition and International Trade*, Oxford: Oxford University Press.

Brander, J. A. and Spencer, B. J. (1985), 'Export subsidies and international market share rivalry', *Journal of International Economics*, February, pp. 83–100.

Buffie, E. J. and Spiller, P. T. (1986), 'Trade liberalisation in oligo-polistic industries: the quota case', *Journal of International Economics*, February, pp. 65–81.

Cassing, J. H. and Hillman, A. L. (1985), 'Political influence motives and the choice between tariffs and quotas', *Journal of International Economics*. November, pp. 279–90.

Cassing, J. H. and Hillman, A. L. (1986), 'Shifting comparative advantage and senescent industry collapse,' *American Economic Review*, 76, June, pp. 516–42.

Cheng, L. K. (1988), 'Assisting domestic industries under international oligopoly: the relevance of the nature of competition to optimal policies', *American Economic Review*, 78, September, pp. 746–58.

Collie, D. and de Meza, D. (1986), 'Inadequacies of the strategic rationale for export subsidies', *Economics Letters*, 22, pp. 369–73.

Daltung, S., Eskeland, G. and Norman, V. (1987), 'Optimum trade policy towards imperfectly competitive industries: two Norwegian examples', Discussion Paper 218, Centre for Economic Policy Research, London.

Deardorff, A. V. (1986), 'FIRless FIRwoes: how preferences can interfere with the theorems of international trade', *Journal of International Dconomics*, February, pp. 131–42.

de Melo, J. and Messerlin, P. A. (1988), 'Price, quantity and welfare effects of European VERs on Japanese autos', *European Economic Review*, September, pp. 1527–46.

de Meza, D. (1989), 'Not even strategic trade theory justifies export subsidies', *Oxford Economic Papers*, 41, pp. 720–36.

Dinopoulos, E. and Kreinin, M. E. (1989), 'Import quotas and VERs: a comparative analysis in a three-country framework', *Journal of International Economics*, February, pp. 169–78.

Dixit, A. K. (1987), 'Tariffs and subsidies under oligopoly: the case of the US automobile industry', in H. Kierzkowski (ed.), *Protection and Competition in International Trade*, Oxford: Blackwell.

Dixit, A. K. and Kyle, A. S. (1985), 'The use of protection and subsidies for entry promotion and deterrence', *American Economic Review*, 75, March, pp. 139–52.

Dollar, D. (1986), 'Technical innovation, capital mobility and the product cycle in North–South trade', *American Economic Review*, 76, March, pp. 177–90.

Donnenfeld, S. (1986), 'Intra-industry trade and imperfect information about product quality', *European Economic Review*, April, pp. 401–18.

Donnenfeld, S. and Mayer, W. (1987), 'The quality of export products and optimal trade policy', *International Economic Review*, February, pp. 159–74.

Dornbusch, R., Fischer, S. and Samuelson, P. (1977), 'Comparative advantage, trade and payments in a Ricardian model with a continuum of goods', *American Economic Review*, 67, December, pp. 823–39.

Eaton, J. and Grossman, G. M. (1986), 'Optimal trade and industrial policy under oligopoly', *Quarterly Journal of Economics*, May, pp. 383–406.

Ethier, W. J. and Svensson, L. E. O. (1986), 'The theorems of international trade with factor mobility', *Journal of International Economics*, February, pp. 21–42.

Falvey, R. E. (1989), 'Trade, quality reputations and commercial policy', *International Economic Review*, August, pp. 607–22.

Feenstra, R. C. (1986), 'Trade policy with several goods and market linkages', *Journal of International Economics*, May, pp. 249–67.

Finsinger, J. (1988), 'Non-competitive and protectionist government purchasing behaviour', *European Economic Review*, January, pp. 69–80.

Flam, H. (1987), 'Reverse dumping', *European Economic Review*, February/March, pp. 82–8.

Flam, H. and Helpman, E. (1987), 'Vertical product differentiation and North–South trade', *American Economic Review*, 77, December, pp. 810–22.

Gasoriek, M., Smith, A. and Venables, A. J. (1989), 'Tariffs, subsidies and retaliation', *European Economic Review*, March, pp. 480–9.

Globerman, S. and Dean, J. W. (1990), 'Recent trends in intra-industry trade and their implications for future trade liberalisation', *Weltwirtschaftlichesarchiv*, February, pp. 25–49.

Godek, P. E. (1986), 'The politically optimal tariff and levels of trade restrictions across developed countries', *Economic Inquiry*, October, pp. 587–94.

Gray, H. P. (1985), 'Domestic efficiency, international efficiency and gains from trade', *Weltwirtschaftlichesarchiv*, August, pp. 460–70.

Greenaway, D. (1986), 'Estimating the welfare effects of VERs and tariffs: an application to non-leather footwear in the UK', *Applied Economics*, October, pp. 1065–83.

Greenaway, D. (1987), 'The new threories of intra-industry trade', *Bulletin of Economic Research*, April, pp. 95–120.

Greytak, D. and Tuchinda, W. (1990), 'The composition of consumption and trade intensities: an alternative test of the Linder hypothesis', *Weltwirtschaftlichesarchiv*, February, pp. 50–8.

Grinols, E. L. (1985), 'International trade and incomplete markets', *Economica*, May, pp. 245–55.

Grossman, G. M. and Eaton, J. (1985), 'Tariffs as insurance: optimal commercial policy when domestic markets are incomplete', *Canadian*

233

*Journal of Economics*, May, pp. 258–72.

Grossman, G. M. and Razin, A. (1985), 'The pattern of trade in a Ricardian model with country-specific uncertainty', *International Economic Review*, February, pp. 193–202.

Grossman, G. M. and Shapiro, C. (1988), 'Counterfeit-product trade', *American Economic Review*, March, pp. 59–75.

Harris, R. (1985), 'Why VERs ar "voluntary"', *Canadian Journal of Economics*, November, pp. 799–809.

Helpman, E. (1987), 'Imperfect competition and international trade: opening remarks', *European Economic Review*, February/March, pp. 77–81.

Helpman, E. and Krugman, P. (1985), *Market Structure and Foreign Trade*, Cambridge, Mass.: MIT Press.

Helpman, E. and Razin, A. (1978), *A Theory of International Trade under Uncertainty*, New York: Academic Press.

Hillman, A. L. and Ursprung, H. W. (1988), 'Domestic policies, foreign interests and international trade policy', *American Economic Review*, 78, September, pp. 729–45.

Hirsch, S. (1989), 'Services and service intensity in international trade', *Weltwirtschaftlichesarchiv*, February, pp. 45–60.

Hirsch, S. and Bijaoui, I. (1985), 'R&D intensity and export performance: a micro view', *Weltwirtschaftlichesarchiv*, May, pp. 238–51.

Hollander, A. (1987), 'Content protection and transnational monopoly', *Journal of International Economics*, May, pp. 283–97.

Honma, M. and Hayami, Y. (1986), 'Structure of agricultural protection in industrial countries', *Journal of International Economics*, February, pp. 115–29.

Horstmann, I. J. and Markusen, J. R. (1986), 'Up the average cost curve: inefficient entry and the new protectionism', *Journal of International Economics*, May, pp. 225–47.

Horstmann, I. J. and Markusen, J. R. (1987), 'Strategic investments and the development of multinationals', *International Economic Review*, February, pp. 109–22.

Horstmann, I. J. and Markusen, J. R. (1989), 'Firm-specific models and the gains from direct foreign investment', *Economica*, February, pp. 41–8.

Hughes, K. S. (1986), 'Exports and innovation: a simultaneous model', *European Economic Review*, April, pp. 383–400.

Itoh, M. and Kiyono, K. (1987), 'Welfare-enhancing export subsidies', *Journal of Political Economy*, February, pp. 115–37.

Jensen, R. and Thursby, M. (1986), 'A strategic approach to the product life cycle', *Journal of International Economics*, November, pp. 269–84.

Jensen, R. and Thursby, M. (1987), 'A decision theoretic model of innovation, technology transfer and trade', *Review of Economic Studies*, October, pp. 631–47.

Kaempfer, W. H., McClure, J. H. Jnr and Willetts, T. D. (1989), 'Incremental protection and efficient political choice between tariffs and quotas', *Canadian Journal of Economics*, May, pp. 228–236.

Kierzkowski, H. (ed.) (1984), *Monopolistic Competition and International Trade*, Oxford: Oxford University Press.

Kierzkowski, H. (ed.) (1987), *Protection and Competition in International Trade*, Oxford: Blackwell.

Kol, J. and Mennes, L. B. M. (1986), 'Intra-industry specialisation: some observations on concepts and measurement', *Journal of International Economics*, August, pp. 173–81.

Kol, J. and Mennes, L. B. M. (1989), 'Intra-industry trade measurement: corrections for trade imbalance: a survey', *Weltwirtschaftlichesarchiv*, November, pp. 703–17.

Kowalczyk, C. (1989), 'Trade negotiations and world welfare,' *American Economic Review*, 79, June, pp. 552–9.

Krishna, K. (1989), 'Trade restrictions as facilitating practices', *Journal of International Economics*, May, pp. 251–70.

Krugman, P. R. (1979), 'A model of innovation, technology, and the world distribution of income', *Journal of Political Economy*, 87, pp. 253–66.

Krugman, P. R. (1984), 'Import protection as export promotion in the presence of oligopoly and economies of scale', in H. Kierzkowski (ed.), *Monopolistic Competition and International Trade*, Oxford: Oxford University Press.

Laussel, D., Montet, C. and Peguin-Feissolle, A. (1988), 'Optimal trade policy under oligopoly: a calibrated model of the Europe–Japan rivalry in the EEC car market', *European Economic Review*, September, pp. 1547–65.

Levinsohn, J. A. (1989), 'Strategic trade policy when firms can invest abroad: when are tariffs and quotas equivalent?' *Journal of International Economics*, August, pp. 129–46.

Mai, Chao-Cheng, and Hwang, Heng (1988), 'Why VERs are voluntary: an extension', *Canadian Journal of Economics*, November, pp. 877–82.

Mai, Chao-Cheng, and Hwang, Heng (1989), 'Tariffs vs ratio quotas under duopoly', *Journal of International Economics*, August, pp. 177–83.

Markusen, J. R. (1986), 'Explaining the volume of trade: an eclectic approach', *American Economic Review*, 76, December, pp. 1002–11.

Markusen, J. R. (1989), 'Trade in producer services and in other specialised intermediate inputs', *American Economic Review*, 79, March, pp. 85–95.

Markusen, J. R. and Svensson, L. E. O. (1985), 'Trade in goods and factors with international differences in technology', *International Economic Review*, February, pp. 175–92.

Marvel, H. P. and Ray, E. J. (1987), 'Intraindustry trade: sources and effects on protection', *Journal of Political Economy*, December, pp. 1278–91.

McAfee, R. P. and McMillan, J. (1989), 'Government procurement and international trade', *Journal of International Economics*, May, pp. 291–308.

Melvin, J. R. (1986), 'The nonequivalence of tariffs and import quotas', *American Economic Review*, 76, December, pp. 1131–4.

Milner, C. (1988), 'Weighting considerations in the measurement and modelling of intra-industry trade', *Applied Economics*, March, pp. 295–301.

Nayyar, D. (1988a), 'The political economy of international trade in services', *Cambridge Journal of Economics*, March, pp. 279–98.

Nayyar, D. (1988b), 'Some reflections on the Uruguay Round in trade and services', *Journal of World Trade*, October, pp. 35–47.

Neary, P. (1988), 'Tariffs, quotas and VERs with an without internationally mobile capital', *Canadian Journal of Economics*, November, pp. 714–35.

Norman, V. D. (1989), 'Trade policy under imperfect competition: theoretical ambiguities – empirical regularities', *European Economic Review*, March, pp. 473–9.

Parry, T. G. (1985), 'Internalisation as a general theory of foreign direct investment: a critique', *Weltwirtschaftlichesarchiv*, August, pp. 564–9.

Rauch, J. E. (1989), 'Increasing returns to scale and international trade', *Journal of International Economics*, May, pp. 359–69.

Rodrik, D. (1986), 'Tariffs, subsidies and welfare with endogenous policy', *Journal of International Economics*, November, pp. 285–99.

Ross, T. W. (1988), 'Movements towards free trade and domestic market performance with imperfect competition', *Canadian Journal of Economics*, August, pp. 50–24.

Rotemberg, J. J. and Saloner, G. (1989), 'Tariffs vs quotas with implicit collusion', *Canadian Journal of Economics*, May, pp. 237–44.

Rugman, A. (1986), 'New theories of the multinational enterprise', *Bulletin of Economic Research*, May pp. 101–18.

Smith, A. (1987), 'Strategic investment, multinational corporations and trade policy', *European Economic Review*, February/March, pp. 89–96.

Smith, A. and Venables, A. J. (1988), 'Completing the internal market in the EC: some industry simulations', *European Economic Review*, September, pp. 1501–25.

Staiger, R. W. (1987), 'The Heckscher–Ohlin theorem in the presence of market power', *European Economic Review*, February/March, pp. 97–102.

Staiger, R. W., Deardorff, A. V., and Stern, R. M. (1987), 'An evaluation of factor endowments and protection as determinants of Japanese and American foreign trade', *Canadian Journal of Economics*, August, pp. 449–86.

Tamor, K. L. (1987), 'An empirical examination of the factor endowment hypothesis', *Canadian Journal of Economics*, May, pp. 387–98.

Thompson, H. (1986), 'Free trade and factor-price polarisation', *European Economic Review*, April, pp. 419–25.

Venables, A. J. (1985), 'Trade and trade policy with imperfect competition: the case of identical products and free entry', *Journal of International Economics*, 19, pp. 1–20.

Venables, A. J. (1987), 'Customs unions and tariff reform under imperfect competition', *European Economic Review*, February/March, pp. 103–10.

Vousden, N. (1987), 'Content protection and tariffs under monopoly and competition', *Journal of International Economics*, May, pp. 263–82.

Wellisz, S. and Wilson, J. D. (1986), 'Lobbying and tariff formation: a deadweight loss consideration', *Journal of International Economics*, May, pp. 367–75.

Winters, L. Alan (1988), 'Completing the European internal market: some notes on trade policy', *European Economic Review*, September, pp. 1477–99.

Yannopoulos, G. N. (1987), 'Trade effects from the extension of customs unions on third countries: a case study of the Spanish accession to the EEC', *Applied Economics*, January, pp. 39–50.

# 8 *Kent Matthews*

# Macroeconomic policy

## Introduction

The last decade has seen a revolution in the theory of macro-economic policy: a revolution in terms of not only the sophistication of the theory but in many ways a return in practice to much of the thinking of the non-Keynesian classical economists. The evolution of the theory has followed one full revolution, in that it began from a basic position of minimal intervention, and evolved into discretionary demand management; it then developed into the ineffectiveness of demand policy, and finally to the application of game theory – the conclusions of which have resulted in a return to long-forgotten policy thinking. The evolution in the theory has mirrored the changing preferences of the policy-makers, who in turn have responded to the changing attitudes and behaviour of the electorate. In fact the theory of macroeconomic policy has altered so radically in the past decade that one would be forgiven for thinking that the conventional wisdom had been turned on its head.

This chapter traces the conditions that originally led to the abandonment of the semi-laissez-faire thinking of policy-makers and the adoption of demand management. It examines the maturing of the theory into a mechanical application of techniques of the engineering sciences to meeting a set of targets. The success of applying the new-found theories is a matter of interpretation. However, the experience of the 1970s led to a reassessment of both the methods and the objectives of policy design. Furthermore, developments in macroeconomic theory, in economic measurement and in statistical techniques led to continuous refinements to the theory in an attempt to salvage the basic demand management paradigm. By the mid-1970s the failure of demand management methods to stem the stagflation-ary process, in combination with the development of the new classical theory, sowed the seeds of disenchantment with the experiment in discretionary policy. By the 1980s the theory had developed game-theoretic perspectives.

The first-generation models of policy design were based on the notion that the economy acted like a mechanical system responding predictably to policy instruments. The second-gener-ation models allowed for uncertainty but still maintained the basic premise that discretionary policy was superior to rules or laissez-faire. The third-generation models, developed over the last decade, and based on the theories of the new classical approach, have altered our view of the response of the economy to policy instruments. The economy is to be viewed not as a mechanical system but as made up of intelligent economic agents responding rationally to changes in government policy. The old debate of rules versus discretion has been raked over once more and on the whole the consensus has come down in favour of rules. The wheel of the theory of macroeconomic policy has turned full circle. This chapter examines this development and applies the theories to examine the government's policy over the decade.

## The historical conditions

Demand management, as both an economic philosophy and a political reality, emerged immediately after the Second World War. Most historians would accept that the immediate post-war period produced the ideal conditions for the development of this philosophy. The war created the precedent by which the govern-ment planned and directed the economy, but perhaps most im-portantly the public had learned to accept and even demand a greater degree of government involvement in the economy. Both the political and the intellectual climate were ready for greater state involvement. Unbridled capitalism was seen as the cause of the world depression of the 1930s, while the organisational framework of the government during the war was viewed as a force for stabilisation. There was a strong political sentiment in the UK that there would be no return to the dark days of the depression when the 'Treasury view' of minimalist intervention dominated the thinking of the economics profession and the political establishment.

After the lean years of the inter-war period and the perceived success of economic planning during the Second World War, a theory had emerged that gave economic planners and politicians the hope that the economy could be managed in such a way as to meet socially desired objectives. A political consensus about the role of the state (meaning government) developed and, despite various criticisms, this consensus remained the dominant view up until the mid-1970s.

The 1950s saw the theory of macroeconomic policy evolve from a statement of principle into a mature force dealing with economic objectives and optimal assignment rules. The principle as stated by Tinbergen (1956) and known as *Tinbergen's principle* stated that, for all targets to be satisfied, the number of independent instruments must be as least as great as the number of targets or objectives. This is a statement of consistency and says nothing about the assignment of instruments to targets. This was provided by Mundell's (1962) *principle of effective market classification*, which stated that each policy instrument should be paired with the policy objective or target over which it has the greatest relative effect. Mundell used this to demonstrate the relative efficacy of fiscal and monetary policy in achieving both internal and external equilibrium. However, underlying this theory was the notion that, through the appropriate application of the instruments available to an economy, socially desirable targets set by the policy-maker could in principle be achieved at a negative net cost to society.

## The case for discretion

The Tinbergen–Mundell principle can be demonstrated in the following way. Consider a closed economy which can be described by the textbook *IS-LM* framework. The authorities have available to them two instruments, namely fiscal and monetary policy. Suppose the two targets are a desired rate of interest and a desired level of real income. Figure 8.1a shows that a combination of expansionary fiscal policy and monetary policy can in principle meet a target rate of interest $R^*$. Similarly Figure 8.1b demonstrates that a combination of expansionary fiscal policy

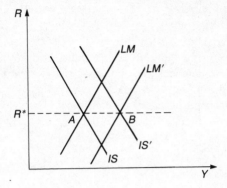

Fig 8.1a

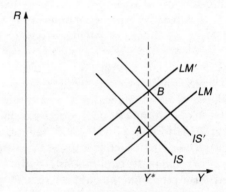

Fig 8.1b

and contractionary monetary policy can, in principle, meet a target level of real income/output, $Y^*$. The combinations of government spending, $G$, and monetary policy, $M$, that meet the interest rate target $R^*$ are depicted in Figure 8.2 and labelled $RR$. The combinations of $G$ and $M$ that meet the real income/output target $Y^*$ are also depicted in Figure 8.2 and labelled $YY$. It is clear that in this instance the Tinbergen principle is satisfied and the authorities can satisfy both targets (although it has nothing to say about the optimal assignment rule, which is dealt with in Appendix 1). However, consider what happens when there are more targets than instruments.

241

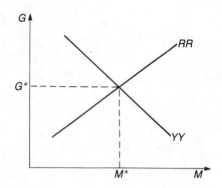

Fig 8.2

Consider the case of an open economy with fixed exchange rates. Figure 8.3a depicts an open economy, using the textbook *IS-LM-BP* analysis, in balance of payments deficit–recession. If capital mobility is imperfect, the *BP* schedule will be upward sloping (perfect capital mobility implies a horizontal *BP* schedule). If the exchange rate is excluded as an instrument, it is clear that, if the balance of payments was a further target, two instruments would be unable to meet three targets except by fluke. A combination of expansionary fiscal policy and contractionary monetary policy could in principle satisfy the external sector target (balance of payments equilibrium). Suppose, however, that our objective is to combine the output target $Y^*$ with external

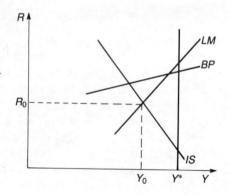

Fig 8.3a

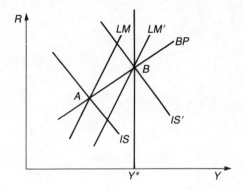

Fig 8.3b

balance. The interest rate target must now be dropped (Figure 8.3b). Assume the *BP* schedule is flatter than the *LM* schedule. Then expansionary fiscal policy has to be matched with expansionary monetary policy. A comparison between Figures 8.1a and 8.3b shows that, for a given increase in government spending, the increase in the money supply needed to bring the external sector back into equilibrium is less than that needed to maintain a target rate of interest. Therefore the fiscal–monetary response schedule labelled *BB* in Figure 8.4a is steeper than *RR*. Except for the special case of the three schedules intersecting at a unique

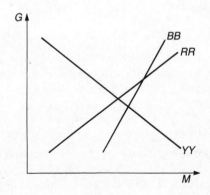

Fig 8.4a

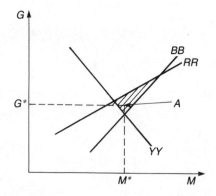

Fig 8.4b

point, it would not be possible to meet all three targets, in the short run.[1] This example illustrates a problem the UK government faced during the 1950s and 1960s. At that time the two most important policy objectives were full employment and balance of payments equilibrium, whereas the only policy instrument that was considered was fiscal policy.[2] Thus, the stop–go cycle of the period can be explained by the attempt to meet two incompatible targets with only one instrument.

One solution to the problem of having more targets than instruments is to weight the deviation of the target variable from its target value and aim to minimise a general loss function as suggested by Theil (1964). This takes the form:

$$L = \sum \alpha_i (x_i - x_i^*)^2 \quad i = 1, 2, \ldots, n, \qquad (8.1)$$

where $x_i$ are the target variables, $x_i^*$ are the targeted variables and $\alpha_i$ are the weights, with the condition that $\Sigma \alpha_i = 1$. In the example used above, the loss function would be:

$$L = \alpha_1 (bop)^2 + \alpha_2 (R - R^*)^2 + \alpha_3 (Y - Y^*)^2, \qquad (8.2)$$

where *bop* is the balance of payments position with a target value set at zero.[3] The minimisation of the loss function subject to the constraints of the economic model will generate optimal values for $(G, M)$, which will push the economy to some point within the shaded area shown on Figure 8.4b.

A similar problem arises in the case of the Mundell analysis of internal and external equilibrium. The Mundell assignment rule is that monetary policy be targeted to maintaining external balance while fiscal policy be targeted to maintaining internal balance. In fact the analysis used to establish this result, by confusing flows with stocks, is flawed at the most basic level.[4] But even if we somehow managed to ignore this, two further inadequacies would remain.

First, it was shown in the late 1960s that fiscal and monetary policy are not independent of each other – they are linked through the government budget constraint.[5] Although it was argued that the lack of independence only occurred in the long run, allowing at least short-run flexibility in exercising both instruments, later developments in macroeconomic theory denied even short-run independence, by recognising the nature of the government's intertemporal budget constraint.[6]

The second problem was that the analysis was entirely in terms of fixed absolute prices. The inflationary experience of the 1970s demonstrated the failure of policies based on fixed-price theories. The targets problem was worsened by the addition of the reduction of inflation to the list.

The recognition that in general there are insufficient instruments to meet all the desired targets led to the development of the flexible target approach. This in essence meant that targets were weighted according to priority and a generalised loss function of the type described by equation (8.1) was minimised, producing a trade-off between the various targets. The notion of flexibility applied to the weights, which could alter according to the political and economic preferences of the authorities. Thus one type of policy-maker may place a higher priority on reducing unemployment and raising output growth rather than inflation and the current account. Another may be willing to tolerate higher unemployment if inflation is lower. But both policy-makers will be trading off between mutually antagonistic targets. For example, if inflation and unemployment are considered to be inversely related, as in the 'Phillips curve' (Phillips, 1958), then the government could choose the rate of unemployment it desires by accepting the rate of inflation that arises.

This concept is demonstrated in Figure 8.5. If both inflation and unemployment are regarded as economic bads and the most

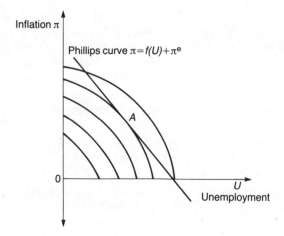

Fig 8.5

preferred combination is zero inflation and zero unemployment, then Figure 8.5 demonstrates the combinations of average inflation and unemployment the government would find equally acceptable. These iso-loss curves can be derived from the loss function, equation (8.1), and describe the preference pattern of the government (and possibly the electorate). The curve that is furthest from the origin is the worst position, whereas curves closer to the origin are more preferred, with the most preferred point being the origin itself. The optimal choice for the government is the point where the Phillips curve is tangential to the iso-loss curve.

Further developments in macroeconomic theory (Friedman, 1968; Phelps, 1967) showed that the Phillips curve was necessarily unstable and shifted for changes in expectations of inflation. The development of the so-called 'expectations-augmented Phillips curve' coincided with gathering evidence of the collapse of the inverse relation between inflation and unemployment. The key point about the expectations-augmented Phillips curve was that the inverse trade-off between inflation and unemployment did not exist. The trade-off was between 'unexpected inflation' and unemployment. In the long run, when unexpected inflation is zero (expected inflation is equalised with actual inflation), the rate of unemployment is at its equilibrium or natural rate. This natural rate is the rate of unemployment that would exist when all markets are in equilibrium. Because of imperfect information and frictions in the labour market,[7] it is not zero.

Unless the point of tangency of the iso-loss curve with the Phillips curve coincides with the natural rate of unemployment, point *A* is only temporary and therefore represents only a short-run policy preference position. In the long run, as expectations adjust to equalise with the rate of inflation, the Phillips curve shifts out and stabilises when inflation is unchanging and unemployment is at the natural rate.

## The case against discretion

The example of the inflation–unemployment trade-off illustrates the case of the policy-maker attempting to reach a social (or political) optimum by balancing out different objectives which may be pulling against each other. The theoretical problem, on the surface at least, looked as if it had been solved. Remaining issues were considered to be of a practical nature. However, it was precisely at the practical level that the earliest criticisms of the 'fine-tuning' approach were based.

The arguments against fine tuning are made at three levels. The first argument is that the government is unlikely to know the full structure of the economy and would underestimate the long-run effects of policy. The second, is that, although it may know what the long-run effects are, it will underestimate the short-run effects of policy. The third is that, owing to a lack of appreciation of the timing of the impacts of policy and the lags in the economic system, the policy could result in dynamically destabilising the economy. The basis of this argument is one of information. The critics of demand management and 'fine-tuning' policy argue that the government does not have the necessary information to dynamically stabilise the economy. On the contrary, attempts to stabilise are likely to make things worse.

This argument is based on the following analysis. Let $x(t)$ be the deviation of real GDP from its trend path at time period $t$ in the absence of government intervention. Let $y(t)$ be the additional deviation of real GDP from trend caused by government intervention. Let $z(t)$ be the deviation as a result of government intervention. Therefore:

$$z(t) = x(t) + y(t). \tag{8.3}$$

If government intervention is dynamically stabilising, the fluctuations of the economy around its trend caused by the policy must be less than the fluctuations around the trend if no policy were applied. Measuring the fluctuations around trend by the variance $\{\sigma^2\}$, it follows that if;

$$\sigma_z^2 < \sigma_x^2 \quad \text{intervention is stabilising}$$
$$> \quad \text{intervention is destabilising}$$
$$= \quad \text{intervention is neutral}$$

The critics of intervention policy argue that any attempt by the government to stabilise the economy will produce greater fluctuations than if the economy were left unhindered.[8] This argument is illustrated in the following way. $x(t)$, in Figure 8.6, represents the business cycle. The government aims to smooth out the business cycle by the application of demand management techniques. The first problem is to identify the position of the economy in relation to its trend. Suppose the economy has been subjected to a negative shock. The authorities have to recognise that the economy is moving away from the trend as a result. The time involved in this operation is known as the *recognition lag*. The second problem is that, once the state of the economy is recognised, the authorities have to devise a response. The time taken in responding is called the *response lag*. The combination of the two is what Friedman refers to as the *inside lags*. A further lag is the time between the implementation of a policy and its effect on the economy. This is referred to as the *outside lag*. Thus, by the time the authorities come to recognise that the economy is on the downturn in response to a negative shock, the economy is already near the bottom of the cycle. Therefore the implementation of policy and its effects occur when the economy is in a mature recovery. The effect of the policy is therefore to cause the economy to overheat by pushing it above its intervention-free path. This is described by the dotted path, $z(t)$, in Figure 8.6.

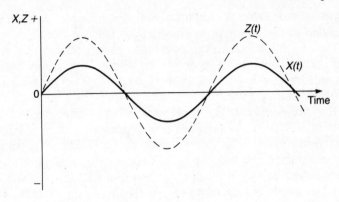

Fig 8.6

A similar description follows for when the economy is recognised to be overheating. Contractionary policy is applied when the economy is already in the downturn, further exacerbating the recessionary force, resulting in a worse recession.[9] It follows that the best policy may be to leave the economy to its own devices – meaning a free market solution. A corollary of this argument is that the best policy is to stick to a well-defined rule rather than engage in discretionary action. An example of a rule is a constant money supply growth.

The example of the expectations-augmented Phillips curve illustrates a further problem with the use of discretionary policy. The benefits do not occur at the same time as the costs. The short-term benefits of reducing unemployment have to be balanced by the long-term costs of higher inflation .

The counter-argument to the rules case has developed along two fronts. Proponents of discretionary policy have long recognised that the target–instrument approach is too simplistic and ignores the inherent uncertainty that exists in the understanding of the economy. The theory of economic policy recognises that, if there are many instruments and there is uncertainty, the optimal policy is to use a mix of instruments in a way that minimises the risk. This is just like a portfolio problem in which an individual attempts to minimise the risk of a portfolio by holding a mix of assets; likewise the policy-makers would diversify their instruments.[10] Thus uncertainty can, in principle, be accommodated in the theory of macroeconomic policy.

The second strand to the counter-argument dealt specifically with the informational problem by using large-scale macroeconometric models to assess the effects of policy in both the short and the long run.[11]

The problem with the theoretical analysis allowing for uncertainty is that it still does not resolve the problem of independent instruments; also, as we shall see later in this chapter, the parameters of economic behaviour are not necessarily independent of the instruments. However, while the debate of rules versus discretion continued in the academic journals, the policy-markers continued in the exercise of policy design confident in the usefulness of the macro-econometric models at their disposal.

## Demand management – the evidence

After all is said and done about the effectiveness of fine tuning, what is the evidence for either case? It has been argued that the transition to the post-war economy was smoothed because of the extension of war-time controls, thus avoiding the boom–slump–boom record of the inter-war years.[12] British economic performance in the 1950s and early 1960s differed sharply from that of the inter-war years. An important consideration is that, unlike the inter-war period, the scope for increasing exports was much greater following the end of the Second World War. Competitor nations had been equally affected by the hostilities and world demand was generally more buoyant and had a stronger impact on aggregate demand at home. The higher level of world trade acted as a benign reinforcer of fast growth following the war, making it difficult to evaluate how much of the improvement was generated by active demand management. The commitment to 'full employment' as a policy objective was embraced by both political parties.

Although unemployment was kept low during the 1950s and only began to rise during the 1960s, it is not clear how much of this can be attributed to demand management. One thing is clear, as Table 8.1 shows: the cycle was not eliminated and the period was punctuated by cycles of four to five years' duration. Demand

Table 8.1 *The UK record, 1950–73*

| Year | Growth[a] % | Inflation[b] % | Unemployment[c] % | Current[d] balance |
|------|-------------|----------------|-------------------|--------------------|
| 1950 | 3.1 | 2.9 | 1.6 | 2.4 |
| 1951 | 3.0 | 9.0 | 1.3 | −2.5 |
| 1952 | −0.4 | 9.4 | 2.2 | 1.0 |
| 1953 | 4.0 | 3.1 | 1.8 | 0.9 |
| 1954 | 4.0 | 1.7 | 1.5 | 0.7 |
| 1955 | 3.9 | 4.6 | 1.2 | −0.8 |
| 1956 | 1.3 | 5.0 | 1.3 | 1.0 |
| 1957 | 1.6 | 3.6 | 1.6 | 1.1 |
| 1958 | −0.3 | 3.2 | 2.2 | 1.6 |
| 1959 | 4.0 | 0.6 | 2.3 | 0.7 |
| 1960 | 5.5 | 1.1 | 1.7 | −0.9 |
| 1961 | 2.6 | 3.3 | 1.6 | 0.2 |
| 1962 | 1.1 | 4.2 | 2.1 | 0.5 |
| 1963 | 3.9 | 2.0 | 2.6 | 0.4 |
| 1964 | 5.6 | 3.2 | 1.7 | −1.1 |
| 1965 | 2.9 | 4.8 | 1.5 | −0.1 |
| 1966 | 1.8 | 3.9 | 1.6 | 0.3 |
| 1967 | 2.1 | 2.4 | 2.5 | −0.7 |
| 1968 | 4.4 | 4.8 | 2.5 | −0.6 |
| 1969 | 2.5 | 5.4 | 2.5 | 1.1 |
| 1970 | 2.0 | 6.3 | 2.6 | 1.6 |
| 1971 | 1.5 | 9.4 | 3.4 | 2.0 |
| 1972 | 2.7 | 7.3 | 3.8 | 0.4 |
| 1973 | 7.1 | 9.1 | 2.7 | −1.3 |

*Notes*:
[a] Real GDP growth average estimate.
[b] Inflation Retail Price Index.
[c] New basis.
[d] As percentage of GDP at market prices.

*Source*: CSO, *Economic Trends*.

management appeared unable to fine tune as was expected. The much noted stop–go cycle was the natural outcome. The overriding principle of fiscal and monetary policy was one of control. Demand was seen to be controllable by monetary measures such as changes in hire purchase regulation, 'moral suasion' on the lending activities of the major lending banks and the use of Special Deposits to control credit growth. With fiscal policy the emphasis was on discretionary changes in taxation. Although government expenditure was not seen as an appropriate instrument for short-term stabilisation policy, it was accepted that it was an important source of domestic demand in the medium term.

Whether fiscal activism and demand management in general actually stabilised the economy is still a matter of debate. The work of Dow (1964), Musgrave and Musgrave (1968) and Hansen (1969) concluded that fiscal and monetary policy were destabilising, although this has been challenged by Little (1966) and Boltho (1981). What is more generally accepted is that by the late 1950s the incompatibility of demand management with other medium-term objectives had begun to emerge. Problems with recurring external constraints and inflation led to further attempts to control the economy in the form of experiments with wage and price controls, starting with the pay pause of Selwyn Lloyd in 1961. However, external considerations began to play a more significant role in the setting of policy in the years leading up to the devaluation in sterling in 1967 and immediately afterwards. The freeing of the economy in 1973 from the straightjacket of fixed exchange rates did not alter the fundamental conclusion that demand policy had failed not only to fine tune but also to maintain its primary objective of full employment. This was seen particularly in the breakdown of the Phillips curve in the late 1960s and early 1970s. The 1970s was a period of policy reassessment. Inflation and unemployment had begun to increase together and economic growth, which had been at an underlying 2.2 per cent in the post-war period, had fallen to an underlying rate of 1.3 per cent between 1973 and 1979.[13]

The slowdown in growth and productivity over the 1970s remains largely a puzzle. Domestic explanations lack plausibility because of the international nature of the slowdown. One obvious explanation is the 'supply shock'created by the sharp rise in oil prices. If oil is a complementary input to production, Bruno and Sachs (1983) argue that a massive rise in oil prices would also affect the productivity of other factors of production. The attractiveness of this argument is that it has the merit of explaining the timing of the slowdown. It is unattractive in that it places the whole reason for the slowdown entirely on the oil price rise.[14] It is not clear whether such a shock could have generated so sharp a decline in world trade performance. The trend rate of growth of world trade fell from around 6.5 per cent in the 1950s to around 4 per cent in the 1970s.

In their exhaustive study of British economic growth, 1856– 1973, Matthews, Feinstein and Odling-Smee (1982) tentatively consider the emergence of supply bottle-necks, but conclude that the period is particularly difficult to explain. They argue that the problems of the 1970s raise doubts about the ability of supply to match a permanent increase in demand. What was thought to be the reinforcement of rapid growth derived from demand-led policy was now seen to be only transitory. An alternative view that emphasises the supply-side argument is presented by Minford *et al.* (1983). They argue that the rising tax burden, union power and unemployment benefits contributed to the slowing down on the supply side and the secular rise in unemployment. Here also it is argued that demand policy had only temporary effects. What cannot be said, however, is that the slowdown in the 1970s was due to a lack of domestic-led demand. Table 8.2 presents the movements of the general government deficit, the share of the public sector, tax revenues and the growth of the money supply. In all respects demand policy was reflationary or at least not contractionary.

## The politics of the business cycle

An interesting development in the theory of policy design begins with the notion that the government is not some disinterested economic planner aiming to maximise the welfare of the people (or the economic planner aiming to minimise a well-defined loss function). Rather, a more cynical presumption is that a democratic government is interested only in maximising the chance of being re-elected. What this implies is that the government in power will court political popularity by engineering a mini-boom in the run-up to an election. The inflationary consequences of such an engineered boom will be felt after the election. So the political business cycle is characterised by popular reflation prior to an election followed by unpopular deflation early in the life of the government. Since both inflation and

Table 8.2 *Indicators of demand*

| Year | PSBR/GDP[a] % | Public Sector[b] % | Tax Receipts[c] % | £M3 growth[d] % |
|------|------|------|------|------|
| 1970 | −0.1 | 36.6 | 37.1 | 8.6 |
| 1971 | 2.3 | 37.0 | 34.9 | 14.0 |
| 1972 | 3.0 | 37.7 | 33.4 | 27.2 |
| 1973 | 5.5 | 37.7 | 32.6 | 27.1 |
| 1974 | 7.6 | 42.5 | 35.7 | 11.0 |
| 1975 | 9.5 | 44.5 | 36.1 | 5.8 |
| 1976 | 7.1 | 42.0 | 35.1 | 9.8 |
| 1977 | 3.7 | 38.1 | 34.7 | 9.3 |
| 1978 | 5.0 | 38.7 | 33.5 | 15.6 |
| 1979 | 6.4 | 39.0 | 34.3 | 13.2 |

*Notes*:
[a] Public sector borrowing requirement as a percentage of GDP at market prices.
[b] Public sector expenditure less debt interest as a percentage of GDP at market prices.
[c] Tax and national insurance contributions as a percentage of GDP at market prices.
[d] £M3 annual rate of growth (fourth quarter).

*Source*: CSO *Economic Trends*.

unemployment are 'bads', the government aims to maximise its popularity by minimising a loss function defined on inflation ($\pi$) and unemployment ($U$) over the time period of the electoral cycle. The problem facing the government is to maximise a voter popularity function $V$ by conducting policies likely to appeal to the floating voter:[15]

$$\text{Max } V = \int_0^T \Phi(\pi, U)e^{-rt}dt \qquad \begin{array}{l} \Phi_\pi, \Phi_u < 0 \\ \Phi_{\pi\pi}, \Phi_{u\theta} < 0 \end{array} \qquad (8.4)$$

subject to

$$\pi = f(U) + \pi^e \qquad f_u < 0 \qquad (8.5)$$
$$D\pi^e = \beta(\pi - \pi^e) \qquad 0 < \beta < 1 \qquad (8.6)$$

where D is the differential operator; $\{Dx = dx/dt\}$.

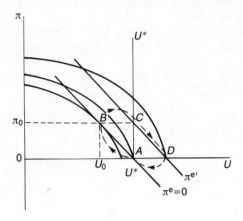

Fig 8.7

The function $V$ which is maximised over the electoral time period $T$ is negative in $\pi$ and $U$ and has the same properties of the iso-loss functions illustrated in Figure 8.5. The maximisation is conducted subject to two constraints. The first is the expectations-augmented Phillips curve. The second is a statement about the determination of expectations, known as the mechanism of adaptive expectations.

Basically, the concept of adaptive expectations is an error-learning mechanism which states that expectations are revised by some fraction $\beta$ of the error in expectations made in the previous period. The political business cycle is illustrated in Figure 8.7. Assume that the economy is at the natural rate of unemployment and actual and expected inflation is zero. Voter popularity is increased by moving on to lower iso-loss curves, with maximum unconstrained popularity being at the origin of the axis. If an election is imminent, the government expands demand from a position of zero inflation, and moves along the short-run Phillips curve to point $B$ on Figure 8.7. This increases the popularity of the government. Inflation is higher than expected but unemployment is lower than the natural rate. However, as expectations catch up, the Phillips curve shifts out to the right until the economy settles at a stable rate of inflation at point $C$, which is less popular than both points $B$ and $A$. The government then attempts to reduce inflation by conducting deflationary policy,

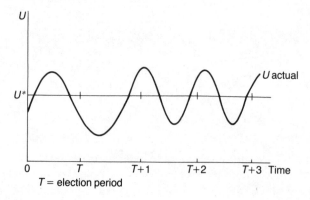

$T$ = election period

Fig 8.8

pushing the economy to point $D$, reducing its popularity further (this can be characterised as the mid-term blues every administration faces). Finally, when expectations adjust, the economy is back at position $A$ in time for the pre-election boom. The path of unemployment between election periods is described in Figure 8.8 Unemployment falls below the natural rate at first and then rises above it, before returning to the natural rate prior to the next election cycle.

Ingenious though this theory is, there appears to be little evidence in its favour. Nordhaus (1975) presented weak evidence for the US, but this has subsequently been refuted by Golden and Poterba (1980). In a similar exercise for the UK, Alt (1979) reported no evidence of a political business cycle. However, it has been found that real per capita personal disposable income is about one-third more likely to accelerate in an election year than in a non-election year.[16] However, this does not tell us whether the government deliberately manoeuvres the economy into a favourable electoral position or that governments carefully choose the timing of the election when the economy is in a favourable position. Thus it is not enough to show that a government stimulates the economy before an election: it has to be shown that it is doing it in excess of what a neutral adviser would recommend. A more damning criticism of the theory is that people are unlikely to be continuously fooled by pre-election booms. By the assumption of adaptive expectations, the political

256

business cycle model shows that the electorate will be continuously fooled by the government and fail to learn from their past errors. In short, the theory assumes that the electorate do not learn to anticipate pre-election booms and the consequent inflationary outcome. This criticism arises out of the development of rational expectations associated with the new classical school.

## The new classical critique

The new classical critique of conventional economics began with the theory of rational expectations originally propounded by Muth (1961) and, in the context of the quantity theory, by Walters (1971). The hypothesis has influenced macroeconomic thinking deeply. In a nutshell, the hypothesis states that people will use all the available information in formulating expectations. They use the information in a way so as not to make systematic errors in expectations. Thus, expectations are the best forecasts that can be made given all the available information. In theory this means that the subjective expectation of economic decision-makers corresponds to the objective expectation consistent with the relevant theory. The relevant theory is the theory used to explain and determine the economic variables of which expectations are made. All the relevant and available information means all the necessary information to make good predictions of the future. In this respect the term 'information set' has to be carefully defined. In general, the information set will include all past observations of economic variables, and some currently observed variables such as the rate of interest, the exchange rate and announcements of current and future policy. The information set defines the state of expectations. Formally what this means is that expectations are *conditional* on the information set.

One of the most significant implications of the rational expectations hypothesis is the so-called policy neutrality result. Loosely stated, this says that systematic macroeconomic policy has no effect on real output. Real effects occur because of non-systematic, unpredictable (random) policy shocks. This result can be demonstrated in the following way. Let aggregate demand be represented by the following log-linear equation:

$$Y_t^{\mathrm{d}} = a + bG_t + c(M_t - P_t) \quad b, c > 0 \qquad (8.7)$$

257

where $Y^d$ is the log of real income, $G$ is the log of government spending, $M$ is the log of the money supply and $p$ is the log of the price level. Let aggregate supply be described by the following equation:

$$Y_t^s = Y^* + h(P_t - P_t^e) + \varepsilon_t \qquad h > 0 \qquad (8.8)$$

where $Y^s$ is the log of output, $Y^*$ is the log of the equilibrium level of output, $P^e$ is the expected log of the price level, and $\varepsilon$ is a random term.[17] Finally let the two policy variables be determined by the following reaction functions:

$$G_t = G^* + \tau(Y^* - Y_{t-1}) + u_t \qquad \tau, \delta > 0 \qquad (8.9)$$
$$M_t = M^* + \delta(P^* - p_{t-1}) + v_t \qquad (8.10)$$

where $G^*$ and $M^*$ are the autonomous levels of government spending and money and $u$ and $v$ are independent random terms.

The first reaction function states that government spending above the autonomous level responds to the gap between the full employment (target) level of output and the lagged level of output and a random term. The second reaction function states that the money supply falls below the autonomous level when the lagged price level is above the target price level.

Expected aggregate demand:
$$Y^{de} = a + bG_t^e + c(M_t^e - P_t^e)$$
Expected aggregate supply:
$$Y^{se} = Y^*$$
Expected fiscal policy:
$$G_t^e = G^* + \tau(Y^* - Y_{t-1})$$
Expected monetary policy:
$$M_t^e = M^* + \delta(P^* - P_{t-1})$$

Substituting for expected $G$ and $M$ and equating $Y^{de}$ with $Y^{se}$ yields the solution for the expected price level:

$$P_t^e = [a + (b\tau - 1)Y^* - b\tau Y_{t-1} + bG^* \\ + cM^* + c\delta P^* - c\delta P_{t-1}]/c. \qquad (8.11)$$

The unexpected level of demand $(Y^d - Y^{de})$ is given by:

$$Y^d - Y^{de} = bu_t + c[v_t - (P_t - P_t^e)]. \qquad (8.12)$$

The unexpected level of supply $(Y^s - Y^{se})$ is given by:

$$Y^s - Y^{se} = h(P_t - P_t^e) + \varepsilon_t. \qquad (8.13)$$

Equating unexpected supply with unexpected demand produces

$$P_t - P_t^e = (bu_t + cv_t - \varepsilon_t)(h + c)^{-1}. \qquad (8.14)$$

It follows that:

$$Y_t - Y^* = \{h/(h + c)\} [bu_t + cv_t + c\epsilon_t]. \qquad (8.15)$$

What the last two expressions state is that systematic fiscal and monetary policy cannot stabilise output or the price level. The deviation both of the price level from its expected value and of output from the full employment or long-run equilibrium value is a function of random terms only. The parameters of systematic policy $\{\tau, \delta\}$ do not appear in either of the expressions. They affect only the expected price level and therefore cannot influence output.

The implications of the policy neutrality result are explored graphically in Figure 8.9. figure 8.9 depicts the aggregate demand curve $(AD)$, the expectations–augmented aggregate supply $(EAS)$ currve and the long-run equilibrium level of output $(AS)$. Full equilibrium occurs when the actual price level equals the expected price level, that is, when $AD = EAS = AS$, shown by point $A$. If there is an unexpected increase in aggregate demand $(\{u, v\} > 0)$, the $AD$ schedule shifts to the right to $AD'$, inter-secting the $EAS$ schedule. The price level is higher than the

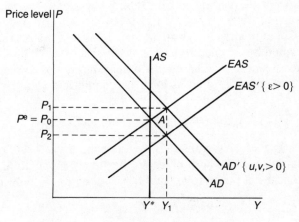

Fig 8.9

expected price level and output is greater than expected. Alternatively, we can consider a positive supply shock ($\{\epsilon\} > 0$) which causes the *EAS* schedule to shift down. Output is higher than expected and the price level is lower than expected. Since these are the result of random and therefore unpredictable shocks, they are treated as transitory and expectations are not adjusted. However, if any of the predictable components of the fiscal and monetary processes were to change, this would cause a permanent shift in both the *AD* and *EAS* schedules. For example, consider the case of the government reducing $M^*$ permanently and setting $\delta = 0$. If this was known in advance, the following adjustments to the *AD* and *EAS* schedules would occur. From an initial position of equilibrium, the *AD* schedule would be expected to shift down to the left. Since the price level is expected to fall, the *EAS* schedule shifts down to the right. Both would intersect with the *AS* schedule at a lower price level but the same level of output.

The policy implication of the neutrality result is that it is only random and not systematic policy that influences output. Governments cannot exploit random policy shocks. If they attempt to conduct continuous surprise reflations, the policy soon becomes predictable and the full neutrality condition will result. If genuine random policy shocks were to be carried out, first this would not meet any sensible policy target and second it has been shown by Lucas (1976) that the slope of the Phillips curve is itself a function of the variance of inflation – the higher the variance the lower the trade-off between surprise inflation and unemployment. Consequently, even an attempt to use genuine random policy would be doomed to failure as the short-run Phillips curve becomes steeper, tending to the long-run Phillips curve. The variance of output around its long-run equilibrium value is given from (8.15) as

$$\sigma_y^2 = \{h + c\}^{-2} [(hb)^2 \, \sigma_u^2 + (hc)^2 \sigma_v^2 + c^2 \sigma_\epsilon^2]. \qquad (8.16)$$

The variance of $Y$ is minimised by following a fixed rule of the Friedman type. If the authorities set the money supply to $M^*$ and $v = 0$, and fiscal policy to $G^*$ and $u = 0$, then (8.16) reduces to:

$$\sigma_y^2 = \{c/(h + c)\}^2 \, \sigma_\epsilon^2, \qquad (8.17)$$

which is clearly lower than (8.16).

It is interesting to juxtapose the informational basis for the fixed-rule implication derived from the new classical school with the conventional argument for rules. The conventional case for rules is based on the argument that the policy-maker does not have sufficient information to appropriately control the economy. The new classical school argues that the fixed-rule result is a conclusion from a model that assumes that both the policy-maker and the private sector have all the available and relevant information. The first assumes minimal information, while the latter assumes maximal information.

The policy neutrality result occurs because of the combination of the assumption of rational expectations with that of market clearing. It is the latter assumption that has caused the most controversy. In fact it has been shown that the policy neutrality result is not robust to changes in this assumption. Taylor (1979) shows that price stickiness that extends over more than one period would be sufficient to restore the relevance of policy.[18] However, the proponents of the new classical school were defending the policy neutrality result not to address a policy rule but to explore the implications of the rational expectations hypothesis. The major implication is that models of private sector behaviour that take into account the effects of policy on expectations will have different properties from models that do not. This is a loose statement of the so-called 'Lucas Critique' of macro-econometric policy evaluation.[19] The Lucas Critique states that the parameters of private sector behaviour are not invariant with respect to the parameters of policy. Consequently, models that do not allow for the effect of policy on the parameters of behaviour will generate misleading policy conclusions. The Lucas Critique therefore lends support to the rules case by identifying a potential failing in the econometric models used by the government to conduct counter-factual policy simulations. Better to have a fixed or simple rule than to fine tune with a model that is necessarily faulty.

A corollary of the new classical model is that announcements of policy will alter economic behaviour by altering expectations. For an announcement to be effective, however, it has to be credible. One of the conditions for fiscal and monetary policy to be credible is that they be consistent with each other on an intertemporal basis. What this means is that loose fiscal policy

261

implies loose monetary policy in the long run and tight fiscal policy implies tight monetary policy in the long run. This conclusion arises out of the analysis of Sargent and Wallace (1981). The starting point for this analysis is the simple observation that the government deficit (defined as public expenditure less tax revenue) plus debt interest must be financed by some combination of monetary and bond issue. The policy-maker is bound by the government budget constraint:

$$G_t - T_t + r_{t-1}B_{t-1} = (B_t - B_{t-1}) + (M_t - M_{t-1}), \quad (8.18)$$

where $G$ is government spending, $T$ is tax revenue, $B$ is the stock of bonds, $M$ is the stock of money, $r$ is the rate of interest and $r_{t-1}B_{t-1}$ is the flow of debt service (debt interest). Sargent and Wallace demonstrate that, if loose fiscal policy is matched with tight monetary policy, one of the two policy variables has to adjust to the other. In the case when loose fiscal policy dominates, at some stage monetary policy has to expand to meet the needs of the deficit. This occurs when all of private sector wealth is held in the form of government bonds.[20] Alternatively, monetary policy can dominate, in which case a deficit has to be offset with a future surplus. This is seen after rearranging equation (8.18) and assuming that the deficit is constant, the rate of interest is constant and the deficit is financed by bond issue only. The latter assumption implies $M_t - M_{t-1} = 0$; then:

$$B_t = (G_t - T_t) + (1 + r)B_{t-1}. \quad (8.19)$$

By continuous forward substitution:

$$B_{t+N} = \sum^N (1 + r)^i (G - T) + (1 + r)^{N+1} B_{t-1} \quad (8.20)$$

after some terminal date $N = 0$, $(B_{t+0+1} - B_{t+0}) = 0$, which implies that either $G - T + rB = 0$ or $M_t - M_{t-1} > 0$. Which of the two possibilities actually occurs is determined by a game of 'chicken' between the fiscal and monetary authorities. One side has to give in before the terminal date. The authority that gives up first is the loser.

Sargent arrives at two conclusions: first, tight money now implies inflation later and, second, tight money now implies inflation now. The latter conclusion arises out of the rational expectations mechanism. Since tight money now implies inflation later, inflation expectations rise, raising the rate of interest and depressing the demand for real balances, If the money supply is held constant, this implies that the price level and inflation must rise today to reduce the level of real balances willingly held. The binding of fiscal and monetary policy destroys the supposed independence of the two instruments, further weakening the basis of demand management.

One of the stated reasons for the announcement of the Medium Term Financial Strategy by the incoming Conservative government in 1979/80 was to influence expectations. A gradual reduction in the rate of growth of the money supply (£M3) was to be matched by a gradual reduction in the ratio of the PSBR to GDP. According to the policy neutrality result, the private sector should have altered its expectations and a low-inflation economy should have come about with minimal effects on output. Does the recession of 1980–1 provide sufficient real-world evidence to reject the market clearing rational expectations model? Not according to Sargent (1986), who argues that although the anti-inflation policy was well announced it was not seen as credible by the private sector. Therefore expectations failed to adjust to the announced policy. The result can be illustrated with the aid of Figure 8.9. The contraction in demand shifts the *AD* schedule down to the left, but, since the policy is not credible, the private sector expects it to be reversed in the future; thus expectations do not change. The *EAS* schedule remains in the same position and the fall in demand is translated into a Keynesian-type recession.[21] Although the recession of 1980–1 can be interpreted using non market clearing models of the conventional Keynesian type as well as the rational expectations type, the market clearing model cannot be rejected so easily.[22] More importantly, the issue of credibility introduces a new development in the theory of macroeconomic policy which dramatically alters our conception of macroeconomic policy and its effectiveness. This new dimension is examined in the following section.

## Policy and games

Up to this point we have continued to assume that the government attempts to meet a set of policy targets and that the private sector responds appropriately. What we have not considered is how the government would react to private sector reactions. Similarly we have not considered the expectations and actions of the private sector that anticipates government reaction to private sector reactions. This sounds very much like one of those 'I know that you know that I know' scenarios, but it is precisely along these lines that the modern theories of macroeconomic policy have developed. The early version of the new classical model assumed that the private sector is made up of rational and smart economic agents while the government continues to attempt to conduct systematic policy even though it knows it would be ineffective. This is an asymmetry in behaviour which does not sit easily with the new classical framework. In keeping with the philosophy of the framework, recent additions to the theory take policy – makers as having objectives and preferences just like private agents, and they also attempt to maximize their utility subject to constraints. This gives rise to a game-theoretic framework in the conduct and appreciation of the role of macroeconomic policy.

The starting point for this analysis is the problem of time-inconsistency analysed by Kydland and Prescott (1977). One of the extensions of the Theil principle of minimising a loss function (or maximising an objective function) was the application of optimal control theory to policy design. This is the use of dynamic optimisation techniques borrowed from the engineering sciences. The view that optimal control techniques constituted a valuable tool for economic policy design was based on the apparent similarity between physical systems used in the engineering sciences and the economic models used by policy-makers. An important principle of optimal control is that an optimal policy designed in time period $t_0$ for period $t_1$ in the future is precisely the same policy that would be chosen in period $t_1$. This is sometimes known as the *Bellman principle*, which states that optimal policy must be time consistent. Whatever situation a policy-maker inherits, the optimal policy in that period is the same one that was chosen for it at some prior date.

Kydland and Prescott (1977) show that, in a world of rational economic agents, optimal policy will be *time inconsistent*. The term time-inconsistency refers to a situation in which a rational private sector is aware that the policy-maker has an incentive to renege on a policy that it has promised to carry out. An example is provided by Kydland and Prescott (1977) in the case of patent policy design. It is generally accepted that some form of patent protection is a socially useful way of encouraging invention. The notion is that more scientific discoveries would occur if inventors knew that they had some monopoly rights to their invention. However, once a discovery is made, society (in the form of the policy-maker) has an incentive to renege on the patent protection so as to reap the full benefits. The problem occurs when the inventor recognises the incentive for the policy-maker to cheat on its promise.

The problem for macroeconomic policy can be analysed using the temporary trade-off between inflation and unemployment that exists in the short-run Phillips curve. A policy of anti-inflation (reduction in inflation), if announced in advance, will reduce inflation expectations and result in a smooth transition to a lower rate of inflation. However, once expectations have adjusted to a lower inflation rate it is optimal for the policy-maker to reduce unemployment by engaging in a pro-inflationary policy. This situation is described in Figure 8.10. Suppose the initial position of the economy is at point $A$. At this point the short-run Phillips curve is tangential to the iso-loss function; therefore this is a sustainable position from which there is no incentive to move.

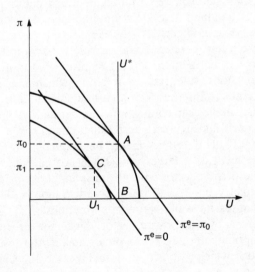

Fig 8.10

Suppose the policy-maker wishes to reach a position of zero inflation as described by position *B*. The optimal strategy is to announce a zero inflationary policy. If expectations adjust to this announcement, the Phillips curve shifts down to the left and intersects with point *B*. However, once this position is reached the policy-maker can reach an even higher utility level (lower loss, higher popularity) by moving the economy to position *C*.

The recognition of the problem of time-inconsistency has led to the development of the use of *game theory* in optimal policy design.[23] It turns out that on the whole simple rules tend to be preferable to discretion, provided that there are sufficient safeguards that stop policy-makers from deviating from the rule. Short of imposing legal or institutional constraints on policy-makers, how is the problem of time-inconsistency solved in an economy where the government is democratically elected? One suggestion advanced by Barro and Gordon (1983a) is that policy-makers value a reputation for not deviating from the announced policy. The model Barro and Gordon use is one in which the policy-maker faces a policy preference function of the following type:

$$Z = (a/2)\pi^2 - b(\pi - \pi^e). \qquad (8.21)$$

The first term is the square of inflation, which enters positively because it is assumed that inflation imposes costs on society which increase non-linearly. The second term is unexpected inflation, which lowers unemployment below its natural rate and therefore lowers costs to society. The problem for the policy-maker is to choose the rate of inflation which maximises its welfare function (minimises $Z$, its cost function). It is assumed that the policy-maker can control inflation perfectly. Assume that the policy-maker aims to reach zero inflation and $\pi = \pi^e$ at point *B* in Figure 8.10. If the policy-maker has a history of discretion, the announcement of a target $\pi = 0$ will not be believed; consequently the private sector will maximise its utility by assuming that discretionary policy will be followed. Similarly the policy-maker maximises its welfare function (minimises $Z$), assuming that $\pi^e$ is given by the private sector. Since the private sector knows the optimal strategy of the policy-maker, the result is the Nash solution, which is position *A* in Figure 8.10. Clearly the Nash solution is inferior to the target rule, in terms of the policy-maker's welfare. If the policy-maker's reputation is a consideration, then the solution for $\pi$ lies at some intermediate position between the discretionary and target positions. The game is played in the following way.

Initially the private sector believes the policy-maker's announcement of the target rule, $\pi = 0$. If the authority breaks the rule, the private sector punishes the policy-maker by assuming that for the next period the discretionary position is maintained. The policy-maker therefore must balance the benefits of cheating on its announced rule against the future costs of being at the discretionary position. The equilibrium to this game depends on the discount rate of the policy-maker, which is used to discount the future costs of cheating now. If the policy-maker heavily discounts the future, then the equilibrium is closer to the discretionary position. If the policy-maker has a low discount rate, an equilibrium closer to the target rule is possible (the solution is examined in greater detail in Appendix 4)

Backus and Driffil (1985) extend this simple model to include uncertainty on the part of the private sector as to the true preferences of the policy-maker. They introduce the possibility of two types of policy-makers: 'wet' governments (pro-inflationary) and 'dry' governments (anti-inflationary). At the outset the true preferences of the policy-maker are unknown. Therefore it will pay a wet government to pretend for some period that it is a dry government, while a dry government may follow a wet policy if the costs of trying to convince the private sector of its true preferences become prohibitive. The policy game in this model is complicated by the private sector trying to discover the preferences of the policy-maker and the policy-maker trying to fool or convince the private sector of its true preferences. A corollary of the Backus and Driffil model is that a dry government will face a period of high disinflation costs (in terms of unemployment) in its attempt to convince the private sector of its true intentions.

The Backus and Driffil conclusion has received further theoretical support from Alesina (1987), who introduces an additional twist to the two-party model. Unlike Backus and Driffil, Alesina assumes that the inflation preferences of the two types of policy-makers are known because they represent different types of supporters. The uncertainty is about voters' preferences. Since wage contracts are based on expectations of inflation and these expectations straddle a future post-electoral period, then expected inflation will be made up of a weighted average of the two possible inflation outcomes. Workers are making 'hedging' pay claims by allowing for the possibility of one of the two outcomes. The weights will be determined by the probability of a dry or wet policy-maker being elected. Once wages are set, they can be viewed as being 'locked in' by the length of the contract. If a wet policy-maker is elected, the economy moves into a boom as inflation is higher than expected, whereas if a dry policy maker is elected the economy moves into a slump because inflation is lower than expected.[24] Alesina shows that there is a third policy (a cooperative policy), which makes both groups of supporters better off in the long run provided both types of policy-maker can be bound to the cooperative rule.

One solution to the problem is to construct binding constraints on the policy-maker. However, it is generally recognised that in a democratic society such constraints may have to be institutionally determined. One such possibility is the Friedman rule of a fixed money supply growth being legally binding. Another is the attempt by Senators Gramm, Rudmann and Hollings to cap the US federal budget deficit. A third possibility is to purchase credibility from a government that already has a strong and credible commitment to an anti-inflationary policy by linking currencies through a mechanism such as the European Monetary System.

Finally there is the possibility that formal constitutional or legal restrictions on a policy-maker may be unnecessary because reputational considerations may produce self-binding commitments. This conclusion, however, is not robust to changes in the structure of the information set or the nature of the game. For example, Canzoneri (1985) considers the possibility of the policy-maker having superior information. In particular, if the policy-maker knows the value of shocks to the demand for money while the private sector does not, then the verification of whether the announced policy rule is being adhered to is problematic.

## Conclusion

The development of the theory of macroeconomic policy over the last decade or so has important implications for the interpretation of policy in that same period. It is generally recognised that the economic policy of the incoming Conservative government in June 1979 represented a radical break from the past. The government of Mrs Thatcher took two important steps. First, it broke away from the post-war consensus that the government be committed to the principle of full employment. The role of the government was seen as to create the conditions for the private sector to achieve high growth and maximum employment but not itself be the instigator. Second, it instituted a policy of announced monetary and fiscal policy targets to bring down inflation – The Medium Term Financial Strategy (MTFS). The policy took the form of an announced gradual reduction in the rate of growth of the money supply, £M3, and the PSBR as a percentage of GDP at market prices. The MTFS embodied the principle of fixed rules but without binding commitments. The prediction of the new classicals was that 'on the assumption that policies are properly understood when they are announced and implemented, the disturbance to output and employment from reduction in the money supply and in the PSBR would be minimised' (Minford, 1980, p. 142). This prediction was spectacularly falsified by the recession of 1980–1.

There are two explanations that employ the rational expectations hypothesis. The non market clearing rational expectations model (Buiter and Miller, 1981a) argues that the anticipated tightening of monetary conditions led to a sharp appreciation of sterling. This resulted in a sharp appreciation of the real exchange rate because of sticky prices in the goods market. Export growth fell back, output declined and unemployment rose dramatically.[25] This view assumes that the announced MTFS was entirely credible and it was only the inherent sluggishness in goods (and labour) markets that led to the negative effects on output.

The alternative argument forwarded by the new classicals has two strands to it. There are those who argue that the policy was not credible because it was assumed that it would be reversed in the future (Sargent, 1986). The second strand to this argument is that, since the announced policy was one of gradualism, this opened up the possibility of the opposition forces gathering in strength to force a 'U turn', buttressing the low credibility problem. Furthermore, the announcement of the MTFS coincided

269

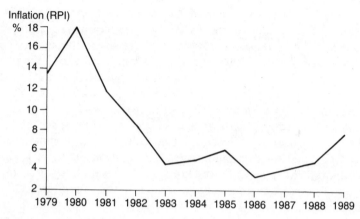

Fig 8.11

with the derequlation of the banking system and the abolition of the Corset. As a consequence the favoured measure of monetary conditions, £M3, grew hopelessly out of control and well outside the announced target range. However, other measures of monetary conditions indicated a sharp tightening of the monetary environment. In particular, the rate of growth of M0, which at the beginning of 1980 was 12.3 per cent, had fallen to 5.8 per cent by the year end. One interpretation is that the government responded to the breach of the monetary targets by tightening the monetary screw even further. Instead of the intended gradual policy, a sharp negative shock was administered. The most severe shock occurred in 1980 but several more were administered before a sufficient stock of credibility was built up.[26] The idea that a government has to build up a stock of credibility stems directly from the Backus and Driffil approach. A government has to convince the private sector the it is 'dry' and not 'wet' in disguise. This can only be done by accepting the high costs of disinflation.

The inflation history of the 1980s is shown in Figure 8.11. The announced target in 1980 was price stability (zero inflation). Although getting fairly close, inflation never actually hit the target. It flattened out between 1983 and 1988 at around 4–5 per cent, before accelerating in the last few years. In the context of recent developments in the theory of macroeconomic policy, the failure to meet its declared target within the space of a decade is a strong blow to the policy-maker's credibility. The longer the government vacillated, in the eyes of the private sector, the greater the likelihood of a cheating outcome. What we have learned from the application of game theory to macroeconomic policy is that, since there are no binding commitments in a democratic society, the government should have acted on a policy of 'sudden death' in the first year of its administration. That is, inflation should have been brought down to zero by administering a sufficiently sharp negative shock to demand. Minford and Rastogi (1989) estimate that the cost of such a policy would have been to have brought forward the increase in unemployment and output loss of the first half of the decade but at a considerable gain in credibility.

The current state of monetary policy can be interpreted as an attempt to restore credibility. However, this policy can be at a significant cost and on the eve of a general election, with the temptation to cheat being even greater, it is unlikely that expectations will alter. Will the government stick to the time-cosistent policy (even at the cost of losing the next election) thus proving that it is indeed 'dry', or will it cave in and go for a pre-election boom and show that it is really 'wet'? Whatever the outcome, the game will continue to be played with interest.

## Notes

1 In the long run, either monetary policy would have to adjust to ensure external equilibrium or the exchange rate would have to adjust. In the case of a balance of payments deficit, the interest rate would be raised (abandoning the interest rate target) or the exchange rate would have to be devalued.

2 This is not strictly true as the government also manipulated Bank rate and HP controls. What governments tried to do was to follow the Radcliffe Committee (1959) recommendation that monetary policy should aim at steady interest rates to facilitate the funding of budget deficits, but increasingly failed to do so as monetary policy was called upon to defend the exchange rate.

3 This refers to the basic balance on the external sector, and is non-zero when the current account is not offset by a net capital flow. Setting a target of $bop = 0$ amounts to targeting the level of foreign currency reserves.

4 The theory was based totally on flows.

5 Based on the work of Christ (1968) and Blinder and Solow (1974).

6 See Sargent and Wallace (1981).

7 For a very clear exposition, see Barro (1990).

8 The most distinguished critic of discretionary policy is Milton Friedman. See in particular Friedman (1953).

9 The informational implications of conducting stabilising macro-economic intervention policy are examined in Appendix 2.

10 See Brainard (1967) for the case of multiplicative uncertainty and Poole (1970) for optimal combination policy.

11 In the UK, the first of the large-scale econometric models was built by HM Treasury, followed by the National Institute of Economic and Social Research to act as an independent check (see Surrey, 1971). Another large-scale model that was developed with a view to fore-casting and policy analysis was the London Business School model.

12 See for instance Matthews, Feinstein and Odling-Smee (1982).

13 Real GDP average estimate source: CSO, *Economic Trends*, Annual Supplement, 1987.

14 Partly for this reason, recent research (Bruno, 1982) has widened the analysis to take into account the price of all primary products.

15 The interested student may refer to Nordhaus (1975) for the first exposition of this view.

16 See, for instance, Alt (1980).

17 For a good explanation for the theoretical arguments that underpin the two functions, see Parkin and Bade (1989).

18 Stickiness in nominal prices arises because of staggered nominal wage contracts.

19 After Lucas (1976).

20 The Sargent and Wallace analysis is carried out on the assumption that government bonds are not net wealth. However, the argument that fiscal and monetary policy are intertemporally bound is independent of that assumption. Appendix 3 demonstrates the link in the two policies even when government bonds are part of net wealth.

21 For an analysis, see Buiter and Miller (1981b; 1983).

22 See Matthews and Minford (1987), who use the Liverpool macro-economic model to explain the recession of 1980–1. The Liverpool model is a rational expectations market clearing macroeconomic model which allows for stickiness in prices caused by nominal wage contracts.

23 For a recent survey, see Blackburn and Christensen (1989).

24 For an examination of the dynamic implications of the two-party policy game in the context of the Liverpool macroeconomic model, see Matthews (1985).

**25** Buiter and Miller (1981b; 1983) assess the effects of the Mrs Thatcher's policy in the first few years of the MTFS.
**26** Matthews and Minford (1987) arrive at this conclusion by using the Liverpool macroeconomic model to simulate the shocks of the past decade. See also Matthews (1989).

# Appendix 1: Optimal assignment rules

The problem of targets and instruments analysed in the main text was looked at in the context of a closed economy. The analysis confirmed Tinbergen's principle that both interest rate and output targets could be satisfied with the two instruments – fiscal and monetary policy. However, assignment of which instrument to which policy depends on the parameters of the model. Consider the following fixed price *IS-LM* set-up:

$$Y = F(r, G) \quad F_r < 0, F_G > 0 \quad IS \text{ schedule}$$
$$M = L(r, Y) \quad L_r < 0, L_Y > 0 \quad LM \text{ schedule}$$

where $Y$ is real output, $r$ the rate of interest, $G$ government spending and $M$ the stock of money. This system is set out in its linearised form as follows:

$$\begin{bmatrix} 1 & -F_r \\ L_Y & L_r \end{bmatrix} \begin{bmatrix} Y \\ r \end{bmatrix} = \begin{bmatrix} F_G G \\ M \end{bmatrix}$$

By Cramer's rule we have the following reduced forms:

$$Y = \{F_G L_r G + F_r M\}/\Omega \quad (1)$$
$$r = \{M - L_Y F_G G\}/\Omega \quad (2)$$

where $\Omega = L_r + F_r L_Y < 0$.

From (1) and (2) we can set the target values of $\{Y, r\}$ $\{Y^*, r^*\}$ so that the *RR* schedule in the main text is derived as:

$$M = (L_r + L_Y F_r)r^* + L_Y F_G G,$$

which has a positive slope

$$\left.\frac{dG}{dM}\right|_{RR} = 1/(L_Y F_G) > 0,$$

and the *YY* schedule is:

$$\Omega Y^* = F_r M + F_G L_r G,$$

273

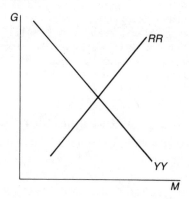

Fig 8A.1

which has a negative slope

$$\frac{dG}{dM}\bigg|_{YY} = -F_r/F_G L_r < 0.$$

Points above the *RR* schedule are $r > r^*$ and points below are $r < r^*$; while points above the *YY* schedule are $Y > Y^*$ and points below $Y < Y^*$. It can be seen by inspection that, if the rate of interest is above its target rate, the policy-maker can meet the target by either increasing the money supply or reducing government spending. If output is below target, the authorities can either raise the money stock or raise government spending. This gives us two possible discrete time assignment rules.

Rule (1)      $M_t - M_{t-1} = \alpha[r_{t-1} - t^*]$
                          $G_t - G_{t-1} = -\beta[Y_{t-1} - Y^*]$

Rule (2)      $G_t - G_{t-1} = -\alpha[r_{t-1} - r^*]$
                          $M_t - M_{t-1} = -\beta[Y_{t-1} - Y^*]$

We have two systems of simultaneous difference equations which can be tested for stability with alternative parameter restrictions. We can, however, get a qualitative feel for the analysis by concentrating on extreme values. The steeper the *IS* curve $\{F_r \to 0\}$ or the flatter the *LM* curve $\{L_r \to -\infty\}$, the flatter is the *YY* schedule. In the limit, *YY* is horizontal. In this situation it can be seen that rule (1) is stable but rule (2) is unstable. On the other

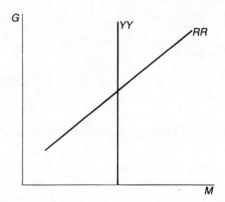

Fig 8A.2

hand, the steeper the *LM* curve $\{L_r \rightarrow 0\}$ or flatter the *IS* curve $\{F_r \rightarrow -\infty\}$, the steeper is the *YY* schedule. In the limit, the *YY* schedule is vertical. It can be seen that in this situation rule (1) will be unstable while rule (2) will be stable.

This can easily be checked analytically. Set out the implied simultaneous difference equations of rule (1) in matrix form.

$$X_t = AX_{t-1} + B,$$

where $X^T$ is the vector $[M_t, G_t]$ as below

$$\begin{bmatrix} M_t \\ G_t \end{bmatrix} = \begin{bmatrix} (1 + \alpha/\Omega) & -\alpha L_Y F_G/\Omega \\ -\beta F_r/\Omega & (1 - \beta F_G L_r/\Omega) \end{bmatrix} \begin{bmatrix} M_{t-1} \\ G_{t-1} \end{bmatrix} + \begin{bmatrix} -\alpha r^* \\ \beta Y^* \end{bmatrix}$$

A necessary condition for stability is that the absolute value of the trace of the matrix $A$ (tr($A$)) should be less than the number equations in the system and that the absolute value of the determinant of $A$ (det($A$)) should be less than unity (see Baumol, 1959, pp. 56–264). Now:

$$\text{tr}(A) = |2 + (\alpha - \beta F_G L_r)/\Omega| < 2$$

iff $(\alpha - \beta F_G L_r)/\Omega < 0$, which is certainly the case.

$$\text{Det}(A) = |1 + (\alpha - \beta F_G L_r)/\Omega - \alpha\beta F_G/\Omega| < 1$$

iff $(\alpha - \beta F_G L_r - \alpha\beta F_G) > 0$.

Let us examine the case when $F_r \to -\infty$.

$$\lim \text{tr}(A) \to 2 \quad \text{as } F_r \to -\infty$$
$$\lim \text{Det}(A) \to 1 \quad \text{as } F_r \to -\infty.$$

Since these are necessary conditions, a violation will imply instability.

## Appendix 2: Optimal macroeconomic policy with uncertainty

Poole (1970) shows that in the context of a Hicksian *IS-LM* model, the authorities can stabilise output by operating on either an interest rate rule or a money supply rule. For certain parameter values one rule can dominate the other. It is also shown that in principle a combination policy exists, where the interest rate and money stock are maintained in a certain relationship to each other such that this combination policy dominate the other two.

Consider the following fixed-price IS-LM set-up.

$$Y = F(r, G^*) + u \quad F_r < 0, F_G > 0 \quad \textit{IS Schedule}$$
$$L(r, Y) = M^* + v \quad L_r < 0, L_Y > 0 \quad \textit{LM Schedule}$$

where $Y$ is real output, $r$ is the rate of interest, $G^*$ is the exogenous level of government spending, $M^*$ is the exogenously given stock of money and $U$ and $v$ are stochastic terms with $E(u) = E(v) = 0$ and $E(u)^2 = \sigma_u^2$, $E(v)^2 = \sigma_v^2$. A linearised representation of the model can be set out as follows:

$$\begin{bmatrix} 1 & -F_r \\ L_Y & L_r \end{bmatrix} \begin{bmatrix} Y \\ r \end{bmatrix} = \begin{bmatrix} F_G G^* + u \\ M^* + v \end{bmatrix}$$

Solving for $Y$ using Cramer's rule, yields:

$$Y = \Omega^{-1}\{L_r(F_G G^* + u) + F_r(M^* + v)\} \tag{1}$$

where $\Omega = L_r + F_r L_Y < 0$.

Taking expectations and solving for $M^*$ produces the optimal money stock policy.

$$M^* = (\Omega/F_r)Y^* - (L_r F_G/F_r)G^*. \tag{2}$$

Substituting (2) in (1) produces:

$$Y - Y^* = \Omega^{-1}\{L_r u + F_r v\}. \tag{3}$$

Defining a loss function $£ = E[Y - Y^*]^2$ and evaluating from (3).

$$£_m = \Omega^{-2}\{L_r^2\sigma_u^2 + F_r^2\sigma_v^2\}$$
$$= \{\sigma_u^2 + (F_r/L_r)^2\sigma_v^2\}/[1 + (F_rL_Y/L_r)]^2.$$

By being willing to buy and sell government bonds in unlimited quantities at a fixed prices, the policy-maker can peg the rate of interest. Pegging the rate of interest at $r^*$ we can obtain, after taking expectations, from the *IS* schedule the following optimal policy response;

$$r^* = \{Y^* - F_GG^*\}/F_r.$$

Substituting (4) into the IS schedule yields:

$$Y - Y^* = u.$$

Therefore the loss evaluation for the optimal interest rate policy is:

$$£_r = \sigma_u^2.$$

The interest rate policy rule dominates the money stock rule if

$$\sigma_u^2 < \{\sigma_u^2 + (F_r/L_r)^2\sigma_v^2\}/[1 + (F_rL_Y/L_r)]^2.$$

We find that a policy of pegging the rate of interest tends to be superior when shocks are primarily monetary in nature ($\sigma_v^2 \gg \sigma_u^2$) and when expenditure is highly sensitive to interest changes ($F_r \to -\infty$). Alternatively, if money demand is strongly responsive to the rate of interest ($L_r \to -\infty$) or if real shocks dominate monetary shocks ($\sigma_u^2 \gg \sigma_v^2$), then the money stock policy is superior to the interest rate pegging policy. However, Poole (1970) shows that there exists a combination policy which dominates both the interest rate and money stock policies. A combination policy takes the form:

$$M = M^* + K_rr + v. \tag{5}$$

Equating (5) with the demand for money, solving for $Y$ in the system above, and taking expectations, we derive:

$$Y - E(Y) = \{(L_r - K_r)u + F_rv\}/[(L_r - K_r) + F_rL_Y]$$

and

$$£_{mr} = [(L_r - K_r)^2\sigma_u^2 + F_r^2\sigma_v^2]/\{(L_r - K_r) + F_rL_Y\}^2.$$

Minimising $\pounds_{mr}$ with respect to $K_r$ yields

$$\frac{\delta \pounds_{mr}}{\delta K_r} = -[(L_r - K_r) + F_r L_Y](L_r - K_r)\sigma_u^2$$
$$+ (L_r - K_r)^2 \sigma_u^2 - F_r^2 \sigma_v^2 = 0.$$

Rearranging and solving for $K_r$

$$K_r = \{F_r \sigma_v^2 + L_r L_Y \sigma_u^2\}/L_Y \sigma_u^2.$$

Substituting the result into the combined policy rule in (5), and solving for the loss value, produces after some tedious algebra a solution that can be shown to be superior to either of the other rules. It is clear that the analysis of the instrument and target problem with uncertainty applies only to situations in which the policy-maker has complete knowledge of the parameters, the structure of the model and stochastic structure of the economy. In practice, this assumption is highly questionable.

## Appendix 3: The link between monetary and fiscal policy

The starting point of the analysis is equation (8.18) in the main text.

$$G_t - T_t + r_{t-1}B_{t-1} = (B_t - B_{t-1}) + (M_t - M_{t-1}).$$

The term on the left is roughly what is described in the UK as the Public Sector Borrowing Requirement. The term on the right is the addition to the stock of government bonds ($B$) and the addition to the stock of high-powered money ($M$) – or M0 as it is known. In a closed economy, the stock of 'outside' financial wealth ($W$) is made up of money and government bonds:

$$W_t = M_t + B_t$$

Dividing the balance sheet constraint by $W_{t-1}$:

$$PSBR_t/W_{t-1} = [(B_t - B_{t-1}) + (M_t - M_{t-1})]/W_{t-1},$$

which can also be written as:

$$\frac{PSBR_t}{W_{t-1}} = (B_t - B_{t-1})B_{t-1}/W_{t-1} + (M_t - M_{t-1})M_{t-1}/W_{t-1}$$
$$= \Phi Db = (1 - \Phi)Dm$$

where D$b$ is the proportional rate of growth of bonds, D$m$ is the proportional rate of growth of money, $\Phi$ is the share of bonds in the private sector portfolio of financial wealth and $(1 - \Phi)$ is the corresponding share of base money. In the long run the economy is assumed to be in full portfolio equilibrium. This is when the portfolio is in equilibrium and all assets are allocated so as to equalise marginal returns. Therefore yields and relative rates of return are at steady-state and are constant. This implies that all assets are growing at the same rate and the PSBR, if non-zero, is being financed by bonds and money in strict proportion $\Phi$ and $(1 - \Phi)$. Therefore D$m$ = D$b$. Consequently the PSBR – GDP ratio and the rate of growth of the money supply have to be consistent to ensure long-run equilibrium. Both items were the subject of the government's Medium Term Financial Strategy in the 1980s. Thus:

$$(\beta)PSBR_t/Y_t = Dm,$$

where $Y$ is the level of money GDP and $\theta$ is the ratio of GDP to total financial wealth.

## Appendix 4: Reputation and credibility

The problem of time – inconsistency is much modified if endogenisation occurs in a framework that allows for the notion of reputation. It is precisely the threat of or loss of reputation which may motivate the controller not to renege on the announced *ex ante* optimal plan.

Barro and Gordon (1983a) assume the following cost function:

$$Z = (a/2)\pi^2 - b(\pi - \pi^e) \quad a, b > 0. \tag{1}$$

The objective of the controller is to minimise the discounted present value of all expected costs. The control variable for the controller is $\pi$ and the choice variable for the private sector is $\pi^e$. Time-inconsistency occurs in this model because, by persuading private agents to hold a particular $\pi^e$, the controller can exploit the gains from unexpected inflation. The model distinguishes three types of policies.

(1) discretionary policy;
(2) the policy rule;
(3) cheating.

Discretionary policy is when agents perceive of the incentive for the controller to renege. This is the outcome under the Nash assumption being time consistent with $\pi^e = \pi^\wedge > 0$. Therefore:

$$\delta Z/\delta\pi = a\pi - b = 0$$
$$\pi^\wedge = (b/a).$$

This is the $\pi$ that minimises costs given that agents perceive $\pi^e$, the Nash assumption being time consistent. Substituting the value of $\pi$ in the cost function produces the cost of conducting discretionary policy, when $\pi = \pi^e$.

$$Z^\wedge = (b^2)/(2a).$$

The policy rule corresponds to the *ex ante* optimal policy, which is time inconsistent. This is the policy that the controller would precommit. Since $\pi = \pi^e$, the optimal value of $\pi = 0$. Hence:

$$\pi^* = 0$$
$$Z^* = 0$$

The third policy is the 'cheating' or time-inconsistent full optimal policy obtained by getting the private sector to have $\pi^e = 0$. Then:

$$\pi^\sim = (b/a)$$
$$Z^\sim = -(b^2/2a).$$

In terms of cost minimisation the three policies can be rated as:

$$\text{first best} \quad - Z^\sim \text{ cheating}$$
$$\text{second best} - Z^* \text{ policy rule}$$
$$\text{third best} \quad - Z^\wedge \text{ discretion}$$

Barro and Gordon (1983b) examine whether the desire to maintain a reputation would be enough for the controller to maintain a sustainable rule. They do this by introducing certain *enforcement rules*. If the controller engineers a higher rate of inflation than people expect, then agents will raise their expectations of future inflation. Thus the cost of cheating is an increase in inflation expectations. Specifically if $\pi_{t-1} = \pi^e_{t-1}$ credibility is enhanced, otherwise there is distrust and the Nash policy is enforced. Therefore the gains from reneging must be judeged against the costs of reputation.

The cost of cheating is the enforcement rule:

$$\eta_c = E[1/(1 + r)] (Z\hat{}_{t+1} - Z^*_{t+1}). \qquad (2)$$

The temptation to cheat is given by:

$$\eta_T = E(Z^* - Z\tilde{}). \qquad (3)$$

Provided $\eta_T > \eta_c$, the controller will adhere to the announced policy. If the inequality is reversed, the solution is unsustainable. The reason for this is because the costs of reneging come later and are therefore appropriately discounted. Since agents know that $\pi^*$ is non-feasible, there has to be positive inflation in equilibrium. This can be seen from (2) and (3) by substituting the appropriate values for the $Z$s:

$$\eta_c = \{1/(1 + r)\} \{b^2/2a - a\pi^2/2\}$$
$$= (a/2)[(b/a)^2 - \pi^2]/(1 + r)$$

$$\eta_T = (a/2)[b/a - \pi]^2$$

These two functions are plotted in Figure 8A.3. People will find the enforced policy credible only if they perceive that the costs of cheating are greater than the benefits. This occurs only in the range between P and Q. Therefore the best enforceable rule is at point $P$ which lies between the ideal rule and the discretionary rule. The minimum cost rule is;

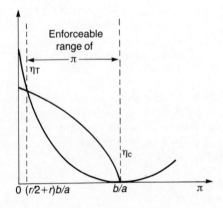

Fig 8A.3

$$\pi^* = (b/a)[r/(2 + r)]$$
$$EZ^* = (b^2/2a)[r/(2 + r)].$$

Notice that as $r \to 0$ this goes some way towards making the ideal rule credible.

## References

Alesina, A. (1987), 'Macroeconomic policy in a two-party system as a repeated game', *Quarterly Journal of Economics*, August.

Alt, J. (1980), 'Political business cycles in Britain', Chapter 6 in P. Whiteley (ed.), *Models of Political Economy*, London: Sage.

Alt, J. (1979), *The Politics of Economic Decline*, Cambridge: Cambridge University Press.

Backus, D. and Driffil, E. (1985), 'Rational expectations and policy credibility following a change in regime', *Review of Economic Studies*, 52.

Barro, R. M. (1990), *Macroeconomics*, 3rd edn, New York: John Wiley.

Barro, R. J. and Gordon, D. B. (1983a), 'Rules, discretion and reputation in a model of monetary policy', *Journal of Monetary Economics*, 12.

Barro, R. J. and Gordon, D. B. (1983b), 'A positive theory of monetary policy in a natural rate model', *Journal of Political Economy*, August.

Baumol, W. J. (1959), *Economic Dynamics*, 2nd edn, New York: Macmillan.

Blackburn, K. and Christensen, M. (1989), 'Monetary policy and policy credibility', *Journal of Economic Literature*, 27, March.

Blinder, A. S. and Solow, R. M. (1974), 'Analytical foundations of fiscal policy', in A. S. Blinder *et al.*, *The Economics of Public Finance*, Washington DC: The Brookings Institution.

Boltho, A. (1981), 'British fiscal policy 1955–1971: Stabilising or destabilising?', *Oxford Bulletin of Economics and Statistics*, November.

Brainard, W. (1967), 'Uncertainty and the effectiveness of policy', *American Economic Review*, Papers and Proceedings, 57.

Bruno, M. (1982), 'World Shocks, macroeconomic response and the productivity puzzle', in R. C. O. Matthews (ed.), *Slower Growth in the Western World*, London: Heinemann.

Bruno, M. and Sachs, J. (1983), 'Input price shocks and the slow-down in economic growth', *Review of Economic Studies*, 50.

Buiter, W. H. and Miller, M. (1981a), 'Monetary policy and international competitiveness: the problems of adjustment', *Oxford*

*Economic Papers*, Supplement, 33.

Buiter, W. H. and Miller, M. (1981b), 'The Thatcher experiment: the first two years', *Brooking Papers on Economic Activity*, No. 2.

Buiter, W. H. and Miller, M. (1983), 'Changing the rules: economic consequences of the Thatcher regime', *Brookings Papers on Economic Activity*, No. 2.

Canzoneri, M. B. (1985), 'Monetary policy games and the role of private information', *American Economic Review*, 75.

Christ, C. F. (1968), 'A simple Macroeconomic model with a government budget restraint', *Journal of Political Economy*, 76.

Dow, J. C. (1964), *The Management of the British Economy, 1945–60*, Cambridge: Cambridge University Press:

Friedman, M. (1953), 'The effects of a full-employment policy on economic stability: a formal analysis', in his *Essays in Positive Economics*, Chicago: University of Chicago Press.

Friedman, M. (1968), 'The role of monetary policy', *American Economic Review*, 58, March.

Golden, D. and Poterba, J. (1980), 'The price of popularity: the political business cycle reexamined', *American Journal of Political Science*, 24, November.

Hansen, N. (1969), *Fiscal Policy in Seven Countries, 1955–65*, Paris: OECD.

Kydland, F. E. and Prescott, E. C. (1977), 'Rules rather than discretion: the inconsistency of optimal plans', *Journal of Political Economy*, 85.

Little, I. D. (1966), 'Review of Dow', *Economic Journal*, December.

Lucas, R. E. (1976), 'Econometric policy evaluation: a critique', in K. Brunner and A. H. Meltzer (eds), *The Phillips Curve and Labour Markets*, Carnegie-Rochester Conference Series on Public Policy, 1, Supp. to *Journal of Monetary Economics*.

Matthews, K. G. P. (1989), 'The UK economic renaissance', *Economics*, 25, 107.

Matthews, K. (1985), 'Policy alternatives before and after the next election', Liverpool Research Group in Macroeconomics, *Quarterly Economic Bulletin*, 6(4), December.

Matthews, K. and Minford, P. (1987), 'Mrs Thatcher's economic policies 1979–1987', *Economic Policy*, No. 5.

Matthews, R. C. O., Feinstein, C. H. and Odling-Smee, J. C. (1982), *British Economic Growth 1856–1973*, Stanford, Calif.: Stanford University Press.

Minford, P. (1980), 'Memorandum', in *Memoranda on Monetary Policy*, Treasury and Civil Service Committee, Sess 1979–80, HC720, London: HMSO.

Minford, P. with Davies, D., Peel, M. and Sprague, A. (1983), *Unemployment Cause and Cure*, Oxford: Martin Robertson.

Minford, P. and Rastogi, A. (1989), 'A new classical programme', Chapter 4 in A. Brittan (ed.), *Policy Making with Macro Models*, London: Gower; pp. 83–97.

Mundell, R. A. (1962), 'The appropriate use of monetary and fiscal policy for internal and external stability', *IMF Staff Papers*, 9.

Musgrave, R. A. and Musgrave, P. E. (1968), 'Fiscal policy', in R. E. Caves (ed.), *Britain's Economic Prospects*, London: Allen & Unwin.

Muth, J. F. (1961), 'Rational expectations and the theory of price movements', *Econometrica*, 38.

Nordhaus, W. D. (1975), 'The political business cycle', *Review of Economic Studies*, 42.

Parkin, M. and Bade, R. (1989), *Modern Macroeconomics*, 2nd edn, Scarborough, Ont.: Prentice-Hall Canada.

Phelps, E. S. (1967), 'Phillips curves, expectations of inflation and optimal unemployment over time', *Economica*, 34.

Phillips, A. W. (1958), 'The relationship between unemployment and the rate of change of money wage rates in the UK, 1861–1957', *Economica*, 25.

Poole, W. (1970), 'Optimal choice of monetary policy instruments in a simple stochastic macro model', *Quarterly Journal of Economics*, 84.

Radcliffe Committee (1959), *Committee on the Workings of the Monetary System Report*, Cmnd 827, London: HMSO.

Sargent, T. (1986), 'Stopping moderate inflations: The method of Poincaré and Thatcher', in *Rational Expectations and Inflation*, New York: Harper & Row.

Sargent, T. J. and Wallace, N. (1981), 'Some unpleasant monetarist arithmetic', *Quarterly Review*, Federal Reserve Bank of Minneapolis, Fall; reprinted in T. Sargent, *Rational Expectations and Inflation*, New York: Harper & Row, 1986.

Surrey, M. (1971), 'The analysis and forecasting of the British economy', Occasional Paper XXV, National Institute of Economic and Social Research.

Taylor, J. B. (1979), 'Staggered wage setting in a macroeconomic model', *American Economic Review*, Papers and Proceedings, 69.

Theil, H. (1964), *Optimal Decision Rules for Government and Industry*, Amsterdam: North-Holland.

Tinbergen, J. (1956), *Economic Policy: Principles and Design*, Amsterdam: North-Holland.

Walters, A. A. (1971), 'Consistent expectations, distributed lags and the quantity theory', *Economic Journal*, 81.

# International monetary economics

The issue of 'What's new in international monetary economics' relates fundamentally to the lessons to be learned from the experience of floating exchange rates. Since 1973 many of the world's major currencies have been floating and the period has been marked by dramatic and unexpected exchange rate volatility, substantial and persistent current account imbalances and severe Third World debt.[1]

Certainly, many advocates of floating rates predicted that a floating rate regime would show some instability early on, but would eventually settle down. However, this has not been borne out in practice: exchange rates have continued to be volatile on a short-term basis and have also displayed long cycles which are hard to explain. For example, during 1980–85 the US dollar appreciated against nearly all currencies (the pound sterling was an exception during 1980–1); then in 1985, the trend was reversed and the dollar depreciated against all major currencies. For example, between the first quarter of 1985 and the second quarter of 1986 the depreciation of the US dollar against the Deutschmark amounted to over 40 per cent. Such sharp changes in the direction and level of exchange rate movements appear to have had significant implications for world trade and have led to renewed interest in issues of international macroeconomic policy coordination, particularly that of exchange rate targets or zones. These matters are taken up in the fourth section of the chapter.

But first, attention is given to the rather more general issue of exchange rate determination. Several models have been devised to try and explain why (flexible) exchange rates have changed suddenly, 'overshot' and finally moved back some way towards their starting position. This observed pattern of exchange rates is so alien to the gradual adjustment expected by the advocates of flexible exchange rates that a large literature has been generated in this field. In general, there are two types of exchange rate movements to be explained: (1) short-run (day-to-day and month-to-month) fluctuations and (2) long-run shifts in the level of exchange rates.

## Variability of exchange rates – is it important?

As noted above, exchange rate variability has been more substantial than expected by the advocates of the flexible exchange rate system; and the observed volatility has led to controversies concerning the appropriateness of such a system for an optimal allocation of resources. Some claim that exchange rates have become excessively variable; and others see nothing special to worry about. Certainly, many problems of the world economy have been blamed upon the variability of exchange rates (see IMF, 1984, for an overview of the issues); but the debate really hinges upon the extent to which causation can be attributed to exchange rate movements alone. There are essentially two issues: (1) do variable exchange rates cause inflation? and (2) do variable exchange rates cause a slowdown in economic growth? These are considered in turn.

### Inflation

It is undeniable that average inflation has been higher during the floating regime than during the Bretton Woods era. What is not so clear is whether this is because monetary authorities, freed from the foreign exchange rate constraint, have exercised less discipline and pursued more inflationary policies or whether the 'dollar standard' (which gave an inflationary bias to the world system during the late 1960s and early 1970s) has continued to be responsible for the large cycles in the inflation rate of the industrial countries. This debate looks set to run (see De Grauwe, 1989).

### Slow growth

Similarly, it is undeniable that the industrialised world has experienced a significant decline in the growth rate of output since 1973. This may be because the increased variability of exchange rates has increased the risks of engaging in international trade and so created an effective non-tariff barrier to trade. Or, on the other hand, it may be that long-term deviations of exchange rates from purchasing power parity – the 'mislignments' – have led to real effects in the economy; for example, by leading to a recession in the traded goods sectors of countries whose currencies have been overvalued and vice versa.[2] In recent years there have been several attempts to gather empirical evidence both on the effect of exchange rate variability on trade (for example, De Grauwe, 1988, DeGrauwe and de Bellfroid, 1987, Kenen and Rodrik, 1986) and on the costs of misalignments. On balance, it seems that there is some discernible negative effect of exchange rate variability on trade, but the empirical evidence is weak; there is much stronger evidence that exchange rate variability has had a negative effect upon growth (see for example, Williamson, 1983), and Bergsten and Williamson, 1983, although we have learned from the European Monetary System that stable exchange rates are not sufficient to obtain better growth prospects (see De Grauwe, 1989, pp. 229–31).

Taken as a whole, it seems that variability of the exchange rates and especially the misalignments that have occurred since the early 1970s has been costly for the world economy. Not surprisingly, then, much recent work in international monetary economics addresses (a) the question of 'what causes high variability of exchange rates? and (b) the more general question of 'how are exchange rates determined?'

### Causes of high variability

There are essentially two schools of thought on the causes of high exchange rate variability: either exchange rate variability reflects variability in the economic fundamentals; or it does not! The 'fundamentalist view' is consistent with the rational expectations (perfect foresight) models in which economic agents calculate the effects of exogenous shocks on the exchange rate, often leading to (requiring) overshooting of the exchange rate. In this view, exchange rate variability will reflect variability of the underlying fundamentals.

The 'non-fundamentalist view' has many versions: perhaps economic agents are irrational and do not attach importance to fundamentals; or they assign some probability to the exchange rate drifting away from the fundamentals solution as in 'rational bubbles'; or, economic agents are so extremely uncertain about the underlying economic model driving the exchange rate that actual exchange rate movements are driven by backward-looking rules or fads. The different views have important implications for policy: in the fundamentalists' view of the world, any attempts to reduce exchange rate variability will usually lead to more variability of other economic variables, e.g. output or prices; this is not the case when exchange rate variability is disconnected from the variability of the underlying fundamentals, in which case one can reduce the variability of the exchange rate without increasing the variability somewhere else in the system. Some awareness of these schools of thought will facilitate an understanding of the ways in which recent research has been directed – the major objective of this work has been to find an acceptable model of exchange rate determination.

## Exchange rate determination

Basic building blocks for many of the current models of exchange rate determination are: the long-run concept of purchasing power parity; short-run interest rate parity; and the notion that efficient markets generate nominal exchange rate changes. It is common to consider the efficient market theory of exchange rate determination as a separate entity, which is the practice followed here. First, we consider the two main views of exchange rate determination – the monetary approach (flex-price and sticky-price) and the portfolio balance (asset) approach.

### The monetary approach

The flex-price model incorporates long-run purchasing power parity (PPP) and continuous uncovered interest rate parity (UIP), and assumes perfect substitutability between domestic and foreign assets. In this case, money is neutral in the sense that changes in the money stock do not have effects on the real economy and the price level in an economy is proportional to the domestic money stock. Thus, if one country unilaterally expanded its money stock it would experience inflation and a depreciation of its currency's foreign exchange value. However, if both countries engaged in monetary expansion, together and at the same rate, both would suffer inflation at home but there would be no change in their mutual exchange rate.

The general form of this model can be expressed, in logarithmic form, as follows:

$$e = p - p^* \quad \text{(the condition for PPP)}$$
$$m = p + cy - dr \quad \text{(money-market equilibrium condition)}$$
$$m^* = p^* + cy^* - dr^*$$

where

$e$ = the exchange rate (the inverse of 'the price of foreign exchange');

$p$ = the price level

and an asterisk refers to the respective variable in the foreign country.

Assuming equilibrium in the money markets both home and abroad,

$$e = (m - m^*) + d^*r^* - dr + c^*y^* - cy.$$

From this expression it can be seen that an increase in the domestic money supply (output/interest rate), relative to the foreign money stock (output/ rate), will lead to an exchange rate depreciation (appreciation). These are strong results, but ones which do not square with the post-1973 experience. In particular, as an equilibrium model, it cannot explain deviations from trend or disturbance to the equilibrium. It cannot explain why, since 1973, there have been short-term deviations from PPP if only because the wide movements in exchange rates have not been matched by movements in relative prices. It cannot explain why, in the UK over the period 1979–81, the sterling nominal effective exchange rate (against a basket of currencies) *appreciated* substantially even though the UK money supply grew rapidly relative to growth in the 'world' money supply. These features, coupled with more general evidence that PPP has not held continuously (see Frenkel, 1981, Taylor, 1988b), has led to the development of models which relax the assumption that PPP holds continuously. This is the essence of the sticky-price version of the monetary model.

## Sticky-price monetary models

These models allow for the fact that there can be sustained deviations from PPP, but retain the assumption of perfect substitutability between domestic and foreign assets. They are associated primarily with Dornbusch (1976) and allow for substantial overshooting of the exchange rate above the long-run equilibrium (PPP) level. The 'sticky' price is the domestic price level, which is assumed to adjust in response to excess (deficient) aggregate demand, but takes time to do so; PPP is violated in the short run but holds in the long run; 'uncovered' interest parity is assumed, which means that any difference between domestic and foreign interest rates has to be compensated by expected changes in the exchange rate. Agents form their expectations rationally (although it should be pointed out that the original Dornbusch, 1976, article has a regressive expectations scheme which is later shown to be consistent with rational expectations in particular circumstances). Uncovered interest parity implies:

$$r = r^* + x$$

where $x$ is the rate of depreciation of the domestic currency.

In this model, consistent with PPP, an expansionary monetary policy will, in the long run, lead to inflation and a depreciation of the exchange rate. However, in the short run, because the domestic price level is sticky, domestic real balances will rise, creating an excess supply in the domestic money market. Assuming output is constant, domestic interest rates must fall to equilibrate the money market, thereby creating an interest rate differential with the rest of the world. This will lead to a capital outflow (thereby depreciating the currency).

The behaviour of asset holders is critical: these agents are assumed to form their expectations of movements in the exchange rate consistent with the condition of uncovered interest rate parity (UIP); they therefore expect the exchange rate to appreciate (see the UIP equation above). When holding foreign currency, these agents will balance the capital gain (from the interest rate differential) against the expected loss (from converting back into the domestic currency on less favourable terms). Short-run equilibrium prevails when the expected rate of appreciation exactly equals the interest rate differential (again, see the UIP equation above). However, since the expected rate of appreciation is positive, PPP has been overshot. The short-run capital outflow must have brought about a sharp depreciation of the currency.

In the medium run, the domestic price level starts to rise, and in the domestic money market the interest rate starts to rise; in the foreign exchange market, the currency starts to appreciate in order to converge with the long-run PPP.

In this overshooting model, it is clear that, from the assumed long-run PPP, the exchange rate needs to depreciate; yet UIP indicates that agents must anticipate an appreciation of the currency. To square these two things, 'the exchange rate must jump immediately in a depreciating direction to a point from which it can appreciate. Since it must have depreciated in the long-run, this initial jump must take it too far so that it can appreciate back to the long-run equilibrium' (Chrystal, 1989, p. 223). This model is currently thought to provide a powerful explanation of the recent volatility of exchange rates (see, for example, Bleaney and Greenaway, 1989, p. 21) and consequently has a central role in current international monetary economics. It does, for example, provide an explanation for the observation that countries with relatively high interest rates tend to have currencies whose exchange rate is expected to depreciate: the initial rise in interest rates leads to a step appreciation of the exchange rate after which a slow depreciation is expected in order to satisfy uncovered interest rate parity (MacDonald and Taylor, 1989, p. 9).

### The portfolio approach

The latest generation of models of exchange rate determination (i) retain the capacity to 'generate' overshooting; (ii) give an alternative derivation which does not rely solely on price level stickiness; and (iii) demonstrate that overshooting is not an inevitable outcome of a monetary shock. These are the portfolio models associated with Buiter and Miller (1981; see Branson and Henderson, 1985, for a survey). The major innovation is typically defined as the incorporation of portfolio or asset stock equilibrium into the analysis of exchange rates – hence the label.

In practical terms, the model relaxes two of the assumptions that are made in the monetary models described above. Domestic and foreign assets are no longer assumed to be perfect sub-stitutes; and the wealth effects of a current account deficit or surplus are no longer assumed to be negligible. Domestic residents are assumed to hold their wealth in a portfolio of money, domestic bonds and foreign bonds. Thus the asset sector of a simple portfolio model contains behavioural equations describing the demand for money, the demand for domestic (non-traded) bonds and the demand for foreign traded bonds. Importantly, real wealth enters both the demand for money equation and the aggregate demand equation (positively). Additionally there is a direct effect of exchange rate changes on the price level: as the exchange rate depreciates, the domestic price level rises as a result of the import content of domestic purchases. The assumption of continuous uncovered interest rate parity is retained, thereby defining the link between foreign and domestic interest rates.

The sluggishness in the dynamics of this system relates to the fact that, following a shock, foreign assets can be accumulated only gradually over time. This is in sharp contrast to the exchange rate, which is free to jump as soon as the shock is felt. Consider again the example of an expansionary monetary policy. Again, there will be an immediate depreciation in the exchange rate (as rational expectations of future current account imbalance prompts agents to enter the foreign exchange market). The economy then runs a current account surplus which involves domestic residents accumulating foreign assets. This additional wealth forces up both aggregate demand and the demand for money, bringing both the current account and the domestic money market back towards equilibrium.

In the meanwhile the monetary expansion will have exerted upward pressure on prices, thereby bringing about a deterioration of competitiveness, again bringing a move towards equilibrium. Thus, in this model, the fact that the exchange rate is free to adjust, while other prices or asset portfolios take time to adjust, gives rise to the possibility of the exchange rate over-shooting its long-run equilibrium.

### Empirical assessments

It is clear that the portfolio model is the most general of the exchange rate theories; however, the question of which theory best fits the facts is an empirical matter. The issue is an important one, not least because of the differing policy conclusions to be derived from the theories. For example, the monetary approach indicates that only non-sterilised foreign exchange intervention is effective, whereas in the portfolio model both sterilised and non-sterilised intervention can be effective (see Genberg, 1981). Much recent research has been directed to such empirical assessments of the theories.

As noted earlier, some studies have been devoted to testing short- and long-run versions of purchasing power parity and resoundingly direct us to a greater focus on models which relax the assumption of continuous purchasing power parity. The main emphasis is therefore on the sticky-price monetary models and the portfolio model; although, for completeness, many investigators retain the flex-price monetary model in their set (see MacDonald and Taylor, 1989, pp. 28–57, for an excellent survey of the evidence on monetary versus portfolio models of the exchange rate).

A major first hurdle for the investigator of the sticky-price monetary model is to model the form of the stickiness in the model. Two different approaches are discernible: for example, Driskell (1981) specifies an equation to describe the time path of prices; and Frankel (1979) splits the interest rate effect of a monetary change into real and inflationary components (now often referred to as the real interest differential (RID) model). The overriding concern has been to derive reduced-form equations from the specified models which permit empirical discrimination. Such equations are relatively easily found (see MacDonald and Taylor, 1989, p. 34); unfortunately there is a potential simultaneity problem in that the dependent variable is the exchange rate and relative money stocks appear on the right-hand side of the equations. To the extent that monetary authorities can and do engage in active intervention in the foreign exchange market, this problem may be severe.

With this warning, it can be noted that the monetary approach appeared to have empirical support for the period 1973–8; but in the 1980s empirical work has cast serious doubt on this model's ability to explain exchange rate movements. For example, Backus (1984) and Frankel (1984) find that the RID model fits poorly, exhibits autocorrelation , coefficients are incorrectly signed, etc.

Indeed, one coefficient magnitude has had special attention since it indicates that an expansionary monetary policy would bring about an appreciation of the domestic currency ('the mystery of the multiplying marks' – Frankel, 1982)! In general, the current assessment of this work is that these reduced-form equations were misspecified (even in the 1970s) and that more work is needed to improve the specification. This has taken the form of: identifying possible omitted variables (in particular, a number of researchers have sought to combine aspects of both the monetary and portfolio models); considering other specifications for the model's dynamics; or, most recently, estimating models structurally (see, for example, Kearney and MacDonald, 1985, and Smith and Wickens, 1988, who estimate the Buiter–Miller, 1981, model).

The latest empirical models of exchange rate determination incorporate some features of the portfolio model together with 'the impact of the current account'. In particular, foreign and domestic assets are modelled as imperfectly substitutable and 'news' of the current account appears as an explanatory variable (see Hooper and Morton, 1982, and Frankel, 1983, 1984). However, even these models cannot outperform the forecasting performance of the random walk model of exchange rates, for the dollar–mark exchange rate, the dollar–yen exchange rate and the dollar–sterling exchange rate, with the possible exception when the forecast horizon is in excess of one year (see Meese and Rogoff, 1983, and Meese and Rogoff, 1984; see also Salemi, 1984, Finn, 1986). The Meese and Rogoff result is devastating: their study involved full pairwise comparisons of the forecasting performance of the flexible-price monetary model, the real interest differential (RID) version of the sticky-price monetary model and the portfolio–monetary synthesis against the random walk model, the forward exchange rate and an autoregression of the spot rate. None of these alternatives outperformed the simple random walk. The only counter-attacks seem to rest on the issue of data frequency or instabilities in the international monetary system. Meese and Rogoff used monthly data, which are inherently noisy, and, as MacDonald and Taylor (1989) argue, it is perhaps unfair to expect the asset approach to perform particularly well on such data (p. 56). Additionally, it should be remembered that the experience of the floating exchange rate regime has been one of turbulent phases with massive interventions by central banks alternating with periods of relative calm. In such an environment, it is difficult to identify issues of cause and effect necessary for estimating and forecasting exchange rate models.

Given the course of empirical discovery in this field, it is perhaps not altogether surprising that relatively little work has been carried out on the most recent of the theoretical models – the portfolio model. However, there are other reasons for the relative dearth of empirical work in this area: bluntly there is a lack of good disaggregated data on non-monetary assets. Nevertheless, some studies do exist which essentially test the hypothesis of whether bonds denominated in different currencies are perfect substitutes. These studies test for a risk premium in the uncovered interest parity equation (see, for example, MacDonald and Taylor, 1988).

The broad conclusion remains that the reduced forms of these models seem to be misspecified. Moreover, they appear to have a weaker forecasting performance than a random walk model of the exchange rate. What's new amounts to continued work in structural estimation of models of exchange rate determination and a new interest in the random walk result. The explanatory power of the random walk model, in part, supports the view that researchers should be relating (and regressing) unanticipated exchange rate movements on surprise/news variables in the asset markets. Some recent work tackles this issue directly and is discussed further in the next section.

## The foreign exchange market and the efficient market hypothesis

The variability of nominal exchange rates under the floating exchange rate regime has been less than the variability of some other asset prices: for example, in the period 1973–80, the average absolute monthly changes in nominal bilateral exchange rates for the seven major currencies were typically smaller than changes in national stock market prices; also, for the period 1973–83, the exchange rate fluctuated less than either short-term interest rates, long-term bond yields, or commodity prices (Bergstrand, 1983). However, the similarity in the movement of

295

exchange rates and other financial asset prices has resulted in more empirical studies of the foreign exchange markets.

One particular aspect of financial asset prices is that they are usually regarded as operating in efficient markets, and it seems natural to ask whether the foreign exchange market behaves in a manner consistent with the efficient markets hypothesis. In practice, this means addressing four questions:

(1) Are forward exchange rates optimal predictors of future exchange rates?
(2) Is the market using all relevant information in forming its expectations of future spot rates?
(3) Are unexpected changes in the exchange rate random?
(4) does the exchange rate follow a random walk?

Answering (1) involves a fairly straightforward linear regression of the change in the exchange rate on a constant and the deviation between the forward rate and the actual exchange rate. Simple hypothesis testing on whether the constant term is zero, the coefficient on the independent variable term is unity and the error term is white noise provides all that is required to test (1). In this way, authors can address the joint hypothesis that agents in the foreign exchange market are risk neutral and rational. Many authors have carried out this exercise (see, for example, Fama, 1984, and Taylor, 1988a). In all cases the joint efficiency/ risk-neutrality hypothesis is rejected by the data.

It is important to recognise that the interpretation placed on rejection depends crucially on a researcher's prejudices. Thus, Longworth (1981) and Cumby and Obstfeld (1984) maintain that agents are risk neutral and that the rejection is due to irrationality – excessive speculation relative to the conditioning information set. On the other hand, Fama (1984) and Bilson (1985) retain the assumption the agents are rational and assert that the rejection result is attributable to time-varying risk premia.

More generally, since most economists would tend to regard the rational expectations hypothesis as a reasonable approximation to the behaviour of participants in asset markets – because such agents have easy access to high-quality information sources and have an incentive to use them effectively – researchers have sought explanations for the rejection of the joint hypothesis outside that of the rational expectations hypothesis. In particular, they have examined the so-called 'peso problem' and 'bubbles', as well as the possible existence of a time-varying risk premium. These are considered in turn.

### Rationalising the rejection

#### The 'peso problem'

At this stage it may be helpful to recall an earlier discussion on two schools of thought on exchange rate determination: the fundamentalists and the non-fundamentalists. The former attribute exchange rate variability to variability in the underlying economic fundamentals, whereas the latter identify other sources of observed variability. The 'peso problem' attributes some explanatory power to agents assigning a positive (typically very small) probability to large step-devaluation in the peso (i.e. assigning a very small positive probability to the outcome of a large change in the market fundamentals; see Krasker, 1980). The term was coined to describe the phenomenon of a consistently non-zero forward premium for the Mexican peso–US dollar exchange rate, even though the spot rate was fixed, prior to the 1976 devaluation of the peso. Other possible examples relate to participants in the foreign exchange market assigning small probabilities to a major change in policy stance (for example, in the run-up to an election); or a major realignment of currencies within an adjustable peg regime such as the European Monetary System. In any of these cases, the regression errors will be distributed non-symmetrically, rendering invalid the econometric theory used to derive inferences in the simple equation above. In this sense, awareness of the peso problem makes it clear that the rejection of the efficient market hypothesis may be an incorrect conclusion.

#### Bubbles

Several authors have offered other reasons why the rational expectations forecasting error may be distributed asymmetrically and therefore why the standard econometric inference used in rejecting the efficient market hypothesis may be invalid. For example, it has been noted that a number of feasible rational expectations equilibria may exist, only one of which is the market fundamentals solution: these alternative solutions have been variously described as 'rational bubble', 'sunspot', 'bootstrap' or 'will o' the wisp' equilibria. A rational bubble may arise where the market exchange rate has drifted away from the fundamentals solution and foreign exchange market participants weigh the probability of a continued deviation from the fundamentals solution against the probability of a return to the fundamentals solution (i.e. the probability of the bubble bursting). The bubble problem for the purposes of econometric inference relates to the case where agents expect that the bubble will burst, but assign a very low probability to it bursting in any one period.

The two problems differ in that in the peso problem the difficulty arises because there is some expectation of a shift in the fundamentals, whereas in the bubble problem the difficulty arises because of a drift away from the fundamentals and agents must form expectations of the likelihood of such a drift being augmented in the future. Their common feature is that they both provide a route by which to rationalise (and dismiss) the econometric rejection of the efficient markets hypothesis within the foreign exchange market. Some recent work attempts to distinguish between the presence of bubbles and other deviations from the maintained hypothesis; both Evans (1986) and Meese (1986) find evidence consistent with the hypothesis that bubbles (and/or the peso problem) exist.

## Tests for foreign exchange risk premia

Given a commitment to the rational expectations leg of the joint hypothesis, some researchers have incorporated rational expectations in their models of exchange rate determination and tested for the existence of time-varying foreign exchange rate premia (see, for example, Domowitz and Hakkio, 1985, Wolff, 1987, Taylor, 1988a). Owing to the difficulties of obtaining tractable estimating equations, these attempts to model the risk premium are, in large part, *ad hoc*. To the extent that they provide evidence on the issue of the existence of risk premia, this is consistent with the view that time-varying risk premia exist (conditional, of course, on the assumption of rational expectations.)

The conditionality of the above results on the assumption of rational expectations is important, not least because there is some evidence that it is the expectations leg of the joint hypothesis which is at fault (see, for example, Frankel and Froot, 1987). This evidence is based on models which use survey data on foreign exchange market participants' expectations, thereby negating the need to specify a particular expectations formation mechanism and allowing a single hypothesis test of the joint null hypothesis. Such survey data have only been available relatively recently; but studies have been reported using expectations of participants in both the US and the UK (see Frankel and Froot, 1987, Dominguez, 1986, MacDonald and Torrance, 1988a). On balance, these findings indicate that the null of the efficient market hypothesis is rejected as a result of the failure of the rational expectations component, although it is possible that some of these results provide evidence of rational speculative bubbles or the peso problem, rather than evidence of agents being irrational processors of information (see MacDonald and Taylor 1989, pp. 97–9).

### The 'economic news' approach

The apparent inapplicability of the efficient markets hypothesis to the foreign exchange market seems to have surprised many researchers. This may well have been the prompt for some researchers to try and model exchange rate movements in models which incorporate 'economic news' (like current account balances, money stock figures, political factors), as an explanatory variable.

Different proxies for news have been utilised – for example, Frenkel (1981) allows for interest rate news; Edwards (1982, 1983) and MacDonald (1983a,b) use measures of unanticipated money supplies, income and interest rates. Other relevant 'news' items relate to the achievement of monetary targets (see the papers by MacDonald and Torrance, 1988b, and Engel and Frankel, 1984). In general, the 'news' approach to the determination of the exchange rate is reasonably supported by the data, although there is one puzzle: Davidson (1985) points out that the volatility of exchange rates appears to be greater than can be accounted for by the volatility of the kinds of variables used in empirical news studies. This may simply reflect the limits of using only the quantifiable elements in news, but it may be that market participants are using a different economic model from that prescribed by international monetary economists! As Dornbusch (1983) has shown, use of the wrong model can introduce greater exchange rate variability than use of the correct model.

All this leads to a rather pessimistic view of what we have learned about the determinants of exchange rate movements, particularly as some authors have already suggested that a rather more *ad hoc* formulation may be relevant; for example, Frankel and Froot (1988) have suggested that exchange rates may in fact be weighted averages of the market fundamentals and of the predictions of chartist analysts.

# International coordination of policy – theory

The growing concern over the performance of floating exchanged rates – excessive exchange rate volatility, prolonged misalignments and persistent large current account imbalances – has led to renewed interest in the general issues of international macroeconomic policy coordination and, in particular, in exchange rate targets or zones. This interest is not just that of academic economists but is also demonstrably shared by policy-makers – witness the Plaza Agreement on coordinated exchange rate intervention in September 1985; and the subsequent series of G7 summits that have reaffirmed cooperation over monetary policy. Perhaps the most significant of these summits was the Louvre Accord,[3] which set a loose arrangement of unannounced exchange rate zones particularly influencing G3 policies (Germany, US and Japan).

### The case for international policy coordination

The case for international policy coordination arises because of policy spillovers between countries. These spillovers are such that some of the benefits of one country's policy action are 'exported' to other countries. With no cooperation amongst countries, there is an incentive to moderate such policy actions as the benefits are not fully internalised. However, with cooperation, an optimal policy stance can be chosen to maximise the joint welfare function of all participating countries.[4] Hence, the Hamada result that non-cooperative outcomes are Pareto-inefficient.

In a series of seminal articles, Hamada (1974, 1976, 1979, 1985) has demonstrated the gains both from full cooperation and from partial cooperation in the form of internationally agreed 'rules of the game'. He adopts a stylised game-theoretic framework which has proved to be the standard framework for analysing macroeconomic policy in interdependent economies. However, other theoretical contributions in this field have demonstrated that the unequivocal superiority of cooperation shown by Hamada now needs careful qualification. Other contributions include analysis of 'games' that may be played by monetary authorities when their countries are faced with an external shock such as an oil price increase (Canzoneri and Gray, 1985; and Turnovsky and d'Orey, 1986); the consideration of the sustainability of the cooperative outcome through time; the question of reputation; and the question of the structural time-dependence of the models.

Several of these developments are considered no further here, not because they are thought to be unimportant, but because they are less crucial for the topic in hand.[5] However, something must be said about reputation and credibility. These concepts relate to the incentive-compatibility of cooperative agreements and come about through the introduction of both strategic dynamics and rational expectations to Hamada's models. Importantly, cooperation is unambiguously superior to non-cooperative outcomes only if policy-makers enjoy a reputation for pre-commitment with their own private sector agents. How countries obtain such a reputation is clearly a major issue for policy coordination.

### Reputation and credibility

The theoretical literature on reputation tackles issues which are a consequence of assuming that private agents form rational expectations. Of crucial importance are the private sector's beliefs regarding future government policy. The issue is not new: it was first highlighted in Kydland and Prescott's (1977) work on time-inconsistency. Private sector agents are forward-looking: if they expect a policy rule to become sub-optimal at some stage in the future, then they will also expect the authorities to change the rule at some stage in the future (irrespective of the government's announced intentions). As a result, the rule must be known by economic agents to be optimal *over the entire future path of the economy* in order to be time consistent. Thus, to have reputation means to have time-consistent policy rules.

If governments could make binding pre-commitments to their *ex ante* optimal policy, time-inconsistency would not be a serious problem; but, since governments are typically free to renge on a time-inconsistent policy, there is a reputation problem. The problem is tightly linked to the issue of credibility. Consider a government which is following a time-inconsistent policy: the government clearly has an incentive to renege; but, if agents can anticipate this future reneging, these time-inconsistent policies lack credibility. Thus the only credible policies are those which are time consistent.

There is some debate about how a government gains a reputation: one route is clearly through the imposition of legal constraints; but it is also possible to achieve this (in a model) through assuming that the private sector will respond appropriately to reneging, that is, by imposing a high penalty on the government should it do so (voting it out of office is one possibility).

Recent work incorporating the reputation problem into studies of international policy coordination shows that cooperation without reputation may be counterproductive (Rogoff, 1985, Levine and Currie, 1987, and Canzoneri and Henderson, 1988). Consider the case of one country capable of engineering a monetary surprise. Because part of the consequent output gains are exported, the incentive to engage in an inflation surprise is much reduced. However, with cooperation, all gains are internalised and the incentive to spring inflation surprises is correspondingly increased, thereby leading to a higher level of inflation. Only if reputation is present could this undesirable outcome be avoided.

Analogous to this result is the possibility that reputation without cooperation may also be counterproductive (both paradoxes are discussed in Canzoneri and Henderson, 1988).

### The application to exchange rate mechanisms

The exchange rate is a shared variable, the domestic impact of which is the same whether exchange rate changes originate at home or abroad. This is in stark contrast with most other variables, whose impacts are significantly smaller internationally than domestically. The need to limit exchange rate spillovers is therefore greater than for other linkage variables and the potential gains for coordination appear correspondingly larger when that is done.

A major problem with exchange rate commitments is that they cannot easily be made time consistent, particularly in a world where national authorities pursue independent inflation and unemployment targets. Consider a two-country model in which the authorities have an exchange rate commitment and agree to set money stocks at the levels $M_a$ and $M_b$ respectively (see Figure 9.1). Suppose there is shock in country A which increases the demand for money: Country A's interest rate rises $(r_1)$, causing B to intervene in the foreign exchange market. The money supply of B falls (via a capital outflow) and its interest rate rises $(r_3)$, which is deflationary for B. If B's authorities are worried about unemployment they will have an incentive to change the rule and devalue or let the currency float. The rule has ceased to be optimal for B. The realisation that this might happen in the future will produce a lack of credibility in the exchange rate commitment and therefore frequent speculative crises. Now, there are only two ways out of this dilemma: either B subordinates all its domestic concerns to the exchange rate commitment (and hopes to retain credibility with its own private agents); or B seeks formulae to soften the commitment to fixed exchange rates, thereby increasing its credibility.

This type of analysis permits a relatively fresh interpretation of the failure of the Bretton Woods regime, as it can now be seen as

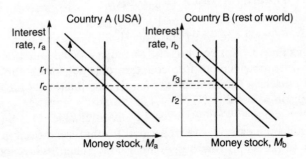

Fig 9.1

a commitment which was too stringent and therefore had low credibility. New versions of fixed exchange rate systems, like the European Monetary System, are in this sense more promising because they are less strict, and therefore more credible.

### The European Monetary System

The EMS is a notable example of international policy coordination in practice and there is a large literature assessing the experience of it, especially on the empirical effect on inflation and exchange rate volatility (see, for example, the papers in Giavazzi, Micossi and Miller, 1988).

The EMS can be viewed as an agreement within which there is an implicit agreement to give the German Bundesbank the role of fixing the system-wide money stock. The general problems for monetary policy-making relate to the difficulties of achieving cooperative solutions which stick. Of course, modern game theory can give some relevant insights because all cooperative agreements suffer from the free-riding problem. Once agreement is struck, incentives remain for individual countries to renege and make themselves better off; the system can only work if partners do not renege in turn. The strength of a cooperative agreement therefore depends upon how well the actions of the partners can be monitored and how quickly retaliation can be expected. If monitoring is easy and retaliatory action can be expected, cooperative agreements have a chance of lasting a long time. If these conditions are not met, cooperative agreements will break down easily.

## International monetary reform

### Williamson's target zone proposal

The most prominent proposals for policy coordination are the target zone arrangement for exchange rates put forward by John Williamson and its extended version (see Williamson, 1983, and Williamson and Miller, 1987). The proposals envisage a set of mutually consistent target zones for real exchange rates pursued primarily by means of monetary policy; nominal income targets are to be pursued primarily by fiscal policy (see Williamson and Miller, 1987, for a detailed analysis).

The idea is that volatility in exchange rates can be reduced by limiting movements of the real exchange rate to lie within pre-specified wide bands. This should come about both through the anchoring of market expectations and through curtailing the ability of governments to rely on exchange rate appreciation to hold down inflation. Both of these routes are seen to be important. It is argued that the former should limit the vulnerability of the exchange rate to the type of speculative bubbles which, it is claimed, have been exhibited in the foreign exchange markets in recent years. Underlying the latter route is a bilief that some governments have relied excessively on exchange rate appreciation to curb general inflationary pressures. In doing so, they have exported inflation to the rest of the world, exerting an important policy spillover, but also generating exchange rate volatility through differences in the timing of such policies.

The important additional features of the extended target zone proposals relate to the supplementation of these target zone proposals with internationally agreed rules for the conduct of domestic macro-policy.[6]

Much recent work has been carried out on these target zone proposals (see, for example, Frenkel and Goldstein, 1986, Currie and Wren-Lewis, 1990). Major criticisms of the proposals which emerge relate to the difficulty of implementation and are two-fold. First, to operate a target zone system, it is necessary to compute equilibrium exchange rates, yet it is not clear how these can be established. Even more disturbing, it is all too likely that estimates of the equilibrium rates that are made will be distributed widely; for example, Loopesko found that expert opinions on the equilibrium dollar–yen rate varied between 100 and 200 yen to the dollar! (Quoted in De Grauwe, 1989.)

Secondly, and rather more fundamentally, it is argued that there is insufficient commitment in the scheme where commitment matters. In particular, there is no rule that governs how large exchange rate adjustments will be in the future and therefore no obvious mechanism by which to anchor expectations.

Other objections to this policy include concern that fiscal policy is too inflexible for successful management of internal demand. An alternative scheme, proposed by Boughton (1989), suggests that fiscal policy should instead be assigned to achieving external current account balance in the medium term, while monetary policy is guided by targets for nominal income rather than for money supply.

## McKinnon's proposal for international monetary reform

In the light of the experience with floating exchange rates, McKinnon has also put forward a proposal for reform of the international monetary system (McKinnon, 1982, 1984). His starting point is that the large shocks which have occurred in the currency preferences of agents have led to large movements of the world money stock. McKinnon suggests that the growth in money supplies should be coordinated on a worldwide basis, leaving fiscal policy available for domestic purposes.

The problem perceived is easily represented in a simple diagram (Figure 9.1). The world is made up of just two countries, A and B. Consider what happens if there is a sudden increase in the demand for A's currency, wholly matched by a reduction in the demand for B's currency (due to a change in currency preferences). If the two countries set their own monetary policy in a non-cooperative policy environment, A's interest rate will rise ($r_1$), whereas in B (the rest of world) the opposite happens ($r_2$). In a flexible exchange rate system, A's currency appreciates. If B wants to avoid currency depreciation, it intervenes in the foreign exchange market, its domestic money stock declines and the interest rate increases ($r_3$). In this case, country B bears the whole burden of adjustment to a demand disturbance in country A! Moreover, the world money supply will contract. Thus a shift in currency preferences leads to worldwide monetary deflation which may lead to recession. Exactly the opposite happens with a shift in currency preference away from currency A.

McKinnon points to the changing popularity of the US dollar through the 1970s and early 1980s as evidence for the importance of this phenomenon. For example, relative to the 1980–5 period, the unpopularity of the dollar during the 1973–9 period was associated with a relatively high rate of expansion of the world money stock, whilst the industrialised countries outside the US experienced a substantial decline in the growth rates of their money stocks. The relatively high demand for dollars in the 1980–5 period brought about the opposite movements in the money stock variables. Thus McKinnon points to the possibility of movements in and out of the dollar having triggered cycles of worldwide monetary deflation and expansion.

According to McKinnon, this uncomfortable feature of the international monetary system is attributable to the system's asymmetry: the US has the right to determine its own monetary policy, independent of movements of the dollar exchange rates, despite its demonstrable influence on monetary contraction and expansion in the rest of the world. He therefore proposes a symmetric system in which the US allows the money stock to be influenced by interventions in the foreign exchange markets.

More precisely, when the dollar tends to appreciate in the foreign exchange market this is a signal that there is an excess demand for dollars, and the Federal Reserve should then increase the US money stock (and conversely). In such a symmetric system, shifts in currency preferences will have no effect on the world money stock. Moreover, provided the authorities of both the US and the rest of the world (McKinnon suggests that an agreement amongst the US, Japan and Germany would suffice) agree to the rule not to sterilise the monetary effects of their interventions in the foreign exchange markets, McKinnon's symmetric system will work automatically.

One criticism of the McKinnon proposal concerns the practicability of his suggestion that the symmetric system could be achieved by an agreement amongst the US, Japan and Germany. More fundamental is the charge that the proposal is nothing but a fixed exchange rate commitment and a very stringent one at that. As a fixed exchange rate system it suffers from the credibility problem outlined in the previous section. Consider an example set out by De Grauwe (1989, pp. 211–16). The starting point is again an increase in the demand for US currency; but now assume that this is due to an upturn in economic activity. Under the McKinnon rule, the Federal Reserve is forced to expand the US money stock, which leads to a credibility problem. Economic agents know that the US authorities are concerned with maintaining low inflation, yet the McKinnon rule has forced the Federal Reserve to fuel a booming economy through liquidity creation. This will be perceived as a suboptimal policy, credibility is lost and the system will quickly break down.

The McKinnon proposal has a fundamental flaw: in order for exchange rate commitments to work, rules must be established for setting the system-wide money stocks (and interest rates). Because stable cooperative agreements (although desirable) are unlikely to come about, so too are credible exchange rate commitments.

### The proposals for reform compared

On balance, recent work on reform of the international monetary system is all rather pessimistic, but it should be remembered that the alternative systems examined above attempt to cope with a whole range of issues which have emerged during the experience with floating exchange rates. Not only have there been pronounced and prolonged deviations from purchasing power parity but, also, the velocity of money has been highly variable. Moreover, during this period, macroeconomic policy has been essentially non-cooperative.

Both of the proposals discussed here seek to stabilise exchange rates through coordination of monetary policy across countries. Both plans are ways of avoiding shocks to velocity while retaining the crucial monetarist principle that monetary stringency must be progressively increased in response to inflation, but notice that in neither case are monetary targets (so popular with the most recent generation of policy-makers) recommended. At the national level, Williamson seeks to stabilise real exchange rates within a relatively wide band while McKinnon proposes to fix nominal exchange rates.

### Empirical testing of policy rules

In the light of the above it is interesting to assess whether these monetary reforms would have improved on the historical performance of the past decade. A number of recent studies do precisely this. In particular, a number of studies look at the extended target zone proposals of Williamson and Miller (1987). For example, Currie and Wren-Lewis (1990), using the Global Econometric Model (a large-scale disaggregated model of the main OECD countries), find that the extended target zone scheme could well have improved on historical performance over the past decade and their conclusion is fairly robust with respect to changes in the objective function. These findings are for the G3 countries alone, supporting an hierarchical structure of coordination; it is not clear whether they would generalise to a larger group of countries adopting the target zone proposal in a non-hierarchical way.

More generally, results suggest that policy cooperation based on the extended target zone scheme can lead to substantial Pareto welfare improvement compared with history, but note that there is evidence that the performance of simple policy rules varies with the nature of the shocks facing an economy (Frankel *et al.*, 1989).

Clearly, an important recent advance in the area of policy coordination and international monetary reform has been the increasing flow of empirically based results. Significantly, it has the potential of making the theoretical research more relevant to policy-makers. However, as Currie and Wren-Lewis note, it is possible that the theoretical analysis is now outstripping the capabilities of our empirical macroeconometric models, not least because issues concerning the Lucas Critique are unresolved for international macroeconometric models.

## Conclusion

Many advocates of floating exchange rates predicted that a floating exchange rate regime would show some instability early on but would eventually settle down. However, this has not been borne out in practive: since 1973, exchange rates have continued to be volatile on a short-term basis and have also displayed long cycles which are hard to explain. Moreover, these movements in exchange rates appear to have had significant implications for world trade and have led policy-makers to discuss international cooperation over monetary policy (viz. the series of G7 summits).

It is not therefore surprising that recent work in international monetary economics addresses the twin issues of exchange rate variability and international monetary policy coordination. This latest work includes a large amount of empirical estimation and testing of models of exchange rate determination; there has been a movement away from reduced-form estimation towards full structural estimation of the existing models. Also, much greater emphasis has been placed on the applicability of the efficient markets hypothesis to the foreign exchange market and the role of 'news' in determining exchange rate movements. With respect to the international coordination of monetary policy, the large and growing literature on macroeconomic policy coordination has become central to the way in which economists assess proposals to stabilise exchange rates. For example, the concepts of reputation and credibility are at the heart of the most recent assessments of proposals for international monetary reform (at both the theoretical and the empirical level).

It is too early to pass judgement on this work, but one disturbing feature is already apparent: it has become increasingly difficult to obtain tractable estimating models which capture the various theoretical developments. This is true both for the models of exchange rate determination and for the macroeconometric models of policy coordination. The fear that the theoretical analysis is outstripping our econometric capabilities is already on the research agenda for the future; it remains to be seen how the challenge will be met.

### Notes

1 This chapter does not explore the issue of Third World debt; rather, the emphasis is on explanations (rationalisations) of exchange rate movements and proposals for reform of the international monetary system.
2 viz. the Dutch Disease phenomenon.
3 See Funabashi (1988) for a review of this period.
4 Note that it is not necessary for countries to share common objectives; indeed there is nothing to prevent the individual objectives of countries being totally at odds with one another.
5 See the recent surveys by Currie and Levine (1989), Hughes Hallett (1989) and Levine (1990) for coverage of these developments.
6 See Currie and Wren-Lewis (1990) for an enumeration of these rules.

### References

Backus, D. (1984), 'Empirical models of the exchange rate: separating the wheat from the chaff', *Canadian Journal of Economics*, 17, pp. 824–46.
Bergsten, C. F. and Williamson, J. (1983), 'Exchange rates and trade policy', in W. Cline (ed.), *Trade Policy in the 1980s*, Washington DC: Institute for International Economics.
Bergstrand, J. H. (1983), 'Is exchange rate volatility excessive'? *Federal Reserve Bank of Boston New England Economic Review*, September, pp. 5–14.

Bilson, J. F. O. (1985), 'Macro-economic stability and flexible exchange rates', *American Economic Review, Papers and Proceedings*, 75, pp. 62–7.

Bleaney, M. and Greenaway, D. (1989), 'Recent developments in macroeconomics', in D. Greenaway (ed.), *Current Issues in Macroeconomics*, Basingstoke: Macmillan, pp. 1–21.

Boughton, J. (1989), 'Policy assignment strategies with somewhat flexible exchange rates', in M. Miller, B. Eichengreen and R. Portes (eds), *Blueprints for Exchange Rate Management*, London: Academic Press, pp. 125–60.

Branson, W. H. and Henderson, D. W. (1985), 'The specification and influence of asset markets', in R. W. Jones and P. B. Kenen (eds), *Handbook of International Economics, II*, Amsterdam: North-Holland, pp. 749–805.

Buiter, W. H. and Miller, M. H. (1981), 'Monetary policy and international competitiveness: the problems of adjustment', *Oxford Economic Papers*, 33, Supplement, pp. 143–75.

Canzoneri, M. B. and Gray, J. A. (1985), 'Monetary policy games and the consequences of non-cooperative behaviour', *International Economic Review*, 26, pp. 547–64.

Canzoneri, M. B. and Henderson, D. W. (1988), 'Is sovereign policy-making bad?', *Carnegie-Rochester Conference Series on Public Policy*, 28, pp. 93–140.

Chrystal, K. A. (1989), 'Overshooting models of the exchange rate', in D. Greenaway (ed.), *Current Issues in Macroeconomics*, Basingstoke: Macmillan, pp. 214–30.

Cumby, R. E. and Obstfeld, M. (1984), 'International interest rate and price level linkages under flexible exchange rates: a review of recent evidence', in J. F. O. Bilson and R. C. Marston (eds), *Exchange Rate Theory and Practice*, Chicago: University of Chicago Press.

Currie, D. and Levine, P. (1989), 'The international coordination of monetary policy: a survey', Discussion Paper 119, University of Leicester, October.

Currie, D. and Wren-Lewis, S. (1990), 'Evaluating the extended target zone proposal for the G3', *Economic Journal*, 100, pp. 105–23.

Davidson, J. E. H. (1985), 'Econometric modelling of the sterling effective exchange rate', *Review of Economic Studies*, 21, pp. 231–40.

De Grauwe, P. (1988), 'Exchange rate variability and the slow-down in growth of international trade', *IMF Staff Papers*, 35.

De Grauwe, P. (1989), *International Money: Post-War Trends and Theories*, Oxford: Clarendon Press.

De Grauwe, P. and de Bellefroid, B. (1987), 'Long run exchange rate variability and international trade', in S. Arndt and D. Richardson (eds), *Real Financial Linkages among Open Economies*, Cambridge, Mass.: MIT Press.

Dominguez, K. M. (1986), 'Are foreign exchange forecasts rational? New evidence from survey data', *Economics Letters*, 21, pp. 277–81.

Domowitz, I. and Hakkio, C. S. (1985), 'Conditional variance and the risk premium in the foreign exchange market', *Journal of International Economics*, 18, pp. 47–66.

Dornbusch, R. (1976), 'Expectations and exchange rate dynamics', *Journal of Political Economy*, 84, pp. 1161–76.

Dornbusch, R. (1983), 'Flexible exchange rates and interdependence', *IMF Staff Papers*, 30, pp. 3–38.

Driskell, R. A. (1981), 'Exchange rate dynamics: an empirical investigation', *Journal of Political Economy*, 89, pp. 357–71.

Edwards, S. (1982), 'Exchange rates and "news": a multi-currency approach', *Journal of International Money and Finance*, 1, pp. 211–24.

Edwards, S. (1983), 'Floating exchange rates, expectations and new information', *Journal of Monetary Economics*, 11, pp. 321–36.

Engel, C. and Frankel, J. A. (1984), 'Why interest rates react to money announcements: an explanation from the foreign exchange market', *Journal of Monetary Economics*, 13, pp. 31–9.

Evans, G. W. (1986), 'A test for speculative bubbles and the sterling–dollar exchange rate: 1981–4', *American Economic Review*, 76, pp. 621–36.

Fama, E. F. (1984), 'Forward and spot exchange rates', *Journal of Monetary Economics*, 14, pp. 319–38.

Finn, M. G. (1986), 'Forecasting the exchange rate: a monetary or random walk phenomenon?' *Journal of International Money and Finance*, 5, pp. 181–94.

Frankel, J. A. (1979), 'On the mark: a theory of floating exchange rates based on real interest differentials', *American Economic Review*, 69, pp. 610–22.

Frankel, J. A. (1982), 'The mystery of the multiplying marks: a modification of the monetary model', *Review of Economics and Statistics*, 64, pp. 515–19.

Frankel, J. A. (1983), 'Monetary and portfolio-balance models of exchange rate determination', in J. S. Bhandari and B. H. Putnam (eds), *Economic Interdependence and Flexible Exchange Rates*, Cambridge, Mass.: MIT Press, pp. 84–115.

Frankel, J. A. (1984), 'Tests of monetary and portfolio balance models of exchange rate determination', in J. F. O. Bilson and R. C. Marston (eds), *Exchange Rate Theory and Practice*, Chicago: University of Chicago Press.

Frankel, J. A. and Froot, K. (1987), 'Using survey data to test standard propositions regarding exchange rate expectations', *American Economic Review*, 77, pp. 133–53.

Frankel, J. A. and Froot, K. (1988), 'Chartists and fundamentalists in the foreign exchange market', in A. S. Courakis and M. P. Taylor (eds), *Policy Issues for Interdependent Economies*, London: Macmillan.

Frankel, J. A., Goldstein, M. and Masson, P. R. (1989), 'Simulating the effects of some simple coordinated versus uncoordinated policy rules', in R. Bryant, D. A. Currie, J. A. Frankel and R. Portes (eds), *Macroeconomic Policies in an Interdependent World*, Washington DC: International Monetary Fund.

Frenkel, J. A. (1981), 'Flexible exchange rates, prices and the role of "news": lessons from the 1970s', *Journal of Political Economy*, 89, pp. 665–705.

Frenkel, J. A. and Goldstein, M. (1986), 'A guide to target zones, *IMF Staff Papers*, 33.

Funabashi, Y. (1988) *Managing the Dollar: From the Plaza to the Louvre*, Washington DC: Institute for International Economics.

Genberg, H. (1981), 'Effects of central bank intervention in the foreign exchange market', *IMF Staff Papers*, 28, pp. 451–76.

Giavazzi, F. S., Micossi, S. and Miller, M. (1988), *The European Monetary System*, Cambridge: Cambridge University Press.

Hamada, K. (1974), 'Alternative exchange rate systems and the interdependence of monetary policies', in R. Z. Aliber (ed.), *National Monetary Policies and the International Financial System*, Chicago: University of Chicago Press, pp. 13–33.

Hamada, K. (1976), 'A strategic analysis of monetary interdependence', *Journal of Political Economy*, 84, pp. 677–700.

Hamada, K. (1979), 'Macroeconomic strategy and coordination under alternative exchange rates', in R. Dornbusch and J. A. Frenkel (eds), *International Economic Policy*, Baltimore, Md: Johns Hopkins University Press.

Hamada, K. (1985), *The Political Economy of International Monetary Interdependence*, Cambridge, Mass.: MIT Press.

Hooper, P. and Morton, J. (1982), 'Fluctuations in the dollar: a model of nominal and real exchange rate determination', *Journal of International Money and Finance*, 1, pp. 39–56.

Hughes Hallett, A. (1989), 'Macroeconomic interdependence and the coordination of economic policy', in D. Greenaway (ed.), *Current Issues in Macroeconomics*, Basingstoke: Macmillan, pp. 182–213.

IMF (1984), 'The exchange rate system: lessons from the past and options for the future: a study by the research department of the IMF', *Occasional Paper*, 30.

Kearney, C. and MacDonald, R. (1985), 'Asset markets and the exchange rate: a structural model of the sterling–dollar rate 1972–82, *Journal of Economic Studies*, 12, pp. 3–20.

Kenen, P. and Rodrik, D. (1986), 'Measuring and analysing the effects of short-term volatility in real exchange rates', *Review of Economics and Statistics*, 68, pp. 311–15.

Krasker, W. S. (1980), 'The "peso problem" in testing the efficiency of forward exchange markets', *Journal of Monetary Economics*, 6, pp. 269–76.

Kydland, F. E. and Prescott, E. C. (1977), 'Rules rather than discretion: the inconsistency of optimal plans', *Journal of Political Economy*, 85, pp. 473–91.

Levine, P. (1990), 'Monetary policy and credibility', in T. Bandyopadhyay and S. Ghatak (eds), *Current Issues in Monetary Economics*, Hemel Hempstead: Harvester Wheatsheaf, pp. 252–80.

Levine, P. and Currie, D. A. (1987), 'Does international macro-economic policy coordination pay and is it sustainable?: A two country analysis', *Oxford Economic Papers*, 39, pp. 38–74.

Longworth, D. (1981), 'Testing the efficiency of the Canadian–US exchange market under the assumption of no risk premium', *Journal of Finance*, 36, pp. 43–9.

MacDonald, R. (1983a), 'Some tests of the rational expectations hypothesis in the foreign exchange market', *Scottish Journal of Political Economy*, 30 pp. 235–50.

MacDonald, R. (1983b), 'Tests of efficiency and the impact of news in three foreign exchange markets: the experience of the 1920s', *Bulletin of Economic Research*, 35, pp. 123–44.

MacDonald, R. and Taylor, M. P. (1988), 'International parity conditions', in A. S. Courakis and M. P. Taylor (eds), *Policy Issues for Interdependent Economies*, London: Macmillan.

MacDonald, R. and Taylor, M. P. (1989), 'Economic analysis of foreign exchange markets: an expository survey', in R. MacDonald and M. P. Taylor (eds), *Exchange Rates and Open Economy Macroeconomics*, Oxford: pp. 3–107. Basil Blackwell.

MacDonald, R. and Torrance, T. S. (1988a), 'On risk, rationality and excessive speculation in the Deutschmark–US dollar exchange market: some evidence using survey data', *Oxford Bulletin of Economics and Statistics*, 50, pp. 107–23.

MacDonald, R. and Torrance, T. S. (1988b), 'Exchange rates and the news: some evidence using UK survey data', *The Manchester School*, 56, pp. 69–76.

McKinnon, R. (1982), 'Currency substitution and instability in the world dollar market', *American Economic Review*, 72, pp. 320–33.

McKinnon, R. (1984), *An International Standard for Monetary Stabilization*, Washington DC: Policy Analyses in International Economics.

Meese. R. A. (1986), 'Testing for bubbles in exhange markets: a case of sparkling rates?' *Journal of Political Economy*, 94, pp. 345–73.

Meese, R. A. and Rogoff, K. (1983), 'Empirical exchange rate models of the seventies: do they fit out of sample?' *Journal of International Economics*, 14, pp. 3–24.

Meese, R. A. and Rogoff, K. (1984), 'The out of sample failure of empirical exchange rate models: sampling error or misspecification?' in J. A. Frankel (ed.), *Exchange Rates and International Macroeonomics*, Chicago: National Bureau of Economic Research.

Rogoff, K. (1985), 'Can international monetary policy coordination be counter-productive?' *Journal of International Economics*, 18, pp. 199–217.

Salemi, M. K. (1984), 'Comment', in J. A. Frankel (ed.), *Exchange Rates and International Macroeconomics*, Chicago: National Bureau of Economic Research.

Smith, P. N. and Wickens, M. R. (1988), 'Assessing monetary shocks and exchange rate variability with a stylised econometric model of the UK', in A. S. Courakis and M. P. Taylor, (eds), *Policy Issues for Interdependent Economies*, London: Macmillan.

Taylor, M. P. (1988a), 'A DYMIMIC model of forward foreign exchange risk, with estimates for three major exchange rates', *The Manchester School*, 56, pp. 55–68.

Taylor, M. P. (1988b), 'An empirical examination of long-run purchasing power parity using cointegration techniques', *Applied Economics*, 20, pp. 1369–81.

Taylor, M. P. (1989), 'Expectations, risk and uncertainty in the foreign exchange market: some results based on survey data', *The Manchester School*, 57, pp. 142–53.

Turnovsky, S. J. and d'Orey, V. (1986), 'Monetary policies in interdependent economies with stochastic disturbances: a strategic approach', *Economic Journal*, 96, 696–721.

Wolff, C. C. P. (1987), 'Forward foreign exchange rates, expected spot rates and premia: a signal-extraction approach', *Journal of Finance*, 42, pp. 395–406.

Williamson, J. (1983), *The Exchange Rate System*, Washington DC: Institute for International Economics.

Williamson, J. and Miller, M. (1987), *Targets and Indicators: a Blueprint for the International Coordination of Economic Policy*, Washington, DC: Institute for International Economics.

# Index